WITHOUT QUARTER

By the same author

Destiny's Daughter: the Tragedy of RMS Queen Elizabeth
George Square 1919
The Hampden Story

Without Quarter

A BIOGRAPHY OF TOM JOHNSTON

'The Uncrowned King of Scotland'

RUSSELL GALBRAITH

MAINSTREAM
PUBLISHING
EDINBURGH AND LONDON

This book is for Bill Lyall and Donald Mackenzie

First published in Great Britain in 1995 by
MAINSTREAM PUBLISHING COMPANY (EDINBURGH) LTD
7 Albany Street
Edinburgh EH1 3UG

ISBN 1 85158 761 6

Subsidised by | THE SCOTTISH **ARTS** COUNCIL

A catalogue record for this book is available from the British Library

Photographs courtesy of the North of Scottish Hydro-Electric Board, *The Herald* and the Scottish Tourist Board
Typeset in Adobe Bembo
Printed and bound in Great Britain by Butler & Tanner Ltd, Frome

ACKNOWLEDGEMENTS

IT HAS BEEN remarked before, over many years, that unlike most statesmen of his seniority, Tom Johnston left few personal papers to assist future generations interested in his career. His daughter, Mrs Mary Knox, believes a natural sense of modesty probably prevailed. Another explanation might be that Johnston, mischievously, wanted to make things a mite hard for anyone wishing to follow the pattern of his life in politics and public service, covering more than half a century, just as he had been forced to dig around in the depths of some half-forgotten archive to produce much of his own work. At any rate, without the assistance and patience of staff at establishments such as the Scottish Records Office in West Register House in Edinburgh, the National Library of Scotland, the Mitchell Library in Glasgow, and the Public Records Office at Kew, a book of this nature would be impossible to achieve. Thanks are also due to Brian Osborne and Don Martin for access to the splendid facilities available at the Kirkintilloch Library where Tom Johnston has been allocated a special archive. A permanent exhibition, which includes his desk and copies of all his major works, also provides an imaginative and lasting memorial to the town's most famous son, and is worth a visit by anyone interested in his career.

Tom Johnston's extensive journalistic output, especially his contributions to *Forward* over many years, provides a fierce and incisive commentary on people and events. Much can also be learned from the early books, including the vituperative *Our Noble Families*, which he later regretted, and *The History of the Working Classes in Scotland*, for which he never apologised. Similarly, speeches in the House of Commons, as recorded in *Hansard*, or delivered elsewhere and reported by contemporary newspapers, offer an immediate response to some of the great events of this century, as well as the abiding issues which beset people everywhere, not least how to overcome poverty and starvation, and avoid war. Sadly, his self-effacing recollections, contained in *Memories*, first published in 1952, adds weight to whatever suspicion might exist that Johnston, the elder statesman, wasn't interested in revealing much about himself. Fortunately, however, this didn't prevent talented contemporaries recording their impressions of the man.

I am also pleased to report that, although much has clearly changed about the workings of the North of Scotland Hydro-Electric Board, the Scottish Tourist Board and the Forestry Commission in Scotland since Tom Johnston's time in charge of all three, a tradition of helpfulness persists. I am especially grateful to staff at the three headquarters for the enthusiasm with which they responded to requests for information and pictures, despite the additional work this involved. *The Herald* in Glasgow also provided photographs, and others who were generous with their time include Mrs Mary Knox, Lord Thomson of Monifeith, Hamish Mackinven, Sir Robert Grieve, Tom Fulton and Lt Col Thomas Riddell. A select bibliography is provided. My thanks to all concerned.

INTRODUCTION

'Do the duty that lies nearest thee which thou knowest to be a duty.
The second duty will already become clearer. And in the doing of
that duty comes the only reward of recompense that endures.'

Thomas Carlyle, *Sartor Resartus*.

NO ONE ELSE this century has dominated Scottish politics quite
like Tom Johnston. When he served as Secretary of State for Scotland
in the wartime Coalition under Churchill, he was able to secure a
degree of power never allowed before or since. A quiet, thrifty, sincere
man of firm opinions, Johnston didn't hesitate to claim the methods
he employed 'got Scotland's wishes and opinions respected and
listened to, as they had not been respected or listened to since the
Union'.

But this uncluttered assessment of his own remarkable career was no
vainglorious outburst, unsupported by outside testimony. Reporters,
acknowledging his popularity, and his power, dubbed him 'the
uncrowned King of Scotland'. From the age of 60 until his death, more
than two decades later, he was, by general accord, 'the foremost Scot of
his day'.

Johnston, who began his serious working life as a journalist, editing
his own newspaper, the abrasive Socialist weekly, *Forward*, was utterly
convinced 'there was very little wrong with Scotland that her sons and
daughters might not speedily put right'. This optimistic view was
expressed in a BBC radio talk broadcast on 23 November 1929 when
Johnston was serving in the second Labour Government as Under-
Secretary of State at the Scottish Office. Nearly 30 years later, in a speech
delivered in Edinburgh on 19 January 1957, he continued to look on the

bright side. Scotland enjoyed 'assets for which many lands would give much. Let us stand up for ourselves. If we do so I have no fear whatever for the future,' Johnston declared.

He first arrived at Westminster in 1922, as MP for West Stirlingshire and Clackmannanshire, along with John Wheatley, James Maxton and David Kirkwood, and other members of the famous Clydeside group. Johnston was then aged 41, with a reputation for strong left-wing views based, largely, on his performance over many years as a councillor in Kirkintilloch, and the opinions he contributed to *Forward*.

Patrick Dollan testified he was 'the best dressed man in the local socialist branches. His suits were tailor-made. He wore a bowler hat designed in the latest style and carried gloves. I was told,' wrote Dollan, 'that next to R.B. Cunninghame Graham he was the biggest swell in the movement.'

A middle-class background was uncommon in Labour circles in the West of Scotland at the time; and it is widely accepted Johnston was raised in comfortable, middle-class surroundings, the son of a licensed victualler, in Kirkintilloch. In fact, he and his two sisters lived with their mother in a small flat above a shop where she also worked. 'His father left Kirkintilloch when his three children were quite young and never returned,' Johnston's surviving daughter, Mrs Mary Knox, revealed. 'I think he was told to leave. But my father wouldn't talk about him, although my sister and I sometimes asked.'

Johnston's own marriage to Margaret Freeland Cochrane, a grocer's daughter, lasted from 1914 until his death in 1963. 'My mother played no part in his public life, apart from sometimes sitting beside him on a platform somewhere. She didn't want to become involved in politics,' said Mrs Knox. 'It was her job to look after the family home while he was away. He relied on her totally. But politics were never discussed at home.'

As a young man, though, Johnston clearly worked at projecting a thoughtful, middle-class image in Labour circles. A bow tie was always part of the meticulously arranged ensemble. But few people knew Johnston had been forced to master the business of tying them, using only his teeth and his left hand, as a result of a schoolboy accident involving a train and some buffers which left him with a permanently impaired right arm.

Patrick Dollan, in his unpublished memoirs, also recalled: 'Tom Johnston preferred writing to oratory and did not take much part in the rough and tumble propaganda of socialism. He was probably right to concentrate on making *Forward* and other publications a success. He was shy and retiring, and liked the study and library rather than the public platform.' Emmanuel Shinwell, another of the 1922 Labour intake from Scotland, also testified that Johnston was never a good speaker. According to Shinwell he was 'awkward and shy'.

Yet the speed with which he caught the Speaker's eye, before delivering his maiden speech on the first working day of the 1922 Parliament, suggests either a diffident man behaving bravely or someone who wasn't at all overawed by his surroundings. Also, in view of Shinwell's evidence, it is interesting to note that, even as a backbencher, when he could have remained silent, Tom Johnston spoke regularly, and at some length, on a wide variety of subjects.

Considering the verve with which he proclaimed his Scottishness, it was assumed in many quarters that Johnston was an ardent nationalist. Including by-elections, Johnston stood for Parliament eight times between 1918 and 1935, winning as often as he lost. But on each occasion Home Rule for Scotland was an important consideration in his appeal to the electors. Twice, in the House of Commons, he seconded Home Rule Bills which never progressed beyond second reading. In addition, he had been a prominent member of the Scottish Home Rule Association for many years and shortly before the outbreak of the Second World War he helped found the London Scots Self-Government Committee.

People with access to secret information were also aware that, as a member of the wartime Cabinet, he wasn't above employing the threat of a nationalist backlash whenever it appeared he was in danger of losing an argument, or it appeared Scottish interests were threatened.

Yet this didn't prevent Johnston from acting swiftly to crush nationalist initiatives which didn't suit his purpose, or threatened the true nature of his own grand design. At the height of the Second World War the nationalist leader, J.M. MacCormick, wrote to Arthur Greenwood, the Minister responsible for post-war reconstruction, to seek a meeting to discuss 'the possibility of the present Government, in consultation with Scottish interests, working out a plan for self-government in Scotland immediately after the war'. It was John MacCormick's case that no substantial measures affecting Scotland could be carried out except through the agency of a Scottish Parliament. By seeking the support of a Minister based in London, however, he avoided the risk of confrontation with Tom Johnston. Except, by his action, he did succeed in delivering a massive snub to the man who governed Scotland from St Andrew's House.

Not surprisingly, if this was his intention, MacCormick's plan quickly backfired. The Minister for Post-War Reconstruction would have found himself at odds with the Prime Minister if he attempted to interfere in Scotland where Tom Johnston had been given virtually a free hand. On receipt of MacCormick's letter dated 14 March 1941 Greenwood simply redirected it to Johnston at the Scottish Office, together with a note asking him to frame a reply. With wry good humour Johnston stifled his anger and offered the opinion that he assumed the Minister for Post-War Reconstruction in London did not wish to receive a deputation from the Scottish National Party to discuss Scotland's future. In which case, he suggested blithely, a reply could be sent to SNP headquarters in Elmbank Street, Glasgow, assuring anyone who wanted to know that Scottish interests were continuously and energetically represented in the Councils of State in London; and wouldn't be allowed to suffer in future 'without vociferous and clamant protest'.

It was never stated but the underlying message was clear, of course: inside the Cabinet room, in faraway London, the people of Scotland could depend on Tom Johnston to protect their interests.

In fact, throughout the whole of his life, Tom Johnston supported the idea of a Scottish Parliament sitting in Edinburgh. But he was never a separatist. What Johnston wanted for Scotland was devolution; although, as Alastair Dunnett, a senior member of his wartime staff, maintained: 'He always thought of Scotland not as a region, or a special area, but as a nation.'

It is clear, however, he would have been happy to settle for a Scottish Parliament, answerable directly to its own electorate for all domestic affairs, operating inside a federally structured United Kingdom; leaving the Westminster Parliament to deal with matters affecting the Empire and the rest of the outside world.

But even this modest ideal was dependent on Scotland achieving a strong economy first. In his judgment this should include all the traditional industries plus a motor industry, an aircraft industry, and a strong tourist industry.

Tom Johnston didn't witness the collapse of shipbuilding on the Clyde, the demise of the Springburn locomotive works, the failure of Linwood and Bathgate, mining villages left to rot, or the abandonment of the Scottish steel industry. But he knew the danger of this happening was always present. As early as 21 June 1945 he warned listeners to the Scottish Home Service that during the period of post-war reconstruction 'people in Scotland had better be extremely careful'.

Johnston always favoured the public ownership of essential industries and public direction of essential services. 'But public ownership to me, and to many thousands of other men and women, never meant vesting the control of industry in some long-distance bureaucracy,' he declared.

According to Johnston, for a year or two during the war there had been a real appreciation in London that 'public ownership is quite compatible with devolved control, and is, indeed, much more likely to succeed if it enlists national and local sentiment in its support, than if it antagonises national and local sentiment and administrative talent'.

Johnston, who had been Lord Privy Seal in Ramsay MacDonald's second Labour Government, preferred persuasion to confrontation. He was, according to his own assessment, a moderate extremist. However, his success at Westminster suggests he was also a tough operator, a machine politician, who could play harder than most when needed.

Like everyone else who was part of that historic 1922 Labour intake from Scotland, during his early years in Parliament, he was 'very radical, with utopian and highly idealistic views about the possibility of revolutionary change in society'. This was a view expressed by Lord Thomson of Monifieth who, as George Thomson, edited *Forward*, represented Dundee in the House of Commons, and served in a Labour Cabinet; all tasks performed in the course of his own career by Tom Johnston.

When they met for the first time Thomson felt he was in the company of 'a man of great moral character, almost a caricature of the canny Scot'. Thomson had been offered a job on *Forward*, as assistant to the editor, Emrys Hughes. But his appointment couldn't be confirmed without Tom Johnston's approval. 'I got the job,' said Thomson. 'But when the bill for coffee arrived, I had to pay half.'

Tom Johnston was then at the height of his fame. He was the man who governed Scotland for most of the war, and the country's leading elder statesman, as well as chairman of the North of Scotland Hydro-Electric Board, the Scottish Tourist Board and the Forestry Commission in Scotland. His plan for the Highlands, and Scotland generally, included the attraction of 'industries which do not depend upon national grants in aid from a sometimes harassed Chancellor'.

Johnston hoped to encourage a post-war programme of all-in national effort similar to the mood that triumphed in the struggle against Hitler. He never abandoned his belief in strength through unity: concurrence, Johnston claimed, offered 'the possibility of great achievement in better housing, better health, better education, better use of leisure, greater security in income, and employment. In barking at each other's heels, in faction fighting and strife over non-essentials, lie frustration and defeat for everybody,' he warned.

Said Lord Thomson: 'I don't think he was ever left-wing in an ideological sense. He was very iconoclastic. But I think his experience of practical politics made him more and more believe you did things best by getting people of ability and good will together.'

History also mattered to Tom Johnston. For years he campaigned against the sanitised, anglicised version served in schools. He wanted people to know that 'when the Norman barons came to Galloway they tore out the tongues of children so that the traditions of ancient freedom should not be bequeathed'.

Thomas Carlyle provided intellectual, political and social inspiration and he considered Robert Burns 'the nearest thing to a miracle that has happened in our recorded history. There is nothing in his heredity to explain him. There is no trace among his forbears on either side of any artistry or genius; no threat or hint of an underground Vesuvius that would one day burst into flame across the world.' Burns, he maintained, rendered Scots a priceless service. 'He saved our language from extinction.'

Churchill, according to his secretary John Colville, considered Tom Johnston 'one of the best of the Labour Party'. The wartime Prime Minister also appeared to revel in the adulation heaped on Johnston by his own countrymen. 'Here comes the King of Scotland!' he announced one evening when Johnston, accompanied by his daughter Mary, arrived at a Downing Street reception; confirming that news of the popular epithet had been circulating at the highest levels in London, and that no one seriously believed any degree of *lese-majesty* attached to it.

According to *The Times*: 'There was a time when he seemed a possible leader of the Labour Party and destined for the highest office. But Johnston himself was almost too disinterested a Socialist, possibly too modest a person also, to aspire to the heights.'

Clement Attlee, the man with most to lose if *The Times* was right in its assessment of Johnston's capabilities, was too big a man not to acknowledge his worth. He looked upon his long-time colleague as a most skilful reconciler of contending factions, who was trusted by people of all political views.

But his wartime press aide, Alastair Dunnett, offered a different view of Johnston from the one advanced in *The Times*. 'For him,' wrote Dunnett, 'life was Scotland, and every single thing he did was to benefit his native land.'

CHAPTER ONE

TOM JOHNSTON traced pride in his Scottishness 'back to the warrior reivers who for centuries kept the Scottish Border, bore the brunt of every English invasion, and preserved Scotland's integrity'. He could claim that, as long ago as the 16th century, historians George Buchanan and William Camden 'described the Johnstouns as the most important of the clans of the west – the great obstacle to the English conquest – and that the King of Scots could always depend upon them for prompt service, loyalty and patriotism'.

Originally, confided Johnston, in what he was pleased to call the Prolegomena to his *Memories*, the family motto on the crest of the Johnstons of Annandale was the somewhat dubious Light Thieves All. This was 'later changed to the more appropriate, or at least more polite wording: Nunquam Non Paratus – Never Unprepared'! Good Scottish stock, as Johnston liked to aver, it mixed well with the Ulster-Irish blood of the Alexanders, who settled in Scotland by way of Wigton and Glenluce; respectable folk who were 'always strong for the orthodoxies, sometimes moving about among the Men of the Covenant, throwing up now and again a kirk elder or an innkeeper'.

Johnston never forgot there was a St Ninian settlement at Kirkintilloch before Columba reached Iona, and Glasgow was still a swamp. 'We were on the maps of Imperial Rome,' he once declared, 'its outmost frontier, at the limits of the then known world, when the wild boar was still rooting among the brushwood on the site where Glasgow now stands.'

The remains of a Roman wall heightened his schoolboy interest in the ancient mysteries which surrounded the town. 'I remember being specially thrilled by speculations that the Syrian bowmen who left their tablets on the nearby Bar Hill were the first cohort of the Hamii who mayhap had in their ranks men whose fathers, uncles, or grand-fathers, were soldiers present at the trial and execution of Christ,' he wrote.

Long before he settled on journalism as a career, Johnston was afflicted with what he called the scribbling itch. Still at school he realised big money could be earned from an interest in writing. His homework was often neglected, or abandoned, while he was still a pupil at Lenzie Academy as he laboured to create pulp fiction, hopefully directed at filling the pages of popular magazines.

If he ever wanted to follow the example set by Charles Dickens, a recent living writer when Johnston was a boy, there was certainly enough to inspire him in the conditions which then existed in the poorer parts of Kirkintilloch. But in early attempts at published fiction Johnston showed no interest in veritas; although, by his own admission, he enjoyed 'sudden bursts of affluence' as a result.

The story-lines Johnston created for *Pluck* and *The Marvel* demanded nothing more than 'high drama on every page, camp fires and pemmican and bison steak, and in the end victory for the righteous and the forces of law and order'. His rampant imagination produced characters who were 'quick on the draw and capable of shooting a midge's wing at 30 yards'. The tyro author, putting aside his homework and labouring nightly to create the mesa and the canyons of the western badlands in the shadow of the Campsie Hills, didn't bother 'to swot up on the geography of the Mexican border'. There was no need for detailed research, as Johnston acknowledged. 'You just invented it, in the sure and certain knowledge that your reading public was as little primed on the matter as you were.'

Johnston had been shaped, educationally at least, by the rigours and determination of his teachers at Lairdslaw Public School, Kirkintilloch, and neighbouring Lenzie Academy. Family and friends, including a succession of dedicated stern Scots dominies who supervised the years of early learning, expected the conscientious, earnest young man with a flair for words and a serious outlook on life to complete his studies with a degree course at Glasgow University. Nobody questioned his capacity

15

for hard work and he was sound enough academically. Indeed, the promising youngster with the vivid imagination was so thoroughly schooled in the rigours of Caesar's Gallic Wars that, more than half a century later, he could boast his ability to recite 'the second book, beginning *Cum esset Caesar*, right through to the end with barely half a dozen promptings'.

But long before he arrived at Gilmorehill, as a mature student, in the summer of 1907 journalism and politics dominated Johnston's sense of himself. Between leaving school and arriving at Gilmorehill as a non-graduating student studying moral philosophy and political economy he engaged in some 'evasive and delaying action' as a junior clerk working in the offices of an iron foundry and an insurance company. He was similarly unenamoured by earlier attempts to interest him in a law career. As he wrote in his *Memoirs*, almost half a century later: 'I had firmly determined I was not going in for law. A brief day in an uncle's office where I was given foolscap sheets of elaborate legal blethers to copy, about first party of the second part and the like, sickened me.'

Johnston despised inherited wealth. Writing in 1909 he maintained 'the present House of Lords is composed largely of descendants of pirates and rogues'. Yet the enterprise which finally shaped his life was a gift of birth; a direct result of his mother's prosperous family connections. *Forward* newspaper, the cornerstone of his working life, owed its existence, almost entirely, to Johnston's foresight and energy. But the circumstances which encouraged this endeavour could be credited, no less significantly, to the beneficence of an elderly relative who was 'persuaded to risk handing over to me one of his many subsidiary enterprises: a printing establishment and the editorship of two weekly papers'. One of the newspapers which had been delivered to his trust was 'a weekly largely concerned with grocers' grievances'. It also 'specialised in fama derogatory to the Co-operative movement' which Johnston supported.

The aspiring editor and future statesman believed there was room in the market for a paper devoted to 'socialist propaganda for key men and propagandists'. The same printing press which had been used to revile some of the most cherished beliefs of the labour movement now targeted its detractors. Johnston enlisted the support of friends, including Roland Muirhead, a tannery proprietor and prominent nationalist, to help finance the venture. The first issue of *Forward* appeared on 13 October 1906: 'We betake ourselves with a light heart to our business,' Johnston wrote.

Newsagents had been targeted in advance of publication with the promise that the first issue of *Forward* would 'mark the beginning of a new era in the progress of Socialist, Trades Unionist and Democratic thought in Scotland'. It would be 'non-sectarian and non-bigot', the editor promised. 'Progressive thought is wide in its sweep and the Truth arises from the clash of opinions. The unpopular will not be boycotted because of its unpopularity.'

Johnston and his backers couldn't be accused of spreading socialism by stealth. The name of the new paper was emblazoned against a dark hillside, the rays of a joyous sun rising behind it. Eight broadsheet pages, six columns across, set in a good clean typeface, supported the challenging masthead. It was exactly the right moment for the new paper to appear, Johnston argued, in an introductory leading article. 'For many a year the massed forces of reaction, the plunderers, the conservers, the old women in trousers, the farthing reformers, have had it all their own way,' he thundered. With one accord, from *The Scotsman* in Edinburgh to the *Evening News* and the *Daily Record* in Glasgow, the capitalist press 'stifles, throttles, sneers, misrepresents and caricatures the wailing shriek of the underdog for justice', Johnston continued savagely. 'Our method will simply be no method and every method. In the slaying of bogus reforms and bogus reformers, in the stirring of public conscience, in creating enthusiasm, in injecting the virus of life in the dull, and discontent (which precedes change) in the dormant, we shall be bound by no hackneyed or cast-iron method. Any method – every method – may be tried. We do not believe in consistency to convention.'

The campaigning young editor refused to permit advertisements for alcohol, or any gambling news, to sully his cherished endeavour. As he recalled later: 'Time and again it looked as if our ship was heading for the bankruptcy rocks, but somehow we always escaped.' A long and distinguished list of contributors, attracted in its early days by the fervour of the editor, no doubt helped to save the paper from ruin. H.G. Wells provided a full-length novel: Keir Hardie, Ramsay MacDonald, James Connolly, John Wheatley and Patrick Dollan wrote regularly for its columns. Other notable bylines, over many years, included George Bernard Shaw, Bertrand Russell, Ethel Mannin and Harald Laski. A friendly Fleet Street rival, the *Daily Herald*, found *Forward* at the height of its powers under Johnston 'full of fact and fire and punch, shining with idealism and sparkling with humour'. Another distinguished Scottish editor, Alastair Dunnett, whose own career embraced long periods at the *Daily Record* and *The Scotsman*, thought *Forward* 'differed from all its dim contemporaries in the fact that it used the popular newspaper devices in a good-humoured way to put over its message. There were comic strips, fiction serials, hilarious footnotes, mickey-taking interviews, gossip columns, reports in depth.'

It was Tom Johnston, one of the most gifted journalists of his day, according to his long-serving deputy and successor as editor, Emrys Hughes, who made the paper. His personality was 'stamped on the front page, on the headlines, and everywhere else'. Johnston always claimed he was flattered when Lord Northcliffe, proprietor of the *Daily Mail*, offered a four-figure salary in return for his services in London. But he declined on the grounds that 'acceptance would mean parting for ever with any capacity I had for usefulness in the affairs of my world'.

Alastair Dunnett, who also worked closely with Johnston as Chief Press Officer in the Scottish Office during the Second World War, believed it was at *Forward* that the future Secretary of State for Scotland 'learned or developed his great flair for getting the facts. Nobody who dealt with him in later years ever risked taking a half-baked story or proposition to him and he was often able to overcome even ingenious opposition by simply a dogged production of facts that refuted flamboyant and emptier claims.'

Johnston revelled in his role as editor and publisher of *Forward* for more than 30 years. The newspaper sold 30,000 copies a week in its heyday and dominated much of his life. 'Millions of words I must have written in propaganda,' Johnston recalled years later. 'But it was a good free life and I do not regret an hour of it.'

As a campaigning young editor, who believed *Forward* could be used to castigate a moronic establishment and flay the rich, Johnston commissioned and cajoled other contributors of similar political stamp, supervised the newspaper all the way through to publication, responded to the inevitable deluge of criticism, and outraged letters, which followed every issue, before proceeding to begin again on the following week's offering of rough and tumble comment, near libel, considered opinion and simple bile.

The Case for Women's Suffrage, a pamphlet written by Johnston in 1907, argued strongly in favour of women's rights. A year later, in a pamphlet dealing with the railways, Johnston advocated full-scale nationalisation with compensation granted to former owners. He believed all land and industry should be owned by the state: in the House of Commons, more than 30 years after starting *Forward,* he argued strongly in favour of the state and local authorities acquiring 'rural and urban land at every convenient opportunity, such acquisition to be based upon fair compensation'. The existing system, which allowed a few people to own the land while the vast majority of people were landless, was wrong and should be abolished, Johnston, by this time a distinguished Member of Parliament and a former Cabinet Minister, insisted. In its place he wanted 'a system of ownership in which we can all be the owners through the State, all inheritors in our native land by virtue of our birth and our service to the community'. It was hardly surprising that for most of his long life he made enemies, especially among the old landowning families of Scotland – 'a selfish, ferocious, famishing, unprincipled set of hyenas from whom at no time, and in no way, has the country derived any benefit whatever'.

Social historian Robert Keith Middlemas considered one series of articles, *Our Noble Families*, written for *Forward*, the 'most caustic arraignment of the Scottish aristocracy ever committed to print'. Emrys Hughes noted with glee how his old chief 'applied every abusive adjective in his extensive repertory to the Scottish landed aristocracy'. Added Hughes: 'With its quotations, references and acid comments it was an extremely informative, readable and devastating book, as effective a piece of polemic as had ever been published in Scotland.'

Hamish MacKinven, one of Johnston's leading latter-day admirers, considered the writing 'vitriolic and redolent of Scottish theological pamphleteering in the 18th and 19th centuries'. MacKinven admits *Our Noble Families* was blatant and inflammatory in style. But he also contends the original articles, and the book which followed, provided 'a philippic powerful and devastating as any in British radical writing'.

Johnston was accustomed to the limitations and pressures imposed on his writing by the demands of a weekly deadline. He probably quite enjoyed the idea of his articles achieving lasting form by becoming a book. As a full-time professional journalist operating in a highly competitive market he was certainly entitled to make whatever money his work merited – without having to justify his actions to anyone but himself, then or subsequently.

Yet, years after *Our Noble Families* achieved considerable, and lasting, notoriety for the rich quality of its invective, Scotland's most distinguished elder statesman maintained he was motivated entirely by the 'earnest requests' he received from a large number of people who didn't want the information buried in the files of *Forward* but 'widely disseminated among all varieties of social reformers'. Priced one shilling, its appearance was deftly timed to coincide with a cherished plan for a Highland Land League, which also appeared in *Forward*, and the so-called People's Budget, presented in Parliament by Lloyd George.

Johnston, the self-declared propagandist, began with a broadside, a ferocious opening indictment, in which he thundered: 'The histories of our land have been mostly written to serve the political purposes and flatter the conceits of our aristocracy. When the historian knew of happenings calculated to cast odium on our landed gentry, he carefully excised the records, and where he did not know, he was careful to assume, and lead others to assume, that the periods of which he was ignorant were periods of intense social happiness, wherein a glad and thankful populace spent their days and nights in devising Hallelujahs in honour of the neighbouring nobleman.' A democracy ignorant of its past couldn't analyse the present or shape the future. 'In the interests of the High Priests of politics and the Lordly Money-Changers of Society, great care has been taken to offer us stories of useless pageantry, chronicles of the birth and death of Kings, annals of Court intrigue and international war, while withheld from us were the real facts and narratives of moment, the loss of our ancient freedom, the rape of our common lands and the shameless and dastardly methods by which a few selected stocks snatched the patrimony of the people,' Johnston claimed. 'Generation after generation, these few families of tax-gatherers have sucked the life-blood of our nation; in their prides and lusts they have sent us to war, family against family, clan against clan, race against race; that they might live in idleness and luxury, the labouring man has sweated and starved; they have pruned the creeds of our Church and stolen its revenues; their mailed fists have crushed the newer thought, and their vanities the arts.'

According to Johnston, writing in 1909, the same privileged class burned and destroyed national records and scorned every principle of morality the people of Scotland considered important. They also gambled and murdered and robbed and foisted numerous children of illegitimate lusts on the granaries of the common people. Mostly, they were 'descendants of foreign freebooters who forcibly took possession of our land after the Norman conquests in 1066. Year after year they still drive the people from the soil, huddling them in stinking cities, bereft of opportunities for the only trade they know: agriculture. And so the poors' rate rises and competition among city labourers for vacant situations becomes keener and wages fall. And so misery and drunkenness and destitution and physical degradation eat like evil ghouls at the very fibre of our national life.'

Ramsay MacDonald, born in Lossiemouth, the illegitimate son of a Scots ploughman and a servant girl, and only a year away from leadership of the Labour Party, contributed a preface in which he echoed Johnston's chief concerns. 'How far has the country as a whole acquiesced in the actions of these favoured individuals, and how far has this acquiescence bound their iniquities like a millstone round our neck?' The future Prime Minister showed nothing but contempt for families 'who have grown rich by laying their hands upon property that belonged to other people and who have increased their estates by a ruthless exploitation of smallholders and peasant owners'. MacDonald believed that 'for such men to talk of land taxation, compulsory land purchase, and the other items of a socialist land programme as injustice, is nothing but impertinence and hypocrisy, which ought to be characterised as such in the plainest of language, both inside and outside the House of Commons.'. Johnston's book, which was based on a wealth of references concerning the early history of 25 leading Scots families, provided a valuable contribution to the scientific side of socialism, MacDonald added. 'The story of the people in history is the best handbook for the guidance of the people in politics.'

Johnston always enjoyed scouring among the dark, dangerous debris of Scottish history. He revelled in the excitement of peering in corners, opening doors and glancing in cupboards shut tight for hundreds of years. Still, the ambitious young editor, intent on building his career and anxious to improve the circulation of his newspaper when *Our Noble Families* first appeared, could be charged with sensationalism, even cynicism, in his account of the histories of many of the families portrayed. Historian Robert Keith Middlemas believed *Our Noble Families* 'played without restraint on the reservoir of real class hatred in the Clyde'. Significantly, in his youth at least, Johnston considered the original articles 'mere preliminary indictments, affording, perhaps, a basis on which future democratic historians will build, but in themselves merely stray leaves from the records of the past, hastily linked together to form a suitable weapon for the campaigns of the immediate future'.

Johnston's view of history, and the various examples of political character assassination contained in *Our Noble Families* evidently appealed to large numbers of ordinary citizens. The modest–looking, brown-backed, 138–page volume was an immediate bestseller. By his own account the delighted author was due royalties on 120,000 copies, 'a phenomenal figure!'.

Emrys Hughes, who joined *Forward* 15 years after *Our Noble Families* first appeared, remembered seeing copies of the book piled high in an office of the Civic Press when he arrived for his first meeting with Johnston. 'It had become recognised as a socialist classic, to be found on every socialist bookshelf, a book well thumbed and passed on,' Hughes recalled. It was reprinted regularly and continued to sell steadily until the author brought its publication to an unexpected halt when he was invited to join the wartime Coalition Government headed by Winston Churchill.

Some years earlier he had been blackballed from membership of the Caledonian Club in London because of *Our Noble Families*; or so Johnston always believed. If his instincts were right the snub was immense. Johnston had been Lord Privy Seal in the second Labour Government. He could expect a place in the Cabinet if Labour won another election and he was still an MP. His sponsors were the Hon. A.D. Cochrane, who defeated Johnston in the Dunbartonshire by-election in 1932, and Walter Elliot, an old friend from Glasgow University, who became Minister of Health and Secretary of State for Scotland in Tory administrations. None of this counted for much with some members of the Caledonian Club, however: the affront caused by the author of *Our Noble Families*, decades earlier, continued to rankle. And, as an amused Johnston later testified, ' there were irate old aristocrats who rose from their corner seats and squelched the nominators and their nominee'.

Many of his old comrades, who remembered the author's pride in his work, and the certainty of his opinions, were dismayed when Johnston, in his memoirs first published in 1952, repudiated a significant portion of what he wrote more than 40 years earlier. They were entitled to harbour a feeling of some surprise when the once-youthful-editor-turned-elder-statesman suddenly averred, 'Although in their heyday many of these old families had ridden their powers with arrogance, selfishness and cruelty, still, looking back upon it, there were at least some descriptions in my collected tracts, *Our Noble Families*, which were historically one-sided and unjust and quite unnecessarily wounding.'

Emrys Hughes believed 'there was something to be said for the young Tom Johnston in reply to the rebukes of the old one'. He conceded the book may have been scurrilous. 'But vehement and vitriolic as it was, was it not for the most part true? Indeed, re-reading it,' Hughes went on, 'I thought it rang truer than the apologia. The fierce, abusive young radical was far more readable than the unconvincing elder statesman.'

In an exercise as strange as it was futile, during his extensive post-war travels in villages and towns throughout Scotland, Johnston never passed a bookshop without inquiring after extant copies of his once precious book. Hamish McKinven, who accompanied him on many of his travels, doesn't doubt he 'put booksellers throughout the country on the alert to buy any copies of the book which came their way and pass them on'. His behaviour intrigued MacKinven who advised readers of a 1991 issue of the *Scottish Book Collector*, 'We do not know what he did with any such copies, how many came his way, nor the total cost of this bizarre book-buying.' MacKinven, a junior colleague, once asked his old chief why he wanted the book forgotten. Johnston shrugged. 'Times change, MacKinven,' he replied. 'Times change.'

CHAPTER TWO

JOHNSTON PROBABLY MADE as much as he wanted from his brief spell at Glasgow University where his contemporaries included James Maxton, O.H. Mavor and Walter Elliot. An essay on freedom and the law, written in 1909 while he was studying at Gilmorehill, clearly pre-empts his later concern with citizenship. 'The state is more than mere geographical area,' he wrote. 'It is more than an agglomeration of people, more than government: it is no alien or antagonistic power compelling us in ways we would not otherwise go. It is the society which gave us our all: gave us great traditions, a finished language, nurtured us in our infancy, gives us a basis in the past, a status in the present and potentialities in the future.'

He already believed that 'behind all law lies the acquiescence of the individuals who obey the law; and even if all coercion were abolished tomorrow, we should, most of us at any rate, regulate our conduct in harmony with the rules or laws beside which the policeman stands today'. To the future statesman trying to articulate his beliefs the rule of law 'guards a man's best against his worst. It is freedom in self-imposed chains. It is the universalising of the best. It is the promotion of machinery for self-government.'

Johnston had been allowed to enrol as a non-graduating student, reading Moral Philosophy and Political Economy. He never intended pursuing a degree. *Forward*, with its punishing, exhilarating schedule, absorbed most of his energy and attention during the two years he spent at Gilmorehill. However, his tactics, as chairman of the University Socialist Society, during a high-profile Rectorial election in 1908, caused particular alarm in high places. Johnston and a group of rebels from the University Fabian Society were pressing the claims of Keir Hardie against

Lloyd George and Lord Curzon. 'At that time the unemployed were being processioned with banners in great numbers through the streets of the city, and the authorities were becoming increasingly anxious about the preservation of public order,' Johnston recalled.

Even within his own camp, few people believed Keir Hardie, although famous as a founding member of the Labour Party, and its first MP, could defeat either Lloyd George, who was about to embark on a seven-year stint as Chancellor of the Exchequer, or Lord Curzon, a former Viceroy of India. But the robust nature of the socialist campaign undermined liberal and conservative complacency in the surrounds of Gilmorehill. The election was finally won by Curzon, from Lloyd George, with Keir Hardie polling enough votes to deprive the future war leader of victory. However, long before the votes were cast, let alone counted, fear of defeat at the polls panicked opponents of Labour who 'let loose the news of their intention to prevent by force the Keir Hardie supporters from recording their votes', an amused Johnston recorded years later.

With an appropriate sense of mischief Johnston and his committee invited 'the unemployed leaders to make a public announcement that they intended organising a march to Gilmorehill to see fair play for Keir Hardie's supporters at the polling booth'. The combative leaders of the city's unemployed, who included Emmanuel Shinwell, a future Member of Parliament and for years a colleague of Johnston on the Labour benches at Westminster, willingly pledged their support. They also added, for the benefit of anyone who questioned the seriousness of their intentions, what Johnston himself considered 'some alarming elaborations' on how students wishing to vote for Keir Hardie in the university elections would be fully protected.

A public declaration of the workers' plans caused fear and alarm in the City Chambers. Johnston and the other committee chairmen were summoned to a meeting with the Lord Provost, the Chief Constable, the Principal of Glasgow University, an officer from Maryhill Barracks and the Town Clerk; all seeking 'assurances from each of us that the other two parties would be allowed to vote. This was an assurance I could cheerfully and easily give without waiting for the Principal's homily about the fear of the beautiful university buildings being destroyed by a mob,' Johnston later recalled.

Johnston would have been less than prudent as a young man if he wasn't seriously impressed with the attitude and presence of the Chief Constable, James Verdier Stevenson. There was nobody in Glasgow who didn't know about Stevenson, a handsome, moustached man with a keen sense of his own importance, and a hardman approach to the job of policing. Stevenson was Irish-born, from County Westmeath, and a man with a reputation for tough tactics long before he gained lasting notoriety for his handling of the police response to the George Square riots more than a decade later. Stevenson wouldn't be standing for any nonsense from any of the lads at Gilmorehill. Principal Sir Donald MacAlister's expression of civilised concern, as Johnston described the scene, was followed by 'the Police Chief's more specific and forthright declaration that he was darn well not going to have it'. In the end, Johnston recorded, the vote passed without incident and everybody was happy.

This cheerful conclusion ignored all hurt suffered by Lloyd George. He had been defeated because of the votes which went to Keir Hardie with Tom Johnston's active involvement. The great Liberal statesman didn't know it then, of course, but he and his young nemesis from the 1908 Glasgow University rectorial election were destined to clash again.

Tom Johnston's interest in active politics centred initially on a desire to play some small part in the governance of the ancient and Royal Burgh of Kirkintilloch. He was just 21 and barely entitled to vote on his own behalf when he first sought election to the local School Board, representing the Independent Labour Party.

The poll which successfully launched his eventful political career was conducted under a cumulative vote system which allowed voters one vote for every available seat. 'If there were seven seats an elector could give all his seven votes to one candidate, or he could distribute them in any proportion he chose among the candidates,' Johnston explained years later. 'The system was PR gone crazy, or, if you like, gone crazier, and it had some curious electoral results.'

As a candidate for the Kirkintilloch School Board his platform included better pay for teachers, a higher school leaving age and evening classes in citizenship. He believed hunger prevented many children from taking full advantage of school. When the 1908 Education Act authorised school authorities to provide meals and clothing for underprivileged children Johnston suggested the money could be recovered from people who, for the moment, preferred to spend their money on 'riotous living, drinking and smoking'. He dreamed of Kirkintilloch becoming a city 'purged from poverty, where the people are strong in mind, healthy in body, sober and industrious, happy and joyous. But if we are ever going to achieve it we must start with the children,' Johnston declared.

It was probably to keep him quiet and out of mischief, Johnston suspected, that, following his election, he was made convener of the Evening Classes Committee. This was generally considered the least important appointment available to those luminaries who had been elected to serve on the Kirkintilloch School Board. Johnston refused to think of the job as a chore; and began a campaign to attract higher Government grants to the town.

Higher grants, to support night classes, were available in direct proportion to the number of people who were registered at the time of the application. Johnston wanted the money to assist the general good. It didn't matter that there was little interest among young people in the town for extra-curricular activities of a serious kind. Johnston employed quiet cunning to encourage their interest: anyone who attended classes in subjects as diverse, and previously unpopular, as maths, sewing, English, mining and building construction, were allowed free admission to dancing classes which he also organised. Johnston, by his own admission, provided a first-class band and a first-class dancing instructor. The pupils formed their own governing committee to maintain discipline and order. 'The experiment was a great success and we had to limit the first dancing class to 100 dancers,' Johnston later recalled. '*Pari passu* the other education classes shot up in number.'

In 1912 he was one of five candidates for two places on Kirkintilloch Town Council. Rejected by the voters, he was unable to play any part in the election of a new provost. However, his failure to win a council seat left him free to castigate the men who had been entrusted with supervising the town's affairs. 'To see the snob class you must go to Kirkintilloch,' Johnston cried, for all to read, in the columns of *Forward*. 'The real, genuine, undiluted, unadulterated, undisguised snob; illimitable in his unconscious class priggishness, encased in unutterable caddishness – the snob unashamed and unrepentant, you'll get him in the Town Council of Kirkintilloch.'

Bailie Daniel Jack, the man Johnston wanted as provost, had been a councillor for 13 years and the acting provost of Kirkintilloch for most of the previous year. A douce, decent Scotsman, according to his friend, Tom Johnston, he was a man of irreproachable character, a lifelong abstainer, well read, a pioneer socialist, quiet and unassuming. However, he was also a working man who returned to his tenement home at the end of his day's work with his hands and face blackened with foundry grime. And it was for this reason, Johnston alleged, that a local businessman was elected provost of Kirkintilloch in his place.

An old working man had been contemptibly insulted, Johnston raged, and through him the working class had been insulted. It was, he claimed, a symptom 'of the desperate length to which middle-class snobbery and middle-class prejudice and middle-class interests will go in their struggles to prevent the working class from getting a square deal'.

Johnston, who was first elected to Kirkintilloch Town Council in 1913, believed a council containing a dozen members was just the right size to serve the interests of a small community. 'Today,' he complained in his *Memoirs*, written after the war, and after years at the centre of great events in the nation's history, 'so much of our business is conducted furth of the town and at daytime meetings, that we have lost a large choice of vigorous personnel for our representatives, and have in part substituted either a professional delegate group, who require the allowances for time off from their daily avocations and whose employers can afford to let them go, or in part a brigade of retired or ornamental personages whose time is their own.'

According to the recollections of its most distinguished former servant, Kirkintilloch Town Council never felt 'unduly bound by use and wont'. As Johnston put it, remembering how the men responsible for the immediate governance of Kirkintilloch conducted their affairs, seated in the little council chamber in East High Street, between 1913 and 1923, 'We pioneered'.

His earliest efforts on behalf of the good burghers of Kirkintilloch included an experiment in cinema distribution. There was no statutory power which allowed the council to run municipal pictures. But Johnston and his colleagues were short of money to fund a diverse programme of civic entertainments. 'The tablets of the law on the subject were frequently and solemnly laid before us,' Johnston recalled, 'but there was nothing the Town Clerk could find in the law books to stop the council fitting up its town hall with cinema projectors, screens and all the appurtenances, and letting the hall so equipped to a small group of councillors who chose to call themselves an Entertainments Committee, and who hired a spare-time manager.'

To the annoyance no doubt of cinema magnates everywhere, including Glasgow, which was already a great cinema city a dozen miles to the south, the bold councillors of Kirkintilloch reduced prices by as much as a third – and immediately filled their makeshift picture palace. Out of the profits the council provided free Christmas treats, galas and fêtes for the children of the town, with 600 prizes for the sporting events. In addition, Johnston recorded, 'we brought first-class lecturers and Beecham opera artists, and we imported the best army bands to play in our public parks'.

Money earned from the cinema experiment was also used on one occasion, following the First World War, to purchase a consignment of surplus civilian suits and army kilts from a warehouse in Bradford at 'phenomenally cheap rates'. The suits were bought at 50 shillings, plus carriage from Bradford, and sold, without profit, for 52 shillings in Kirkintilloch. They were splendid suits, made of good material, Johnston attested. 'The Provost always wore one when he was giving official interviews, saying it gave him elegance and dignity.'

Johnston believed a community was obliged, in all good sense, to capitalise on its own resources to the general advantage of all its citizens. Troubled times lay ahead, however, when, in 1920, as convener of the Law and Finance Committee of Kirkintilloch Town Council, he persuaded a majority of his colleagues to extend the principle of free municipal enterprise to banking.

A similar venture, the brainchild of Neville Chamberlain, and the first of its kind in Britain, had been launched with great success in Birmingham in 1919. However, as Tom Johnston observed in his memoirs published more than 30 years later: 'Had we sought to go through the hoops that Lord Mayor Chamberlain and his Birmingham City Council had to jump ere they got their parliamentary powers to start a municipal bank we should have been jumping at these hoops still, and with a pretty bill in legal obfuscation for our citizens to meet.'

Kirkintilloch didn't need parliamentary approval to register a majority of its members as a limited liability banking company. 'I had only to persuade a majority of the council to agree to have the majority registered as a company under the Companies Act 1908 to 1917 and to agree that the company when formed should be called the Kirkintilloch Municipal Bank Ltd.,' Johnston recalled.

A loan from the Common Good Fund covered the £40 cost of floating the company. Paid-up capital amounted to seven shillings, subscribed by Johnston and six other councillors. Johnston, as convener of the Law and Finance Committee, was appointed chairman. Council staff, including the Burgh Treasurer, added banking duties to their customary labours. 'Once a municipal bank company is registered,' Johnston explained in his 1934 book, *The Financiers and the Nation*, 'its modus operandi is simple. The shares in the new company can only be held by members of the council, and no member may hold more than one share, which he must give up to his successor when he demits office; no profit or dividend is, or can be, paid on the shares, and no "director" can get remuneration for his services.'

The Kirkintilloch Municipal Bank opened for business on 22 March 1920, complete with ledgers, safes, passbooks and all the other paraphernalia essential to such an important undertaking, not least a shiny new nameplate attached to the grey sandstone wall of the municipal building in the centre of the town. Invited to invest their precious savings in an untried enterprise run by members of the local council, operating under another name, the good burghers of Kirkintilloch were entitled to consider their proposals carefully.

Security against a run on funds was obtained from the Scottish Co-operative Wholesale Society. However, as Johnston insisted in *The Financiers and the Nation*, 'as the municipal bank is bound by its constitution to invest its monies only with municipal departments which have the security of the rates behind them, the savings of the worker deposited with the municipal bank are absolutely guaranteed'.

When the Kirkintilloch Municipal Bank began seeking accounts potential customers were also reminded that interest on savings deposited in a Post Office or Trustee Savings Bank earned no more than 2.5 per cent. However, when the town council 'borrowed money for gas works, or public parks, or water works, or any other statutory purpose, they were compelled to pay anything from 3.5 per cent upwards, and for temporary and short–term period borrowings as high as 5.5 per cent'. Johnston and his fellow directors offered a half per cent improvement on the rate offered by all the main Scottish banks. They also proposed charging the town only three per cent on its borrowings. Both rates contrasted hugely, and favourably, with anything on offer elsewhere. As money poured into the Kirkintilloch burgh coffers at an encouraging rate, the douce Scots town in the shadow of the Campsie Hills was able to clear its debts; and eventually achieve a threepence reduction in the rates.

'Of course there are objections,' Johnston admitted in *The Financiers and the Nation*. 'It is always much easier to suggest and imagine difficulties than to conceive and carry through any change which relieves the community of a portion of the financial incubus which strangles and paralyses municipal effort today.'

Despite repeated appeals from the Association of Municipal Corporations and the Institute of Municipal Treasurers and Accountants, the Government refused to allow other municipalities in England and Wales to follow the example set by Birmingham. But in Scotland, where the Government had been unable to prevent the Kirkintilloch Municipal Bank opening its doors to the public in 1920 under existing legislation, other towns, such as Irvine, Clydebank, Motherwell, Peebles and

Selkirk, soon followed their example – with 'phenomenal' success, according to Johnston.

In its accounts for the year 1932–33, the Kirkintilloch Municipal Bank, which served a population of only 12,000 and faced fierce competition for the townspeople's loyalty and funds from a thriving Trustee Savings Bank, revealed deposits totalling £68,354. That same year in Motherwell, where the council didn't launch themselves in the banking business until 1924, the municipal bank was the custodian of £315,101 belonging to local savers.

Johnston found himself 'introduced to public meetings as chairman of one of the Scottish banks, and no doubt perhaps when eminent functionaries in Edinburgh heard of the description,' he observed wryly, 'it but added to their displeasure and disgust at the entire municipal banking project'.

His brainchild was just six years old when the financial establishment in London – the high priests of moneylending, as Johnston called them – reacted forcibly to prevent the spread of municipal banking throughout Britain. Birmingham, in particular, alarmed the Treasury not least perhaps because in that major city of the empire, when it started, the municipal bank was headed by a prominent establishment figure, the Rt. Hon. Neville Chamberlain MP.

A committee of inquiry, headed by Lord Bradbury, was appointed to report on this dangerous and unpredictable phenomenon; and wasted no time bringing some cheer to those major financial institutions, with their headquarters in London and Edinburgh, who feared their continued happy existence might be threatened. When the report of the Bradbury Committee appeared, with unusual speed, in 1928, Tom Johnston wasn't at all surprised by the negative nature of its conclusions. In *The Financiers and the Nation* he maintained: 'From its composition the report was almost as predictable as would be one from a committee of butchers set to inquire into vegetarianism.'

To the relief of the clearing banks especially, Lord Bradbury and his colleagues suggested the Treasury should seek to secure an early Government ban on the use of the word municipal in the title of any banking company; or any other term which might suggest connection with a local authority.

The Bradbury Committee opposed the general policy of allowing municipal banks under any circumstances. However, they appeared reluctant to tackle the well-established, and successful, Birmingham Municipal Bank head-on. It might have been difficult, and at the very least awkward, for Lord Bradbury and his colleagues to recommend closing an enterprise started by Neville Chamberlain, former Chancellor of the Exchequer and future Prime Minister. But neither did they wish to see another municipal bank sanctioned for at least ten years – 'the precise period recommended to them by the Governor of the Bank of England', Johnston claimed.

The committee's recommendations were duly enshrined in the Companies Act of 1929. This allowed existing municipal banks in Scotland to continue largely as before. However, the use of the word municipal in the title of any new bank was no longer permitted. Whoever else happened to be converted by the findings and recommendations of Lord Bradbury and his Committee of Inquiry, at least one knowledgeable reaction was typically bleak. Tom Johnston, the original driving force behind the Kirkintilloch Municipal Bank Ltd, believed the financial establishment was telling the country that municipal departments needed to avoid the peril of cheap money. Otherwise local councils might become spendthrift and reckless. Now the public had been warned off the banking course, time-dishonoured methods of exploiting the ratepayers would continue, he claimed.

The final and conclusive recommendation he offered, as late as 1934, for a wider adoption of municipal banking was his unequivocal insistence that 'there is not a single town councillor of any political party in any city or town where a municipal bank has been established who would propose to disband that bank. Not one. Whatever else there may be local disagreements about, there is none over the desirability of maintaining and developing it.' A municipal bank, once established, offered 'a standing illustration of the developing civic spirit, an essential support to all the other municipal enterprises and a partial relief to the community from the terrible exactions of private banking', Johnston argued.

It pleased him that every £1 million, or every multiple of £1 million, raised from the citizens for the citizens' business was another block of capital removed from the orbit of the private speculator in finance. He acknowledged readily enough that it was difficult to estimate what proportion of municipal bank money was so-called new money. Neville Chamberlain estimated the total amount of new money deposited with the Birmingham Municipal Bank at between 75 and 80 per cent; a figure the Bradbury Committee refused to accept. They claimed it was no higher than 25 per cent. 'Even so,' Johnston observed, in *The Financiers and the Nation,* 'that extra saving of 25 per cent indicates clearly that by municipal banking we can get into effective municipal use about £100 million presently retained in jugs or in pockets.'

His interest in local government survived the years. Despite his high place in the affairs of the nation during the final months of the second Labour Government, Johnston continued to believe firmly in the importance of government at the narrowest community level. As Lord Privy Seal he defended 'parish pump patriotism' on the grounds it took account of community experience where the interests of the citizens were common and obvious. These interests could include family traditions and personal association, Johnston explained; even, he suggested dreamily, 'affinity bonds through the hill, the stream, the bridge, or the mould of the old churchyard'.

At a ceremony in Kirkintilloch Town Hall on 4 July 1931, at which he became the first freeman in the history of the ancient burgh, Johnston claimed there had been a misguided attempt at the destruction of local government, in parish and burgh, in recent years. Local knowledge had been replaced with an impersonal county authority, with no time or desire to acquire it. And an area of opportunity for the generation of new ideas had been wantonly and foolishly limited, Johnston complained.

Councils which met in the evening could draw their personnel from wide sections in the community, the Lord Privy Seal explained. But only a small and diminishing class of representative could attend meetings during the day. Because of this, he believed, vast numbers of men and women of administrative talent would be lost to local government in the years ahead.

His audience, which consisted largely of councillors, officials and their wives, was also invited to consider the likelihood that waste and inefficiency would be the inevitable result if local government affairs were passed to salaried officers, operating at county level, who were physically unable to supervise the detailed work of a widely scattered territory. 'The time has come when we must take a firm stand against any further encroachment upon burghal rights and upon the essentials of democratic and effective local government,' Johnston declared.

CHAPTER THREE

JOHNSTON REACTED BITTERLY, on grounds of conscience, to the First World War. His writing mixed hatred and contempt of the power élite he blamed for starting it with compassion and humanity for the great mass of people who suffered because of it. There was nothing ambiguous about his methods, or the message he wished to convey, expressed angrily for as long as the conflict lasted in a running series of front-page updates, 'Socialist War Points'. There was never any flag-waving rhetoric from the editor of *Forward*. Quite the reverse! The week it all started he warned his readers that Britain was going to war 'in a cause in which we have no interest, in which we were never consulted, and from which by no conceivable result can we derive any advantage – only starvation, hungry children, crying in the streets, bones lying in the battlefields, widows, orphans, tears'.

In one wartime pamphlet he employed raging, colourful invective to condemn the European nations' reliance on secret diplomacy to settle their differences before the war. If negotiations had been conducted openly, guided and controlled by public opinion, 'Europe would not have rocked as with an earthquake, nor would the lurid flames of a million burning homesteads have licked upwards to the heavens, nor death and disease and sorrow have come so unexpectedly and so unbidden into the lives of common men'. Men were no longer prepared to murder one another for the Love of God or Bonnie Prince Charlie, Johnston suggested. 'Nowadays they will organise murder for nothing less than fair interest upon investment and more opportunities for extending that investment.'

Worried about the course of the war and the need to increase armaments production on the home front, the Minister of Munitions,

David Lloyd George, arrived in Glasgow on 24 December 1915 to address a workers' rally in St Andrew's Hall. On his appointment to the new and crucially important Ministry of Munitions from the Treasury eight months earlier, Lloyd George had been ordered 'to ensure such supply of munitions for the present war as may be required by the Army Council or the Admiralty, or may otherwise be found necessary'.

Britain continued to depend on a volunteer army – 'drawn almost exclusively from the better class of artisan, the upper and middle classes' – to hold the line against Germany. Lloyd George favoured conscription. He also wanted 100,000 skilled munition workers released from active service and returned to their civilian occupations with all possible speed. Without the services of essential war workers, Lloyd George warned, he couldn't possibly succeed.

Special powers bestowed on the Government by the Munitions of War Act 1915 were predictably draconian. Factories producing munitions were placed under complete Government control. The movement and supply of labour was restricted by means of a system of leaving certificates. There was a ban on strikes and strike leaders faced the threat of prosecution in the criminal courts.

Skilled workers, encouraged by the Government to move voluntarily to other parts of the country, as required by the demands of the war, reacted indifferently. As the official history of the Ministry of Munitions suggested, 'family ties, local connections and prejudices, difference in manners, mode of living, and dialect, the craftsmen's expectations, and conservative habits' all contributed to the scheme's failure. Faced with a serious shortage of skilled labour, Lloyd George and the rest of the Government, headed by Asquith, were forced to rely on unskilled workers to keep the troops supplied with guns and ammunition. So-called dilutees, including a conspicuous number of women, began appearing in yards and factories, either to replace or augment skilled workers. Not surprisingly, the pay and conditions of the new workforce attracted the attention of trade union leaders who were determined to maintain their members' hard-won differentials and other rights.

Tom Johnston sympathised with craftsmen who 'saw their little safeguards disappearing'. He also acknowledged 'there was great apprehension about the high-handed way in which the Ministry of Munitions appeared to be importing thousands of dilutees'. Although writing about his feelings years after the war ended, Johnston continued to believe the diminution in differentials when 'added to the impact of thousands of strangers on an already overcrowded and inadequate housing system, created in every union branch a steadily growing resentment'.

However, as Robert Keith Middlemas noted in *The Clydesiders*, shop stewards who saw the necessity of using dilutees in wartime 'objected to women working on the same terms as men'. According to Middlemas they also claimed certain rules contained in the Defence of the Realm Act 'tied a man to his work as if he were a slave. That no dragooning could compare with the military discipline which they had been spared seems not to have occurred to them.'

The Government-sponsored rally attended by Lloyd George in St Andrew's Hall, Glasgow, on the afternoon of 24 December 1915 was carefully ticketed: trade union members who wished to attend were paid six shillings, in lieu of lost time, for their interest. The nation's future war leader was perhaps the greatest orator in the land, famous for his powers of stern persuasion and endless charm. On this occasion at least, however, there weren't many among the capacity audience of trade union members, stamping their feet and roaring their disapproval, who were prepared to give him a hearing. Long afterwards Tom Johnston commented: 'A more unruly audience surely never gathered in Glasgow.' Lloyd George was accustomed to mesmerising audiences of all shades and sizes. However, struggling to make himself heard above the din, he was finally forced to stomp from the platform, defeated by the anger of his trade union audience, his speech unfinished.

The public humiliation heaped on Lloyd George, a senior member of the Cabinet, demonstrated a serious measure of disillusionment, on Clydeside at least, with the Government's conduct of the war; and with the future war leader's view of himself as a man of the people. Fortunately for the Government, and Lloyd George's peace of mind, wartime censorship rules allowed officials to impose their version of the day's events on newspapers. An official hand-out, written in advance, offered a sublime version of what occurred. Tom Hutchison, a reporter from *Forward,* told a different story.

He assured his editor that the 'smoothly fabricated and all-was-well stuff' issued to the newspapers by the men who manipulated the Whitehall news machine didn't square with his own verbatim account of what happened. This appeared in the New Year's Day issue of *Forward.* All references to military affairs had been removed but otherwise 'we published the lot', Johnston declared proudly.

The report, spread across several columns, detailed the distinct lack of respect which had been shown to Lloyd George on his visit to Clydeside. Johnston enjoyed himself hugely at the Minister's expense. From the reporter's notes, he utilised amusing examples of the heckling and rough good humour which accompanied the great man's speech. As the editor of *Forward* soon learned, however, his idea of a joke differed greatly from that of the man who was destined to lead Britain to victory in the war. When the 1 January 1916 issue of *Forward* reached London the subject of its main report 'completely lost his sense of proportion and ordered a complete raid of all copies of the *Forward* in every newsagent's shop in Scotland'. A party of plainclothes policemen arrived at the offices of the Civic Press in Howard Street and took command of the building. They were acting, the House of Commons learned later, under the Defence of the Realm Regulations at the instance of the Minister of Munitions.

Lloyd George was adamant: the raid on *Forward* was totally unconnected with the paper's treatment of his St Andrew's Hall speech. That, said the future war leader, was 'a childish, fatuous, silly suggestion'. The ban had been imposed because *Forward* was guilty of publishing, in cumulative fashion, several articles designed 'to stir up friction among workers in the most important munitions district in the country'.

Few people appeared to believe the Minister of Munitions' version of events. But the ban on *Forward,* which lasted five weeks, wasn't lifted until Johnston and his lawyer, Rosslyn Mitchell, signed an undertaking 'not to issue or publish any matter calculated to prejudice the military interests or safety of the country in the present crisis'. They also agreed that *Forward* wouldn't impede or interfere 'with the production or supply of munitions of war or cause disaffection with the Munitions of War Acts or with the policy of the dilution of labour'.

Johnston took the whole of the front page and much space inside the 5 February issue to deny the main thrust of Lloyd George's charge. He also wanted compensation. None was forthcoming. In fact, as Johnston was the first to admit, his row with the future Prime Minister brought *Forward* thousands of pounds worth of free advertising. It also guaranteed a substantial increase in circulation when the paper next appeared: an additional 10,000 copies a week was a useful measure of its new-found notoriety.

Two years before the war ended Johnston also outraged big business, and anyone else making money from the war, with a hard-hitting pamphlet entitled *The Huns at Home*. A nation's hour of distress and extremity was capitalism's hour of greatest opportunity, Johnston declared. With the nation fighting for its life, 'Capitalism will raise its rate of interest upon money loans; it will increase its shipping freight charges; it will raise land rents; it will increase its charges for coal, iron and food; it will hold up supplies of vital commodities; it will, in short, exhibit itself even more nakedly than it does in time of peace, as the real enemy of the people'.

Within days of the Armistice which brought the First World War to a stuttering, bitter conclusion, the Prime Minister, David Lloyd George, announced a general election which was a historic occasion in its own right. It was the first one-day election ever held in Britain and women over 30 were voting for the first time.

Lloyd George had been the architect of victory in the war: six weeks after the Allies were able to secure the end of hostilities, a contorted electoral pact with the Tory leader, Andrew Bonar Law, virtually guaranteed he'd add the people's endorsement to his year of triumph.

It is probably impossible for anyone who is part of a generation approaching the millennium to imagine a general election campaign anywhere in the world without television. But in 1918 the first public demonstration, by John Logie Baird, of the invention which made him famous was eight years in the future. Almost half a century of political scheming, rancour, debate and noisily failed ambition, together with another global conflict, separated candidates in the first election following the First World War from the television age.

Anyone who aspired to the House of Commons then was obliged to meet their would-be constituents face-to-face. Election issues were the subject of fierce and serious debate involving a wide cross-section of the community. Well-attended open meetings were held in public halls across the country. Heckling was considered a cherished part of the democratic process and no one attending a meeting was evicted for disagreeing with the platform party; or showing any signs of disrespect for the important personages seeking the favour of their support.

Tom Johnston was a Labour star, famous as the crusading editor of *Forward* and author of *Our Noble Families.* Pressured by James Maxton to become a candidate, he represented the Independent Labour Party in West Stirlingshire and was immediately a major attraction in the village halls which provided the main venues on the campaign circuit.

Although, with his handsome presence, he could occupy a room, or command the rowdiest audience as he walked on stage, he was never a good public speaker in the accepted rousing, declamatory sense. His delivery was often dull and uninspiring. It would have been folly, considering his dour perseverance, to compare him with any of the great public speakers of his time. Among his contemporaries Lloyd George, Churchill and Maxton himself were acknowledged masters of the art. Johnston always assembled a strong case and an army of facts before launching an attack. He relied on the peculiar, biting, savage quality of his words and the force and decency of his argument to floor an opponent. But his assaults on people and policies were always most effective when delivered in print.

During the 1918 election Lloyd George was seeking to return to Downing Street at the head of a Coalition Government in which his natural political foes, the Unionists, would be the hugely dominant party. The once and future Prime Minister was anxious to prevent the war becoming an excuse for passion or bitterness during the general election campaign; a view supported by the *Glasgow Herald.* It believed the total absence of any such feelings on polling day 'was a tribute to the good sense and serious mood of the new electorate called, as it was, to decide the most momentous issues in the long history of the country'.

Yet, for most of the campaign period, the spectre of an evil war was never far from people's minds. A large proportion of the population blamed Germany for the catastrophe and showed little sign of forgiveness. Lloyd George, hounded by the newspapers for his opinion, was alert to the public mood. He acknowledged the war was a crime, a frightful and terrible crime, for which the Kaiser must be prosecuted. 'The men responsible for this outrage on the human race must not be let off because their heads were crowned when they perpetrated the deed,' the victorious Prime Minister declared to general acclaim.

In the mixed rural and mining constituency of West Stirlingshire and Clackmannanshire, in central Scotland, two other candidates offered themselves for election in opposition to the reluctant Tom Johnston who held out nothing for Labour's chances. Harry Hope, who won the seat for the Conservatives four years earlier, had been endorsed as the official Coalition candidate. This endorsement was part of the highly destructive electoral pact agreed between Lloyd George, on behalf of his own supporters in the Liberal Party, and Bonar Law for the Conservatives. It was thought to bestow a considerable advantage on the nominated candidate and was highly prized. Harry Hope believed Germany should be made to pay for the war; although, as his Labour opponent noted, without rancour, many years later, 'how they were to pay, whether in ships, coal, or free labour, or what' was never clear.

However, the barely remembered Unionist serving the Coalition cause in West Stirlingshire wasn't alone with this dilemma. Some of the most famous names in history, contesting the 1918 election, appeared equally baffled. Winston Churchill, campaigning successfully on behalf of the Liberals in Dundee, thought it might be an idea 'not to take ships from the Germans, but to make them build for us'. A doubtful strategy – militarily, economically, industrially and, not least, socially – which Sir Eric Geddes, the First Lord of the Admiralty, was quick to condemn. *Forward,* the unequivocal voice of the Labour candidate in West Stirlingshire, also condemned the idea. Its dismissive verdict: 'Mr Churchill is only a political charlatan who talks claptrap.'

43

Lloyd George, who would be pursuing Britain's interests and claims for reparation at Versailles, believed 'Germany must pay the cost of the war up to the limit of her capacity. The only restriction is that she must not pay it in such a way as will inflict more damage to the country that received than the country that pays.'

No one expected Tom Johnston, representing the ILP, and his Tory opponent to find common cause on a matter of any importance affecting the long-term good of the country. But this was never the case with his Liberal opponent, R.B. Cunninghame Graham, an old friend. Graham was an aristocratic adventurer and former Liberal MP, descended from King David. For more than half a century he contrived to pursue several different careers in politics, writing and business. Successful as a writer of travel books, short stories and essays based on his experiences in Spain, Morocco and the Argentine, he was known respectfully as 'Don Roberto' across two continents, and counted George Bernard Shaw, Joseph Conrad and W.H. Hudson among his friends.

The elegant, bearded figure of Don Roberto was once a familiar, if unlikely, sight in West Stirlingshire when he owned an estate at Gartmore. On a morning's ride to Lake of Menteith, on the fringe of the Trossachs Hills, dressed in full South American riding garb, cavalry-style hat, a large scarf, arranged with casual exactitude, long tunic and high-boots, with sharp-pointed spurs, he looked the perfect man of the plains, a real gaucho, astride Pampa, his favourite horse.

Despite his exalted line, Graham had been treated kindly in *Our Noble Families*. Johnston called him an intrepid Socialist leader who went to gaol for the unemployed; referring to an incident in 1887, early in his erratic and eccentric political career, when the laird of Gartmore, along with John Burns, pioneer socialist and Labour MP for Battersea, had been imprisoned for taking part in an 'illegal assembly' in Trafalgar Square.

A year later Graham, who was the Miners' Justiceman during his time in the House of Commons, was elected first chairman of the Scottish Parliamentary Labour Party. According to Johnston in *The History of the Working Classes in Scotland*, the SPLP, which was eventually suppressed in its original form by the National Labour Party, emerged at a time when there was 'a slow but steadily growing tendency to a working-class political party – a party suffused, stimulated and inspired by an incessant socialist propaganda'. Its near-revolutionary aims included free education, state insurance against sickness, accident, death or old age, an eight-hour working day, with a minimum weekly wage, supported by adult suffrage, payment of MPs, Home Rule for Scotland, abolition of the House of Lords and a sweeping programme of nationalisation to cover the banks, mining and all means of transport; plus land taxation and a cumulative income tax beginning at £300 a year.

Writing, with obvious whimsy, in *Our Noble Families,* the editor of *Forward* informed his readers that friends and acquaintances of 'this direct descendant of the Earls of Menteith, in the male line of succession' often hugged themselves imagining what might happen if the Stuarts returned and Graham was elevated to the Scottish throne.

When the errant Scots nobleman brought the Irish trade union leader, James Larkin, to Glasgow on 10 December 1913 the editor of *Forward* chaired the 'fervently enthusiastic' meeting which welcomed Graham and Larkin to the City Hall. At this meeting, held during the course of a long strike involving the Transport Workers Federation, Johnston proposed a resolution calling on the Government 'to withdraw military and police support from our capitalist enemies'. A few weeks later Johnston offered his support when Graham became a candidate for the Lord Rectorship of Glasgow University in opposition to Andrew Bonar Law and Lord Strathclyde. In the end all three candidates withdrew when Britain declared war on Germany, and the Rectorship was bestowed on the President of France, unopposed.

Before the war Graham considered Germany a civilised nation, not unlike Britain; maintaining blithely, 'If we go into battle and she beats us, honour to the better man. In dealing with civilised men you may expect honourable terms.' Now, as a Liberal candidate for Westminster, he placed himself squarely on the side of hardline opinion: the Allies were entitled to make Germany pay 'to the uttermost farthing' for the war. The man once described as an intrepid socialist leader also maintained, 'This was not a war of capitalists. It was the working men of Germany who sang the hymn of hate.'

Graham claimed he was contesting West Stirlingshire, in direct opposition to Tom Johnston, because his Labour opponent was a pacifist. In fact, Johnston, strictly in accordance with ILP policy, had been a conscientious objector during the First World War. He was never at any time in his life a pacifist: a pacifist would have been hard-pressed co-existing with Churchill in the Second World War.

However, in December 1918, at the end of a long and bloody war, few people understood or bothered to learn the difference. R.B. Cunninghame Graham did. But that didn't stop him offering to make a present of petticoats, openwork silk stockings and suspenders to anyone who had been a 'conchie' during the war; most notably his Labour opponent. In *Cunninghame Graham*, a critical biography, two of his most recent biographers, Cedric Watts and Laurence Davies, offer the opinion: 'This basely emotive attack must have cost Johnston many votes; a correspondent to the local paper urged working men and women to vote for Graham rather than for the pacifist who had failed to support the war against barbarism.'

Graham had been too old for service when the war started and remained a civilian, in the pay of the War Office, who 'sent him to South America to buy horses for the Western Front. In terms of his knowledge of horses and South America, he was the best man for the job, with unrivalled experience; the bitterness lay in the fact that Graham, who so often protested against the inhumanity of man to the animal kingdom, should now select the animals to die in the mud, gas and shellfire of the European war.'

Watts and Davies concede their subject's treatment of Tom Johnston during the 1918 campaign was a blot on his record; similar to 'some act of cruelty or treachery' found in accounts of the conquistadors, written by Graham himself.

Johnston, who didn't believe for a moment he could win, preferred to avoid becoming ensnared in 'loud yelling exercises' with opponents; although he acknowledged 'partisan controversies and strifes' were a routine hazard in politics. By dismissing his chances of success in the 1918 election he demonstrated a properly developed sense of political reality following the war. It would have been foolish in the extreme not to ignore almost any insult hurled in his direction by an ungrateful old comrade with a sense of mischief and no more chance of winning. Petticoats, openwork silk stockings and suspenders were dangerous props in any political debate or age. However, there is nothing in his own brief account of the 1918 election campaign to suggest he harboured any grudge against Graham who was later elected first president of the Scottish National Party. Cedric Watts and Laurence Davies acknowledge it was his rival's magnanimity, and cheerful good humour, which eventually erased the blot they perceived in Graham's campaign record. As Johnston saw it, with wicked good humour, Mr Graham, representing the Liberals, 'enlivened affairs by denouncing the late William Ewart Gladstone and telling the electors that if they could not see their way to vote for Graham, to vote for Johnston and not for Hope'.

When the votes were finally counted in the 1918 general election there were few surprises anywhere; not least in West Stirlingshire and Clackmannanshire. Tom Johnston and R.B. Cunninghame Graham couldn't muster enough support between them to defeat Harry Hope, the defending MP. Hope was the man favoured by Lloyd George and Bonar Law, chief architects of the Coalition. He also appealed to more than half the voters in West Stirlingshire. The number of votes cast for Hope totalled 6,893, giving him nearly 52 per cent of the poll and an impressive 23.2 per cent majority over Johnston. With 3,809 votes he attracted less than 30 per cent of the poll, while Graham, who had been struggling throughout the campaign, with no endorsement from Lloyd George, finished last with 2,582 votes, representing 19.4 per cent of the poll.

Tom Johnston, the reluctant candidate, had been right. The seat was unwinnable – then!

CHAPTER FOUR

ALTHOUGH HE RETREATED finally from some of the wilder pronouncements contained in his original arraignment of Scotland's flawed nobility, *Our Noble Families*, Tom Johnston never abandoned any of the conclusions he reached in *The History of the Working Classes in Scotland*. This was a bleak, thundering crusade of a book which appeared two years after his first assault on the House of Commons and more than a decade after Johnston used the pages of *Forward* to blast Scotland's hapless aristocracy.

Mostly it was used to deliver a hard, savage indictment of irresponsible and unrestrained capitalism. A catalogue of misery, full of anger and contempt for a system which treated ordinary working people without regard, it recounted the horrors of working-class existence across several centuries of bitter struggle. In it Johnston maintained: 'No pen will ever paint even a dim picture of the horrors of the early years of the capitalist system in the factory towns. A plethora of labourers, cottars from the soil, handicraftsmen from the villages, driven to little, over-crowded, bleak and cheerless hovels, hastily erected around the factory walls; compelled to sell their toil in foul and filthy working conditions, and for the barest pittances; from dawn to sunset bullied and oppressed, the last ounce taken from their bodies by scarcely less oppressed over-seers; hunger, misery, dirt; no sanitary or factory regulations; no machinery fenced; their children killed off like flies, and they themselves emaciated, consumptive, and without hope; no trade union or friendly society benefits; no co-operative societies; no holidays at the seaside; no part in citizenship; the only relaxation being on the Sabbath, when a clergyman, voicing the desires of his chief paymaster in the raised pew, would urge submission to the present Hell as a qualification for the Paradise to come.'

According to Johnston 'recurrent trade crises, panics, over-productions, slumps, market gluttings were all used to crush the worker back to the barest level of physical existence, consistent with his ability to stand at a machine, and indeed not always that'. In the early years of the 19th century the pauper children of Edinburgh had been dispatched to David Dale's cotton mills in Lanarkshire 'where they slaved from six a.m. to six p.m., and all over Scotland the master handloom weavers were indebted to the Poor Law authorities for a supply of cheap child labour'.

Johnston also found that an Act of Parliament, passed in 1840 to 'prevent poor little boys and girls from being sent up sooty chimneys as brushers or cleaners by enterprising chimney sweeps', was only partially observed more than 20 years later. To his amazement it was reported by the Children's Employment Commissioners that boy-sweepers were on the increase in 1863 'because the fine of £5 levied upon the master who employed them was so harsh that magistrates were indisposed to convict'.

The *Glasgow Weekly Herald*, never a left-wing sheet, writing about Johnston years later, commended *The History of the Working Classes in Scotland* as 'one of the grand and deliberately unbalanced publications of our time'. Its author clearly intended to cause offence and stimulate fury; even a degree of class hatred. But unlike the embarrassment he suffered in later years over *Our Noble Families*, the celebrated elder statesman never felt obliged to apologise for any part of the monstrous succession of 'slaveries, robberies, murders, class cruelties and oppressions' which stained almost every page of this brutal account of the lives of ordinary people throughout the long span of recorded history.

From 1760 onwards great mechanical inventions transformed the basis of industry from the domestic circle to the factory floor. But even before that happened, Johnston demonstrated, capitalist practices were not unknown. In 1663, for example, the old Scots Parliament conferred special powers upon manufacturing companies which allowed them, with the support of parishes who had been relieved of the burden of the unemployed, to seize vagabonds and set them to work, for periods of seven years, as they alone deemed fit. And there was no mistaking 'the nefarious intent' of some early statutes. Anyone who refused to accept a decreed wage was liable to imprisonment and punishment at the discretion of the magistrates. The price of foodstuffs might rise, Johnston noted, but wages were stationary. However, with the years, 'municipal regulations curtailing wages naturally evoked bitter resentment among the labouring classes and the jails were not built which could accommodate the strikers'.

Johnston was editor of *Forward* – intent, as he once admitted, on providing socialist propaganda for key men and propagandists – when he wrote the original book. A quarter of a century later, when the Unity Publishing Company, with an address in Civic Street, Glasgow, approached him with plans for a fourth edition, he was a Privy Counsellor with a distinguished parliamentary and Cabinet record, and a public figure of considerable importance. It would have been unsurprising if he refused to sanction a new edition of his corrosive early work. However, when a new edition of *The History of the Working Classes in Scotland* appeared in 1946, Johnston contributed a prefatory note in which he proclaimed himself 'rather proud' that nothing had been withdrawn, or amended, from the original. He was also pleased to relate that, despite their diligence, historical pundits and apologists for the existing order of society had been unable to find anything upon which to base a charge of inaccuracy in fact, or of error in interpretation.

With his endorsement of the original text, more than 25 years after its first publication, Johnston was quite clearly reasserting his belief in socialism; and allying himself, to the benefit of his own lasting reputation at least, with the aspirations of the working class. 'Labouring folk all down the ages have clung to communist practices and customs, partly the inheritance and instinct from the group and clan life of our forefathers,' Johnston contended, 'and partly because these customs were their only barrier to poverty; and because without them social life was impossible.'

The 'conscious socialist movement' was barely a century old when he wrote *The History of the Working Classes in Scotland*. 'The horrors of the capitalist system at the beginning of the 19th century generated and nourished in the minds of men of goodwill a passionate desire for more equitable social conditions,' Johnston maintained.

Slavery was the common condition of the overwhelming mass of the working classes from the period of the earliest authentic records down to the later years of the 13th century. Serfs enjoyed 'no rights, no privileges, and no family name and were rated equally with the cattle that browsed upon the meadow and the deer that bounded through the glen'.

Before the coming of steam-power and the industrial revolution, the recurrent wars, famines and dearths produced a great army of migratory starvelings who maintained themselves in their itinerancies upon the charity and generosity of the settled, though scarcely less-starved, peasantry, Johnston reported. He also felt able to insist: 'Modern apologists for the ruling castes in post-Reformation and neo-capitalist times may descant as they will upon the rebirth of learning and upon the industrial and commercial developments of the 17th century; but it is impossible to disguise the fact that the period was one of extreme misery and degradation for the working class – a misery and a degradation so severe and so humiliating that the working class refused to be a working class, preferring the greater part of it, a life of vagrancy and theft.'

The 17th century had been a hard, hard age for Reformers. 'Daring spirits who challenged iniquity and tyranny were assured of martyrdom, each ruling class standing firm and four square, prepared to stick at nothing in defence of its privileges and powers.' But it was the industrial revolution, and the growth of a capitalism unregulated either by law or by sentiment in the early years of the 19th century, which 'began a massacre of human life beside which the casualties of the medieval battlefields and plagues were as farthing dips to the noon-day sun'.

Working conditions, offering starvation wages, which could be as low as 1s 3d – about seven new pence – per day for a miner in 1868, delivered the average city worker to the grave two years ahead of his 50th birthday. Workers who believed conditions could be improved with trade unions were prohibited by law from attending meetings designed to raise wages. Trade union agitators could be imprisoned for three months on the testimony of a single witness. 'Combinations among workmen were naturally driven underground amid a network of secret passwords, signs and grips,' Johnston noted. 'Sabotage, arson and vitriol throwing were substituted for the strike.'

But even these extreme tactics failed to achieve much in the end. There were long periods, Johnston claimed, when activists, who sought to maintain wages by means of a general strike, might as well have struck against the law of gravitation. For 'at every factory and workshop gate there struggled a mass of starvelings eager to be employed at any wages'.

Acute trade depression occurred during the years 1810, 1816, 1819, 1825 and 1826 when 'the social consciousness of the upper classes did not run to much in the way of charity or relief works, so long as the weaker among the working class died with a minimum of inconvenience to their masters'.

Property was sacred and theft, particularly working-class theft, was considered the most heinous of crimes. Little more than half a century before Johnston started writing *The History of the Working Classes* a man who stole 14 shillings was transported for 14 years and a woman who stole a pair of boots was sentenced to seven years' transportation. In 1864, at the Spring Circuit Court in Glasgow, the theft of a lorry cover was punished with eight years' penal servitude; a woman who stole three yards of drugget from a hedge was sentenced to six years; and a man who helped himself to a cloth cap left hanging on a shop door was gaoled for three years. The same eccentric sentencing policy evidently permitted the same Spring Circuit Court to imprison a woman, charged with stealing fourpence-halfpenny worth of copper, to 15 months; which was exactly one and a half times longer than the incarcer-ation ordered for one Alexander Still who struck and killed a man with a poker. Meanwhile, or so it appeared to the angry author of *The History of the Working Classes in Scotland*, 'peculation on a big scale from the public, gambling in food-stuffs, rent-raisings, market riggings by the rich, these, when not openly commended as good business, were privately excused'.

Mandatory trucking, which obliged workers to purchase the necessities of life from stores owned by their employers, had been established in monopoly areas throughout the country. No other shop was allowed to open in the vicinity of a trucking store, and any thrifty housewife who sought to purchase her goods in some neighbouring town discovered that her husband or her son was promptly discharged from employment. Necessities were usually sold at a 20 per cent profit by the store owner, 'and as none durst complain, the storekeeper could make an extra illicit profit by adulteration and under-weighing'. One truck shop manager with premises in Lanarkshire left an estate worth £10,000 when he died 'which indicates something of the profits made, as most of that sum would be extra robbery on his own account after the coal owner had been satisfied', Johnston claimed.

Trucking also allowed employers to conduct business at no great expense to themselves. In one case uncovered by Johnston from the files of the *Glasgow Herald* a workman who sued the Shotts Iron Company in 1859 received only 12s 10d – about 65 new pence – for three years' work. The rest of his wages had been issued in the form of credit lines which were only redeemable in the company store. As Johnston explained, 'Twenty pounds a month kept a large works operating, the wages passing from the pay office to the truck store and from the truck store to the pay office, and sometimes the payment of wages was suspended until the first men who had been paid had purchased goods at the store and thus enabled the store manager to send up the cash to the wages office again.'

The collier had everything trucked to him, except his coffin. 'If he went on strike his children ceased to be educated, for the schoolmaster was trucked, supplied by the employer but paid by the worker, out of levies on his wages.' Workers, paid monthly, were usually in lasting debt to the company store; with interest charged at a shilling on the pound or a penny on the shilling. According to Johnston this 'iniquitous truck theft' was the workers' chief grievance during the middle 1850s 'and against it the workers waged unrelenting war'.

He also found housing conditions vile – 'almost beyond belief' – for most of the period not long preceding the first publication of *The History of the Working Classes in Scotland*. Every new development in machinery, every failure in the crops or the fishings, every fresh importation to the industrial districts, of famished Gaels or starving Irish, submerged another section of the workers. Between 1831 and 1841 the population of Lanarkshire increased by over 37 per cent, 'mostly starving Highlanders or Irishmen, and all of them living precariously in squalor and dirt in ramshackle hovels; the death rates there were never specially collected, and today we can only surmise at the extent of the callously regarded massacre'.

The 1861 census showed more than a third of all families in Scotland inhabiting a single room with a single window: thousands existed in similar circumstances minus the luxury of a solitary window. The wynds of Glasgow had been called the unhealthiest places in Europe. Children of working-class parents inherited only an evens chance of surviving to the age of five.

'During the last 30 years of the nineteenth century there were energetic efforts made to improve the insanitary conditions in which the working class lived and died,' Johnston noted. 'The design was to wipe out contagious diseases, which had the inconsiderable habit of spreading to the habitations of the well-to-do. Cholera and typhus especially were marked out for attack for they notoriously were no respecters of persons; and in the closing years of the century,' Johnston went on, 'when the opinion spread that tuberculosis was contagious, the upper classes took alarm, and tuberculosis, too, was put upon the index. The result has been a decline, due to increased and improved sanitation, in the adult death rate. But infantile mortality among the poor, which is not easily, if at all, transmissible to the cradles of the rich, shows no decline.'

Anyone unfamiliar with Tom Johnston's early career and discovering *The History of the Working Classes in Scotland* for the first time might have been surprised, in 1946, to find a leading member of the wartime Government heartily belabouring the peacetime nobility for the sins of their ancestors. Although Johnston was prepared to admit that some of the descriptions in *Our Noble Families* were 'historically one-sided and unjust and quite unnecessarily wounding' he made no attempt to excise his contempt for 'proud families, whose fortunes rest upon alleged national heroisms, sacrifices, and services rendered by an ancestor in the twelfth, the thirteenth or the fourteenth centuries' from *The History of the Working Classes in Scotland*.

From the comfort of his home at Monteviot, Kirkintilloch, he cast a jaundiced eye on families whose 'hired minstrels and lackey historians still provide schoolbook lies'. It also still cheered him to conclude such families were not 'over kindly disposed to the pitiless and searching analysis to which the modern investigator subjects the Norman struggle for the Scottish throne and its prerequisites'.

Similarly, given an ideal opportunity, with his prefatory note to the fourth edition of his savage early work, Johnston didn't try to suppress, or alter, with the benefit of any hindsight, his original opinion that the 'greater part of the drum and trumpet history and ruling caste ancestor worship' which had been used to prime generations of Scottish children was ridiculous and irrelevant.

The rebel historian's revisionist opinions didn't spare Scotland's greatest hero, Robert the Bruce. His unsentimental view of the soldier-king, as portrayed in *The History of the Working Classes in Scotland*, was bound to antagonise traditional nationalist opinion. Bruce, the victor of Bannockburn, was an icon of lost nationhood. He was revered in classrooms across the land as Good King Robert, the man who persevered; learning, in adversity, from a spider to try, try and try again. As Johnston was careful to point out, however, a close reading of various ancient sources supported his claim that Robert de Brus, the new Anglo-Norman-Scottish noble who had climbed to the throne of Scotland after the battle of Bannockburn, 'played a most despicable, vacillating, and traitorous part' in the drama of his times.

In accordance with his theme, Johnston bestowed the main battle honours at Bannockburn on the working class – the sma' folk and the *poueraille*, or poor people, fighting without armour, who threw themselves on the English host and smashed it to chaotic rubble. 'This light reserve division has been smeared off the battle-picture: not fighting men, only ghillies, only camp followers! An aristocrat lie!' Johnston declared vehemently. 'They were not mail-clad, but they had come to fight, and they were deliberately held in reserve until the first shock of the mail-clad men was over. They were the working class and it was their charge that won the battle of Bannockburn.'

A close study of parish records and other sources also suggested that during the years of the Highland clearances at least 200,000 people had been driven from their homes to make way for sheep. The evictions were conducted with so great a barbarity and on so colossal a scale, according to Johnston, they aroused the anger and disgust of the whole civilised world. A general disposition of the time to regard the Highlanders as a wild, hungry, thievish race, whose extermination would be a national gain, meant he could only provide an approximate arithmetical estimate of the scattering of the Celtic people by the landlords of the north, Johnston admitted. However, as he endeavoured to explain, almost every rural community in Scotland suffered from the clearances – 'from Orkney and Shetland in the north to Galloway in the south, cottagers, cottars, run–rig crofters, and small farmers were swept ruthlessly from the soil, factors scorning their tears and courts of law their rights'.

Thus a steady stream of destitutes arrived in the industrial towns 'owning no capital but their muscles, knowing no trade but that of tilling the soil and herding cattle – destined, if fortunate, they and their children, to the miserable, half-starved drudgery from which an unregulated capitalism wrung fabulous profits; if unfortunate, to a nameless pauper's grave'.

Johnston, with a solid lack of detachment, claimed it was impossible to know for certain how many people were evicted and driven from the glens during the period of the clearances. A few pamphleteers travelled to the Highlands from cities in the south to see for themselves what was happening. But even when writing of clearances within their own cognisance, Johnston maintained, such witnesses 'were always far more concerned to expatiate upon the savagery of the eviction methods and upon the piety and peacefulness of the evicted than upon the actual numbers of people swept from the soil, or upon the brave, determined resistance which thousands of them undoubtedly offered to the destruction of their homes'.

As Johnston explained in 1920: 'To appeal successfully for public sympathy 100 years ago, it was deemed necessary to minimise in every way the turbulent, rebellious occurrences which scared the northern sheriffs and sent many a policeman and estate officer home with a broken head.'

CHAPTER FIVE

FOLLOWING THE BENCHMARK general election of 1922 the most famous group of left-wing standard-bearers ever dispatched from Scotland to the House of Commons arrived in London. Immortalised in Labour lore, they are remembered still, with affection and pride, as The Clydesiders. The political map of Glasgow, where Labour won ten of the 15 seats, was transformed by the 1922 result. But right across the industrial heartland of Scotland, from Lanarkshire to Dundee, people who seldom saw the Clyde put their trust in Labour to change and improve their lives.

Caused by the collapse of the Lloyd George-inspired Coalition, it was the first 'real' general election since the First World War. For the second time Tom Johnston's name appeared on the ballot for West Stirlingshire. But he was pessimistic about his chances. Johnston believed his old adversary, Sir Harry Hope, who had been knighted since the last election and was now appearing openly for the Conservatives, was assured another few years' grace in the House of Commons. For all anyone knew he might be offered a place in the next Government formed by Mr Bonar Law, acting for the Conservatives as well as the King.

Without benefit of hindsight, and the record of history, his colleagues in the ILP, privy to his views and rightly irritated by the gloomy nature of his forecasts, could have been forgiven wishing to replace Johnston with another, more optimistic candidate. More than anything then Tom Johnston derived enormous satisfaction from his work as a journalist: finding a seat at Westminster could never match the joy and excitement of editing *Forward*!

His lack of interest in pursuing serious politics at the highest elected level exasperated James Maxton. Maxton even threatened to disengage himself from Bridgeton, ahead of the 1918 election, if Johnston continued to ignore his responsibilities to the Labour movement and did not become a candidate. 'Not until then did I fall for the apparently "hopeless" seat of West Stirling,' Johnston acknowledged.

In the previous election 13,284 votes had been divided between three candidates in West Stirlingshire. This time it was a straight fight between the Conservative candidate, Sir Harry Hope, and Tom Johnston, representing the Independent Labour Party.

Another 500 people had been added to the voters' roll. In a close fight their votes could be crucial. An improved turnout was also expected. Tom Johnston was the beneficiary on all counts. A combination of voters from the Liberal side, together with most of the people who didn't vote last time opting for Johnston on this occasion, pushed his share of the vote from 28.7 per cent in 1918 to an impressive 52.4 per cent four years later. Of the 17,023 people who finally voted 8,919 favoured the ILP candidate, a majority of 815.

Johnston affected surprise and dismay at the result. It was a harmless bluff: he was entitled to feel pleased with his performance. His 4.8 per cent majority over the Conservative in West Stirlingshire and Clackmannanshire was an important milestone in Labour Party history.

One small consequence of the result certainly amused him. Henceforth, as the Member of Parliament for West Stirlingshire and Clackmannanshire, he could 'irritate the country gentrice' by asserting he represented the Duke of Montrose and Lord Younger, the chief Tory Whip, both of whom kept estates in the constituency'.

The highly charged but far-from-cohesive group who arrived at Westminster in 1922 included the serious-minded and highly respected John Wheatley, representing Shettleston. Many people believed Wheatley should be leader of the Labour Party in preference to Ramsay MacDonald. The long-haired former teacher, James Maxton, was among his most ardent supporters. Maxton, elected in Bridgeton, was an outstanding public speaker and easily the most charismatic figure in the entire Labour group.

Emmanuel Shinwell, the tough union boss imprisoned three years earlier for his part in the George Square riot, was also among those charged, following the 1922 election, with pursuing the Labour cause at Westminster. A natural schemer who outlasted, and outlived, the rest, Shinwell won Linlithgow. Alongside him, Davey Kirkwood, a kindly and impulsive man who shared a High Court dock with Shinwell, was elected in Dumbarton.

'There was no question of us staying in posh hotels, only the cheapest digs,' Shinwell recalled. 'Tom Johnston and Davey Kirkwood shared a flat. None of us ate much and what we did needed to be cheap.'

Free travel for MPs between Westminster and their constituencies didn't exist: £400 a year combined salary and expenses. Most people, including Tom Johnston, couldn't afford the heavy cost involved in a regular round trip between London and Glasgow. Johnston never forgot 'the boredom and weariness of the weekends we Scots MPs from the Clydeside had to spend in London'.

Johnston was widely admired for the bold, attacking style he imposed on *Forward*; and the skill and energy he displayed as a propagandist spreading socialist ideals throughout the country. However, he always insisted he never wanted to be an MP. 'Upon my soul and conscience I never wanted the life Parliamentary, and most assuredly not in London,' he wrote.

When the new Parliament met for the first time on Monday, 20 November 1922, Labour was easily the second largest party in the House of Commons. Bonar Law and the Conservatives, with 347 seats, enjoyed a huge overall majority. Labour, however, for the first time in its history, could assemble the support of 142 MPs, which was comfortably more than the Liberals combined, counting 60 Independent Liberals and 57 of the National variety.

Led once again by Ramsay MacDonald, who had been out of Parliament since 1918, when his anti-war views cost him his Leicester seat, Labour was a party in the process of change. In his biography of MacDonald, historian David Marquand has claimed the man from Lossiemouth was trying to make Labour a movement of opinion rather than of class. If that could be achieved, Marquand argued, Labour could also present itself for the first time as a government in waiting.

It was an eventful first week due, almost entirely, to the unpredictable nature of the fresh Labour intake from Scotland. Summoned by Black Rod to the House of Lords for the Royal proclamation, rough-and-ready Davey Kirkwood, former militant shop steward and MP for Dumbarton Burghs, surveyed the red plush benches, with their ageing occupants resplendent in ermine, and announced fervently to John Wheatley, 'We'll soon change all this!'

The men from the Clyde wasted no time making themselves heard on the country's main political stage. On Thursday, 23 November 1922, on the first day of the opening debate following the King's Speech, John Wheatley, Emmanuel Shinwell and David Kirkwood all delivered their maiden speeches ahead of the new MP for West Stirlingshire and Clackmannanshire.

Philip Snowden, who became Labour's first Chancellor of the Exchequer in 1924, congratulated Wheatley on the best speech of the day. It was also generally agreed that Shinwell, along with another Labour newcomer, Clement Attlee, MP for Stepney, demonstrated a ready grasp of Parliamentary practice.

Davey Kirkwood, in passionate, angry mood, showed little regard for his surroundings, however. As historian Robert Keith Middlemas noted, in his account of the Clydesiders' first day at Westminster, after it was 'disentangled from his broad dialect' Kirkwood's speech was 'almost totally out of order'.

The Government benches were almost deserted, and the few MPs present, tired of baiting Kirkwood, were already calling for an end to the day's business when Tom Johnston rose, around nine o'clock on Thursday, 23 November 1922, to address the House of Commons for the first time. The theme of his maiden speech, unemployment and the plight of the working class, was vintage Johnston.

'We have pleaded with the Government to do something immediately to relieve the agonies, the slow torture and starvation in hundreds and thousands of homes in this country. We are met by laughter, mockery and jeers,' he complained. He was prepared to admit that some who spoke in support of the Labour view hadn't addressed the

House in the polished accents of Oxford or Cambridge. 'We do not pretend to come here to throw about Latin maxims, to utter any pleasantries, or to offer meaningless courtesies. We have come here to ask reasonably and courteously that the Government should face the fact that the common people of our land are in a state of starvation.'

Johnston, who had been called by the Deputy-Speaker to address a near-empty House of Commons, reminded anyone who cared to listen that Britain ended the First World War with a huge debt: between £7 billion and £8 billion. The annual interest on that debt was about £350 million a year, or £1 million a day. 'That taxation has to come from somewhere and the only class who have paid so far have been the working class,' Johnston thundered.

Laughter from the Government benches didn't deter him. Figures issued by the Ministry of Labour showed there had been a reduction in working-class wages amounting to £10 million a week: a £500 million per annum reduction in the purchasing power of the working classes meant the workers hadn't the purchasing power necessary to enable them to buy back in the home markets the goods that labour produced.

'The life, the social happiness of the people, has been destroyed,' Johnston persisted. 'In addition to the £500 million a year cut in their wages, the Government of this country has levied another £180 million of indirect taxation upon the working classes. They have levied on their tea, sugar and tobacco, and also on the beer of those who drink beer, and these taxes are another method of getting the people to pay the interest charge upon the war.'

He evinced no surprise that, on the same day on which the Government increased tax on beer, they reduced taxation on sparkling wines and champagne. Still, he wondered if any answer would be 'forthcoming from the Government benches to the statement that the workers have had their capital levy, that the workers have had to bear, in addition to reduction of wages, short-time employment or unemployment, a huge extra increase in indirect taxation'. He also wanted to know: 'Is there any answer to the fact that while the nation is broken, while the workers have no purchasing power, they are refused the right to produce for themselves, for their own use, and that unless they can produce for the profit and aggrandisement of the trusts and combines and monopolies, they must starve?'

His performance impressed the Labour-controlled *Daily Herald*. According to the party's lone voice in Fleet Street the MP for West Stirling was someone of whom 'great things may be expected'.

Early in the new Parliament one leading Labour figure, Philip Snowden, went out of his way to praise the efforts of the Scots contingent at Westminster. 'They are all socialists to the backbone,' Snowden declared, 'and fearless in expressing their socialist views. They are a fine body of men, with clean minds and healthy appetites.' Snowden believed the solidarity and team spirit demonstrated by the Scots helped other new Labour members develop a sense of comradeship. Thanks to them, Snowden went on, 'the whole Labour Party has been permeated with an *esprit de corps* which it has sadly lacked in the past'.

Snowden, a future Labour Chancellor, also noted how many of the new members were teachers. 'In no part of Great Britain has the socialist movement attracted the teaching profession so largely as in the West of Scotland,' Snowden explained. 'All political parties know that the political influence of the teachers is enormous. The fact that there are so many teachers in the Socialist movement in Scotland no doubt accounts to a considerable extent for its progress.'

According to Snowden people in the public galleries were soon attracted by the appearance of a handsome, dark-haired, clear-featured young man seated on the second Labour bench. This was Tom Johnston, the editor of *Forward*, who had done much to bring about the Socialist success in Scotland. Claimed Snowden: 'His success at the general election was thrust upon him. He has never been much of a platform man, preferring to wield the weapon of the pen. But he was swept into Parliament by the tidal wave, and already has astonished his friends by his ability of speech.'

But not everyone was as kind as Philip Snowden, then. Beatrice Webb found Johnston dour. But she also acknowledged he was 'the best of the Clyde lot'.

During the first few weeks in the House of Commons the new men from Scotland were patronised endlessly. A gallery reporter working for the *Daily Sketch* recorded the opinion that 'Labour members of the present Parliament seem to be particularly well tailored'. It appeared Tom Johnston and Emmanuel Shinwell each owned a blue suit and a grey suit. However, readers of the *Daily Sketch* were informed gravely, both men never appeared in the House of Commons wearing the same colour of suit. 'Some day they will appear in the same colour at the same time,' the writer suggested, 'and so disillusion anyone who may have dared to imagine that Communal principles have invaded the realms of dress.'

But like so much from his life and career Tom Johnston confided little from the period to his self-effacing *Memories*. However, the mischievous nature of some of his early questions suggests the Member of Parliament for West Stirlingshire didn't mind making a nuisance of himself on a wide variety of topics.

He wasn't long an MP before he obtained an apology from the Prime Minister, Andrew Bonar Law, over a high-level gaffe in official correspondence with the French Premier, Raymond Poincaré. Several times, in a letter dated 21 February 1923, Johnston complained, the word England had been used when Britain was correct. He wanted an assurance that 'in all diplomatic correspondence on behalf of the British people care will be taken that the inclusive term British is used, and not the sectional term English'. Canadian by birth, and an iron merchant in Glasgow before he became an MP, Bonar Law apologised at once. 'I committed a grave error which I shall try not to repeat,' he said.

Johnston also questioned moves to hang a painting, depicting the introduction of Viscountess Astor to the House of Commons, in a place of honour at Westminster. She was the first woman MP in history to take her seat at Westminster and many MPs thought the occasion should be recognised. Concerned as always about the facts of a case, Johnston wanted to know when and by whom the decision to hang the painting was taken; and for MPs to be given a say in the project. As his friend and flat-mate, David Kirkwood, reminded the House of Commons, the American-born socialite was only the second woman elected to Parliament. A year before she won her seat at Plymouth in 1919, a Sinn Fein candidate, Countess Markievicz, was elected in Ireland. Lady Astor arrived in the House of Commons to predictable cheers: Countess

Markievicz, who had been sentenced to death for her part in the Easter Rebellion and reprieved, didn't bother to attend.

By his own account, in his first few months at Westminster Johnston wasn't noticeably anxious about the importance of the personages he offended. Early in his Parliamentary career he inquired about Government loans, totalling £3.5 million, to a company irrigating cotton estates in the Sudan. This was the prosperous Sudan Plantation Syndicate which included Brigadier-General A.M. Asquith, a son of the Liberal leader and former Prime Minister, Henry Asquith, among its directors. Johnston professed himself amazed when he learned that Asquith and J.R. Clynes, the former Labour leader, had been at the head of a deputation which approached the Government seeking support for the syndicate months before the loan was granted.

As the former Member of Parliament for West Stirlingshire later recalled, the question and answer raised a howl of indignation. 'Mr Asquith promptly made a personal statement that he had no financial interest in the syndicate, and that he had gone with the deputation, as Mr Clynes had gone, in the interests of his constituents employed in the cotton industry.'

In fact, the former Prime Minister and MP for Paisley was furious with Johnston who hadn't bothered to warn him – 'as is prescribed by the inveterate and honourable traditions of Parliament' – that a question, which was bound to offend against etiquette and also encourage wild speculation concerning his role in the affair, was pending.

Asquith missed the original acrimonious exchange between Johnston and the Government front bench. This occurred during a late-night sitting on 4 December 1922, at the committee stage of the Trade Facilities and Guarantees Bill. Johnston's Parliamentary career was barely a fortnight old and he pronounced himself 'surprised at the absolute lack of information supplied by the Treasury Bench regarding the investment of £3.5 million in the Sudan'.

Told by the Under-Secretary of State at the Foreign Office, Ronald McNeill MP, that all the great textile interests in Lancashire had been pressing urgently for this investment, Johnston demanded to know why the Government was prepared to risk £3.5 million in the 'far Sudan, over which they have no means of direct control, when they continually object to financing similar enterprises in this country on the ground that such enterprise is inimical to the benefit and well-being of the British people'. Johnston also wanted to know what happened in the event the enterprise failed and the money was lost. 'Is the guarantee or provision made so that certain favoured cotton interests in this country can get a cheap subsidised supply of cotton at the expense of the British taxpayer?' he demanded. People were entitled to be told if any of the great cotton interests in this country had been promised a cheap subsidised supply of raw material for their future operations, Johnston insisted.

During one exchange the Chancellor of the Exchequer, Stanley Baldwin MP, claimed he was puzzled at Johnston's use of the word charges. He wished to ask him 'straight out' if he had any charge to make against Asquith. Johnston replied stonily that he never made any charges against the former Prime Minister. 'I asked for explanations,' he declared.

By the time Asquith learned of Johnston's late-night inquiries concerning the activities of the Sudan Plantation Syndicate, and whatever part he'd played in its future prosperity, the mood on both sides of the House of Commons was explosive. Asquith claimed his inclination was to disregard the matter and treat it with contempt. Except there were people outside the House of Commons who believed, not illegitimately, he said, that statements of this kind 'must be made with some measure of knowledge and some sense of responsibility'. Addressing a rapt House of Commons the former Prime Minister denied he had been actuated by 'personal and indirect motives and interests'.

Asquith said he didn't normally attend deputations. Two reasons persuaded him to depart from his usual practice on this occasion. In the first place he had been Prime Minister at the time of the original loan to the Sudan which 'provided the fund under which this great scheme, vital to the cotton industries of this country, was initiated and reached a certain stage of development'. Secondly he had been asked to attend by his constituents in Paisley where the principal industry was heavily dependent on 'the kind of cotton that is grown in Egypt and the Sudan'. The original fund was entirely expended, and the scheme incomplete, when Asquith, together with Lord Derby and the former Labour leader,

J.R. Clynes, approached the Government with a request for assistance. They wanted additional funds allocated 'not to any company, not to any syndicate, not to any body of private undertakers, but to the Sudan Government itself, which alone was responsible, both for the payment of principal and the payment of interest and the supervision of the whole thing', Asquith declared.

Johnston acknowledged he was at fault for not informing the Liberal leader of his question in advance. But he didn't believe the former Prime Minister had been able to controvert in any way whatsoever 'any statement of fact or question of fact made inferentially in the questions I addressed to His Majesty's Government this morning. No single statement of fact, no single figure, has he attempted to controvert in any way,' Johnston declared.

An unidentified MP protested: 'He has repudiated the insinuations!' Minutes later, and much more seriously, he was challenged by no less a figure than Sir John Simon to repeat 'his allegation of corruption or withdraw it'.

Johnston was rescued finally by his leader, Ramsay MacDonald. 'My honourable friend appears here for the first time,' MacDonald, who had been an MP for 16 years, reminded everyone present. 'Those of us who have been longest here know how very difficult it is to observe, with the most perfect rectitude, the relationships that exist between honourable members on all sides of the House. Therefore I am perfectly certain that the House will view with fairness and generosity the incident, the rather painful incident, that has just taken place.'

In the din that followed Johnston appeared to begin an apology of sorts. But he still hadn't managed to comply with his leader's request when the Speaker called the third reading of the Trade Facilities and Loans Guarantee Bill. It was probably a narrow escape for Johnston. Inexperienced in the ways and nuances of the House of Commons he could have been judged guilty of abusing Parliamentary privilege – although he continued to insist, at a meeting in his constituency a few days later and in his own account of the affair published in *Forward* on 16 December 1922, that it never crossed his mind to imagine Asquith had been motivated by any direct financial interest in Sudanese cotton. And many years later, long after anyone could suggest Johnston was unwise in the ways of the House of Commons, his position hadn't changed: it was the Government, led by Andrew Bonar Law, and not he, 'who first introduced Mr Asquith's name as leading the deputation which had urged the Treasury guarantee'.

But in the midst of so much rancour he was probably surprised to find the leading Tory weekly magazine of the period among his few supporters. *The Spectator* acknowledged that Johnston's attack on Asquith was somewhat crude. But the magazine also believed nothing could have been more unsatisfactory than the way in which 'an overwhelming majority of the House of Commons, the party leaders, and the chief person concerned' combined to fall upon the MP for West Stirlingshire. 'One would have imagined from reading the headlines and the summaries that Mr Johnston had been found out in some act of political turpitude and was guilty of the most shameful conduct. Yet, in reality, the worst that can justly be said of him is that he had made a bad blunder in manners.'

The Spectator also maintained: 'If Members of Parliament are to be howled down merely on a point of bad manners when they show an interest in their duty as watchdogs over the public purse Parliament not only ceases to be the Grand Inquest of the nation, but becomes devitalised. In money matters nothing is more necessary than the antiseptic of what we may call reasonable suspicion,' the magazine added. 'No doubt such antiseptics, if used too freely, may burn and injure the skin or the tissue of the body politic. But that is a reason not for roaring out curses on the antiseptic, but rather for discretion in its use.'

In an article which appeared in the *Socialist Review* a month later, the leader of the Labour Party, Ramsay MacDonald, made no attempt to conceal his disapproval of anything that might be deemed unparliamentary behaviour. 'If the party fails in Parliament, it fails in the country,' MacDonald warned, 'and the dream of a Labour Government will vanish for a generation.'

Johnston was not disposed to allow the activities of the Sudan Plantation Syndicate to vanish from public scrutiny, however. More than a year later he complained in Parliament when the first Labour

Government, with Ramsay MacDonald at its head, proposed allocating a further £3.5 million to the same group. A business which paid a 35 per cent dividend the previous year didn't 'require the benevolent support of the British Government, particularly a British Labour Government', Johnston complained.

Neither was Johnston long an MP before he found himself at odds with official Labour Party policy concerning the Empire, later the Commonwealth. Johnston refused to accept the general assumption that 'all colonial development was imperialist and anti-socialist and liable to embroil us in international strife'. The fact so many different people from so many different lands already acknowledged the Crown as a single symbol of unity, and were even prepared to settle difficult inter-nation disputes before the Privy Council, was important and shouldn't be discarded lightly, Johnston believed. In his view, if common purpose and action couldn't be achieved at this level, 'then there was but a poor chance of our succeeding with a League of Nations outside the Empire'.

Johnston claimed it was in everyone's interests for countries inside the Commonwealth to exchange marketable surpluses in production. Such a scheme, properly organised and developed, might lead to an 'advance in human well-being almost beyond our imagining'.

As an example of what he hoped to achieve Johnston once suggested salted herring from Scotland, where there was heavy unemployment among herring fishermen due to the loss of sales to Russia and the Baltic countries since the end of the First World War, and in which millions of pounds worth of public capital invested in the herring towns was at risk, could be swapped for Jamaican citrus fruits. In the West Indies the population was 'avid for salted fish, and possessed of a means of payment in their great surplus production of limes and other citrus fruits. Could not the surplus herring somehow be exchanged for the surplus fruits?' Johnston wanted to know.

Although ambitious and out of the ordinary, viewed positively Johnston's suggestion could be judged sensible enough – assuming the means of delivery and a modest level of commitment on the part of those involved in the business of selling herring and citrus fruits at different sides of the same ocean.

A series of meetings and reports involving the Empire Marketing Board, the Colonial Marketing Board, the Jamaican Chamber of Commerce, the President of the Board of Trade and the Herring Industry Board followed. However, despite this resolute flurry of bureaucratic activity nothing much happened. As Johnston himself noted, ruefully, years later, 'Neither this country nor the West Indies were yet ready for the orderly disposal of surpluses in production.'

Johnston also found himself seriously out of step with some of his colleagues, during his early years in the House of Commons, when 'the very mention of the word tariffs was a blasphemy and defilement in the temple of labour'.

He appeared to identify a serious contradiction in his party's attitude to the use of 'sweated' labour whether at home or abroad. 'There we were as a party struggling to raise standards of living among the producing classes, urging factory Acts and all manner of restrictions and penalties upon employers who underpaid labour and worked child labour for long hours, yet as a party committed to an extreme free trade in the importation of sweated goods, always provided of course that these goods were produced abroad,' Johnston complained.

With the powerful support of John Wheatley and Arthur Greenwood he persuaded the Labour Party to appoint a committee, under the chairmanship of Philip Snowden, to consider and report upon Sweated Imports and International Labour Standards. Child labour in Bengal, prisoners in Belgium and labourers working 13 hours a day, seven days a week, for low wages in China and Japan, were all identified by Johnston and his supporters as the makers of goods against which British manufacturers, and legitimate employers located in other parts of the Empire, were obliged to compete.

It was familiar, well-worn ground for the editor of *Forward* and author of *The History of the Working Classes in Scotland*. The final report, unanimously approved by Snowden and the rest of the committee, which emerged from these deliberations 'did more to shift the Labour Party away from traditional Whigism [sic]' than anything else Johnston could remember. Its main aim was an international boycott of goods produced by countries which failed to implement the Washington Hours

Convention regulating the length of the working day. 'There were only 24 hours a day anywhere in the world,' Johnston explained. 'The number of hours worked could not be confused as could money values and exchange rates and purchasing values.'

The proposals approved by Snowden and the other members of the committee included certain restrictions designed to placate inveterate free traders in Labour's ranks. The committee hoped to achieve an absolute ban on certain imports. They weren't seeking tariffs or imposts upon price to make them dearer. And only commodities with alternative, acceptable sources of supply were affected.

Johnston was happy to tackle the problem one clear step at a time. He was also entitled to believe he had been instrumental in changing traditional Labour attitudes in an important area of human endeavour: seeking to improve the status and conditions of labour in other lands was a new concept in the affairs of men.

Of course, as the editor of *Forward* also recognised, a major improvement in living standards in other countries would lead, inevitably, to an accompanying increase in purchasing power. And that offered Britain and its workforce the chance of developing new and expanding markets.

CHAPTER SIX

IT WAS THE hotly debated issue of free trade which inspired the 1923 general election – 'one of the strangest election campaigns in British history', according to one historian, David Marquand. Bonar Law had been committed to a policy of no tariffs during the lifetime of the previous Parliament. But he had been forced to retire, due to ill-health, after barely eight months as Premier. His successor, Stanley Baldwin, believed some form of protectionism was vital to safeguard the domestic market and help reduce unemployment.

There had been barely enough time since the last election for voters to deliver fair and lasting judgment on the performance of individual MPs elected only a year ago; although in West Stirlingshire, at least, anyone who helped send Tom Johnston to Westminster probably noticed the practised ease with which their man made headlines. They also knew from experience that he wasn't afraid to make himself unpopular with established Parliamentary opinion in his pursuit of social justice, some-times at risk to his own career; a quality he shared with the Clydesiders group who were busy gaining notoriety for the unpredictable nature of their performance at Westminster.

On 4 July 1923, less than six months ahead of the election Prime Minister Stanley Baldwin deemed necessary to protect British trade and employment interests, four Scottish MPs (James Maxton, John Wheatley, Campbell Stephen and George Buchanan) had been suspended from the House of Commons by order of the Deputy-Speaker for calling Sir Frederick Banbury, Conservative MP for the City of London, and other Tories, murderers.

Maxton alleged a Government circular dated March 1922 denied needy mothers and infants milk; and that babies suffering from whooping cough had been refused admission to hospital. 'In the interests of economy they condemned hundreds of children to death and I call it murder. I call the men who walked into the lobby in support of that policy murderers. They have blood on their hands – the blood of infants!' Maxton declared. Maxton, as many listening to him understood, was referring to the death of his own first wife when he said, 'I saw a mother struggling with the last ounce of energy to save an infant life and in saving it she lost her own.'

According to one listener, the MP for East Stirlingshire, L. MacNeill Weir, 'the House listened with the keenest interest for Maxton was making the greatest appeal of his life, an appeal for the underdog and the children of the poor'.

Statistics didn't interest him, Maxton continued movingly. 'I am interested in the tens of thousands of fathers and mothers tonight watching over cots of little babies wondering whether they are going to live or die. If I could strike the public conscience to see that this is absolutely wrong and unjustifiable in a Christian nation I should think I had rendered some service to my country.'

After he called fellow MPs murderers, the Labour leader, Ramsay MacDonald, and the Deputy-Speaker tried in vain to find a form of Parliamentary expression which would save Maxton from suspension. 'I absolutely decline to withdraw,' Maxton insisted. 'The whole business is a matter of historical knowledge.'

It was a moment of deep hatred unusual in the House of Commons. Outside its privileged precincts the remark would have been considered slanderous; although at least one opponent, Walter Elliot, then MP for Lanark, later described Maxton as 'one of the most sincere, most sympathetic, and in many ways, one of the finest characters in the House'.

A motion to suspend Maxton and his friend and political ally, John Wheatley, who repeated the charge of murder directed at the Tory benches, was carried by 258 votes to 70. During the division Tom Johnston urged Maxton not to apologise. 'Every MP who took part in that shameful decision to cut the milk grants to the local authorities, and therefore caused the deaths of children, is himself in fact and in deed a murderer,' Johnston claimed.

Johnston was amongst those who voted against suspension. He later wrote: 'I would rather have died that afternoon than refrain from showing by every means in my power my sympathy and agreement with Maxton. And that evidently was the view taken – perhaps it was not a view at all but an uncontrollable human impulse – by every Scots MP present.'

There was little Ramsay MacDonald could do but sit and fume as Maxton, followed by John Wheatley, and later by Campbell Stephen and George Buchanan, was ordered from the chamber. According to a reporter from *The Times*, the Labour leader was 'white with anger at the folly of his own followers'.

Seeking to present the acceptable face of Labour to the electorate, Ramsay MacDonald set himself two objectives. 'The first was to ensure, if possible, that politics revolved around a struggle between the Conservative and Labour Parties, in which the Liberals could be dismissed as irrelevant,' one major biographer, David Marquand, argued. 'The second was to ensure that the Labour Party presented itself as an alternative government, capable of winning and holding power, not in some remote classless society, but in Britain in the 1920s.'

His methods caused a great deal of heart-searching and no little exasperation among many of his followers. Tom Johnston acknowledged readily enough that MacDonald had been given no easy task making Labour an effective and homogeneous fighting force. But he was equally adamant that differences of opinion regarding tactics and policy should be permitted.

Writing in his *Forward* column, following the suspension of the four Scottish MPs, Tom Johnston complained that Labour was becoming obsessed with the idea of winning power at the next general election. But he also noted the party was required not to scare anybody, in its attempt to win power, especially the middle-class voter. 'Anything in the cargo we carry likely to frighten off a sympathetic bourgeois must be jettisoned,' Johnston, with undisguised sarcasm, went on. 'The *sturmtruppen* must be hidden away with camp followers in the rear; the host that is to march forward to the destruction of capitalism is to be disguised as voluntary welfare workers with elastic-sided boots out for an excursion: we are to promise to do nobody any harm: every change is to be so gradual that no exploiter need be unduly worried: the kingdom of man is to come by stealth.'

But power without the active support of a politically educated working class would last a fortnight, Johnston warned. Unless the Labour Party was successful in 'creating socialist opinion, and not merely an opinion that we are tame and harmless substitutes for the old Liberal Party, we shall only get office and not power. And office without power to do anything with it means disaster.'

During the election campaign Johnston's agent predicted victory for his candidate with an increased majority in West Stirlingshire and Clackmannanshire. The constituency spread across much of central Scotland and Labour had been unable to establish election committees in rural villages and hamlets where Johnston needed to be heard. But the constituency had been well nursed by Johnston and 'there has been a tremendous propaganda which is bound to tell on election day', the agent claimed. Largely for the benefit of the converted who were regular readers of *Forward* he also maintained: 'The Tory candidate, after announcing himself as an anti-Socialist candidate and nothing else, has discreetly dropped all talk of socialism – he doesn't mention it in his election address – but the Liberal candidate has taken up the running in this respect, and he knows as much about the subject as a babe unborn.'

Tom Johnston appealed to the voters on a manifesto which claimed the election wasn't a contest between Protection and Free Trade but between capitalism and socialism. It also maintained: 'The unregulated scramble for private profit, in which thousands of men and women perish, must give way to an orderly pursuit of the common good, achieved by common service. To this end the State must control the nation's credit power, industry must become a public service and land a national heritage.'

Johnston's share of the vote in West Stirlingshire actually dropped in the 1923 general election. However, there was an increase in the number of people voting Labour and Johnston was entitled to consider 51.9 per cent in his favour a satisfactory response to his first period as an MP. The intervention of a Liberal candidate was a blow to the Conservatives. A year earlier, in a straight fight, only 815 votes separated Johnston and Sir Harry Hope. But on 6 December 1923 the same Tory candidate trailed Johnston by 3,060 votes. The figures were: Tom Johnston 9,242; Sir Harry Hope 6,182; and R.I.A. Macinnes, the Liberal candidate, 2.390.

Johnston and another 189 Labour MPs followed Ramsay MacDonald to Westminster where the Conservatives could now muster only 259 seats in the House of Commons. This put them comfortably ahead of Labour, the second largest party with 191 seats – but considerably short of an overall majority given the presence of 159 Liberals under the leadership of H.H. Asquith.

The Times thought the Conservatives and the Liberals should unite in coalition. Other voices, who feared the prospect of a Labour leader in 10 Downing Street, argued for a government of national trustees. Some inside the Labour Party also thought it would be a mistake for Ramsay MacDonald to form an administration in the prevailing circumstances. The veteran trade union leader, Emmanuel Shinwell, who had been returned with an increased majority in Linlithgow, believed there was little 'prospect of promoting beneficial legislation in the interests of the working class with a majority of Conservatives and Liberals in opposition'.

A week after the result of the poll was known, William Stewart, writing in *Forward*, insisted: 'The Labour Party has no right or claim to become the government of the country. It is in a minority in Parliament. When it secures a majority – as it will, in due course – it will put in its claim and exercise its rights to govern the country. Till then we must expect to have a capitalist government.'

Stewart was presumably acting with the knowledge and support of his editor, Tom Johnston. It was certainly Johnston who allowed this trenchant analysis of the choice facing the main political parties to appear high on the front page, in a position of considerable prominence, beneath a two-decker headline, 'To be, or not to be? Socialism or ruin?' It also insisted: 'The business of the Labour Party in Parliament is to prevent them from misgoverning the country, and if in the ensuing clash and struggle, government of any kind becomes impossible, and there is another appeal to the country, it will be the duty of the workers to send the Labour Party back to Parliament in sufficient numbers and with an effective mandate to take office in a straightforward manner without regard to any of the customary tactical – or tactless – manoeuvres and intrigues. It is for this opportunity that Labour in all its sections must now prepare.'

Whatever his critics felt, Ramsay MacDonald believed he was right to claim Downing Street for the Labour Party, assuming Baldwin was unable to command a majority in the House of Commons. If the Liberals were allowed to assume power, the Labour leader argued, most of the opposition benches in the House of Commons would be filled with Tory MPs, reducing the Labour Party presence to the status of a group.

G.D.H. Cole, in his *History of the Labour Party from 1914*, acknowledged that it would have been difficult for MacDonald to refuse office. His failure to accept the challenge of Downing Street 'would have been widely misrepresented as showing Labour's fears of its own capacity, and it would have meant leaving the unemployed to their plight'. In addition, it would have meant 'doing nothing to improve the state of international relations or to further European reconstruction and recovery' – and this, Cole believed, weighed even more heavily than the plight of the unemployed with many Socialists.

At any rate, following the election, Ramsay MacDonald and his supporters moved fast to ensure Labour would form the next government, lobbying furiously anyone of importance and influence who supported Labour. By 13 December 1923 the National Executive, the General Council of the TUC and the executive committee of the Parliamentary Labour Party were all agreed that, 'should the necessity for forming a Labour government arise, the parliamentary party should at once accept full responsibility for the government of the country without compromising itself with any form of coalition'.

Two days later, in a front-page article in *Forward*, Tom Johnston declared: 'There's going to be no Lib-Lab alliance or coalition or understanding. We can dismiss the very possibility of it from our minds.' The Liberal Party was a capitalist party, financed, secretly, by capitalists, Johnston insisted. 'If the Labour Party, which has been formed to get rid of capitalism, were to betray the working class by allying itself with a capitalist party, the Labour Party is finished,' he thundered.

Johnston acknowledged that Ramsay MacDonald 'would require to get a majority before he could carry his budget or take over the mines and the railways. To secure that majority the Labour Party should, in my opinion, fight upon a narrow front. They ought not to load their programme with the work of a dozen sessions.' As he saw it: 'One or two simple issues such as measures for the relief of unemployment, nationalisation of banks, mines and railways, widows' pensions and amendment of the Old Age Pensions Acts, prefaced with a statement that the Labour Cabinet did not propose to take any salaries, would capture the imagination of the country and compel our capitalist opponents to fight upon ground where we would have every chance of success.'

Alongside Johnston, on the same page, John Wheatley, who had been safely returned as MP for Shettleston, following a straight fight with a Liberal, dismissed any thought of coalition with one of the other two parties in the House of Commons. 'The measure of social progress in the future will be the extent to which competitive capitalism is destroyed,' Wheatley argued. He envisaged circumstances in which a Labour Government might introduce a bold socialist policy in the House of Commons, without the support of any other political party, and then seek agreement from the electorate. 'These proposals would be accompanied by measures for the better distribution of national wealth,' Wheatley explained. 'It should never be forgotten that the people of this country are rightly more interested in what they are going to get than in what others are going to lose.'

In his opinion it would be political madness to discourage people from thinking the Labour movement didn't intend to menace vested interests. 'These interests are keeping our people in the depths of poverty and are now actually threatening to throttle our national existence,' Wheatley insisted. 'We must destroy them rapidly in self-preservation. The people of Glasgow will support us in this task, and so will every other section of the populace, if we nail our colours to the mast and leave timidity in the rear.'

Writing in the same issue of *Forward*, another Glasgow MP, James Maxton, professed himself 'not keenly interested' in how the country would be governed during the next few months, since no party had a sufficient majority to rule on its own. 'An immediate general election would suit Labour admirably,' Maxton suggested. 'The party did not have to stretch itself to its limits in the contest just concluded, and, with a fortnight's rest, will be quite fit to fight and capture the 150 seats that are obviously waiting to be seized.'

Johnston, Wheatley and Maxton, writing on the same page, on the same day, in the same newspaper, barely a week after polling, were bound to cause maximum embarrassment to their leader. MacDonald could hardly ignore the demands of three prominent backbenchers, with constituencies in the new Labour heartland of Scotland. MacDonald hoped to achieve socialism by stealth. Johnston, Maxton and Wheatley were men in a hurry. And they wanted to change society now!

His dependence on Liberal support probably worked to MacDonald's short-term political advantage in 1924. A minority government, unwilling to risk defeat in the House of Commons, could never hope to pursue any of the 'simple issues' demanded by the editor of *Forward*.

It was in 1924 that Johnston first encountered Emrys Hughes, his long-serving deputy and eventual successor as editor of *Forward*. Hughes, son-in-law of Keir Hardie, was a fierce pacifist who had been forced to serve with the Third Battalion of the Welsh Regiment during the First World War; and spent most of the war in prison for refusing to comply with service regulations.

A former teacher, Hughes had been working as an ILP organiser when he heard there was a vacancy on *Forward*. His experience of journalism was limited to submitting articles to various periodicals and he travelled to Glasgow from Wales to meet the editor, with no great expectations of landing a job on the paper. At the top of a six-storey building in Howard Street, behind the St Enoch Hotel, he found 'a glass door with *Forward* printed on it and in a tiny room, thick with tobacco smoke and strewn with newspapers, discovered Tom Johnston'.

Johnston was then in his early forties, with 'a mop of black hair, which was going a little grey, a shrewd, rather gloomy, lined face which reminded me a little of the portrait I had seen of Carlyle in his early years: grim, stern, rather fanatical until he smiled. He wore a Gladstonian collar, and a blue spotted bow tie, and was smoking a big pipe. He came to the point immediately.'

Tom Dickson, who had been assisting Johnston on *Forward*, was now an MP, representing Lanark, and they 'needed somebody to bring out the paper during their absences in London'. Hughes was surprised to learn there was no one in Scotland the editor of *Forward* wanted to recruit as his deputy. Johnston evidently thought he was up to the job and wanted him to start immediately. His salary would be £5 10s a week, the editor added. Hughes realised this was the minimum rate for the job permitted by the National Union of Journalists. But he was happy to accept. 'Right,' said Johnston, shaking his hand, 'let's go to Cranston's and meet the boys!'

Hughes remembered: 'Cranston's was the regular lunchtime meeting place of the Clydeside Socialist MPs. There they met, discussed, argued and exchanged experiences.' The group commandeered a round table in a corner of the room. 'With each new arrival,' wrote Hughes, 'the circle grew wider, and the table receded, until they sat with their plates and cups of tea in their hands, or on their knees, interested only in the conversation and the arguments.'

On the occasion of that first visit to Cranston's, in the company of Tom Johnston, the young Welshman was introduced to most of the Clydeside luminaries who were then the scourge of the Westminster Parliament.

'James Maxton was there with his long black hair down to his shoulder and over his forehead, dark face and bushy eyebrows, deep-set blue eyes, looking very grim and sinister,' Hughes noted, 'until his face lit up with a charming smile and one realised that this outward appearance of being the stern revolutionary was really a pose.

'Next to him,' Hughes went on, 'sat John Wheatley, bland, inscrutable behind a thick pair of glasses. He did not say a lot but when he spoke they listened to him.

'George Buchanan, the most youthful of them, red-headed and headstrong, a pattern-maker from the shipyards, had the most to say.'

He also met big Davey Kirkwood, and the Rev. Campbell Stephen, as well as Neil Maclean 'who had been in Parliament for six years and had been censured by the Parliamentary Labour Party for remaining seated when everybody else had risen to cheer Lloyd George on his return from Versailles'.

Later they were joined in Miss Cranston's by others – not MPs – such as 'Hugh S. Roberton, an undertaker and leader of the Glasgow Orpheus Choir, Walter Leishman, a lawyer with long hair and a big head who looked like Karl Marx and was the terror of magistrates in the Glasgow courts, Rosslyn Mitchell, a different type of lawyer, dressed like a dandy, very good looking and very keen.

'It would have been difficult to find anywhere in the country,' Hughes suggested, 'such a collection of colourful and forceful characters as those who used to meet at Cranston's in those days. Some were to make their mark at Westminster, some to disappoint, some to fade out.' Reflecting on the man who introduced him to Miss Cranston's Hughes added: 'Nobody thought he'd become a national institution one day.'

It was typical of the ILP group in Glasgow, and their loudly proclaimed dislike of strong drink, that they should adopt a tearoom as their headquarters; not just any tearoom, of course, but perhaps the most stylish establishment of its kind in what was then a splendid Victorian city.

Temperance was a way of life in the ILP. As the end of the First World War approached and Labour's chances of achieving power at Westminster increased, a survey conducted by the Rev. James Barr showed almost universal support for prohibition among prominent members of the party. Commenting on Barr's findings Emmanuel Shinwell declared: 'If Labour is true to its ideals it must take a firm stand on the liquor question.' James Maxton maintained: 'Recent public house restrictions have shown us that the persons who appreciate the restrictions most are men who are victims of the alcoholic habit. This leads us to the belief that any legislation bringing further restriction would not be felt as harsh, repressive legislation by any considerable section of the community.'

Tom Johnston didn't doubt there had been a hardening of Labour opinion in Scotland in favour of prohibition. People who suggested the average working man was prepared to suffer anything rather than lose his pint were talking nonsense, Johnston averred. Usually, the idea was propagated by people with a financial interest in alcohol, such as brewers and publicans, Johnston claimed. In his view it was an insult for people to talk about ordinary, decent working men in this way.

For almost half a century Johnston's influence helped keep an entire town dry. Six deed polls held in Kirkintilloch between 1920 and 1961 all favoured prohibition. It wasn't until 1968, five years after Johnston's death, that a majority voted to allow licensed premises in the town.

In fact, Johnston was known, on rare occasions, to drink a glass of sherry and Compton Mackenzie claimed he witnessed him drink two large whiskies following a rally in St Andrew's Hall!

CHAPTER SEVEN

RAMSAY MACDONALD had been agonising at his home in Lossiemouth over the names of the men he thought could be trusted with a place in the first Labour Government. MacDonald was determined to appoint people who wouldn't cause any great offence to the established order. 'As he saw it,' David Marquand noted, 'he and his colleagues were there not to defy or even subvert the established order but to infiltrate it – to prove that they, too, could carry on the King's Government if they were given the chance, and in doing so, to consolidate their lead over the Liberal Party.'

On 21 January 1924, more than six weeks after the election, the Government was defeated on a Labour amendment to the address and Baldwin resigned as Prime Minister the following day.

Only a few days earlier, the *Red Flag* and the *Marseillaise* had been sung at a victory rally attended by hundreds of Labour supporters in the Albert Hall. Some MPs wanted to celebrate their leading role in the Government's defeat in the House of Commons by reprising that occasion, complete with revolutionary anthems. To no one's great surprise there were important people, inside and outside the Labour movement, who disliked the connection. Ramsay MacDonald was barely able to keep his ecstatic supporters under control; or so he told the King.

Tom Johnston's omission from the first Labour Government, even at junior ministerial level, was a surprise and a shock to his friends. Some thought it was punishment deferred for his behaviour at the time of the Sudan cotton row and his attack on Asquith.

John Wheatley had been appointed to the Cabinet, with responsibility for health and housing, following a brief trial of strength and bluff with the Prime Minister who wanted him to accept a similar position outside the Cabinet without the same powers; and considerably less status. In his history of the Clydeside group Robert Keith Middlemas commented: 'It would seem that MacDonald was swayed between the obvious dangers of leaving out so prominent a figure, and the fear of having a left-winger of republican views and Clyde wartime background in a Cabinet he wished above all else to be respectable.'

To the bemusement, even horror, of many of his supporters, in seeking respectability the Prime Minister insisted on his chosen Ministers wearing Court dress to meet King George V. According to his biographer, Sir Harold Nicolson, the King 'attached to correctness of vesture an importance that to some people seemed exaggerated'. MacDonald was happy to comply. A gold coat meant nothing to him but 'a form of dress to be worn or rejected as a hat would be in relation to the rest of one's clothes. Nor do I care a fig,' MacDonald confided to his diary on 12 May 1924, 'for the argument that it is part of a pageantry of class, or royalty or flunkeyism. If royalty had given the Labour Government the cold shoulder, we should have returned the call. It has not.'

Tom Johnston took a different view. He disapproved of pacifists who went to levees in knickerbockers and swords. At the height of the row over Court dress he asserted: 'There are people who say this "galoshan" business does not matter. Why worry about it, let us get on to serious business. Alas, the "galoshans" are but the outward sign of an inward dry rot and a party which tamely accepts the mediaeval circus and participates in, and takes a delight in participating in, useless, costly and stupid mummeries, is a party that is not in the way of serious business.'

His treatment of one old comrade, James Brown MP, was particularly harsh. Brown left Annbank Public School in 1874, at the age of 12, to work in the mines. He spent more than three decades working underground before becoming a full-time union agent. A seat at Westminster followed in 1918 when Brown was elected MP for South Ayrshire. After six years in Parliament Brown moved with pride to the Government side of the House of Commons. His appointment as Lord High Commissioner to the General Assembly of the Church of Scotland was another grand step.

Almost entirely self-taught, by way of night school and the Annbank village library, Brown was a voracious reader who acquired a huge knowledge of English and Scottish literature. He was also a strict teetotaller, an elder of the Church of Scotland and a Sunday school teacher for more than 50 years. Brown was the first commoner in nearly 300 years to become Lord High Commissioner to the General Assembly of the Church of Scotland. Ramsay MacDonald probably believed he was acting democratically when he offered the job to a former miner: the post was usually reserved for members of the Scottish nobility.

The ceremonies which he would be required to observe during his stay at Holyrood Palace didn't appear to bother James Brown. But to his Parliamentary colleague, Tom Johnston, he was a sad case. After a long, dignified and honourable career as a representative of the Ayrshire miners Brown was now expected 'to dress himself up in knee breeches and silk stockings and paste buckles on his shoes and a cocked hat with feathers', Johnston complained. He would carry a sword and be called Your Grace! He would 'ride in a coach with outriders and postillions and trumpeters and who knows what useless trash. And thus attired and guarded,' Johnston added, 'he will process up the Royal Mile, through the streets of Edinburgh, to auld Holyrood where he will sleep for 14 glorious nights in a great state bed.'

Johnston hoped the new Lord High Commissioner, who had been given an allowance of £2,000 to cover expenses, would break with centuries-old tradition by refusing to hold what he called 'levees' during his stay at the Palace. There should be no free wine and champagne, only non-alcoholic drinks, for the clergymen and elders of the Church of Scotland. However, as Johnston also noted, if the former miner was able to break with these traditions, 'he might just as easily have broken with the other traditions as well and gone in his Sunday clothes and opened the General Assembly without the waste of public money and flummery and guzzling'.

Johnston's own attendances at church, he later revealed in a letter to the *Glasgow Herald* dated 22 June 1925, had been few and discriminatory since he discovered that a Church which professed to suffer the little children could consistently throw its weight against the feeding of hungry schoolchildren by the community. His interest 'somewhat evaporated when the battleships were blessed in the name of the Prince of Peace and when the pulpits rang with the declamation, not against greed and oppression, and the grinding of the faces of the poor, but against those who were given to change a social system which mocked the very idea of a brotherhood of man or Thy kingdom come on earth'.

However, a year earlier, when he lambasted the ancient ceremonials surrounding the Lord High Commissioner to the General Assembly of the Church of Scotland, he was careful to avoid being critical of the Kirk itself, or James Brown personally. 'To James Brown, as a loyal son of the Kirk of Scotland, and as a ruling elder in her counsels for years, there could be no greater honour than to represent the state at the opening of the General Assembly,' Johnston wrote. 'That is quite an understandable and laudable ambition. But it might have been carried through in a dignified way. If James Brown had gone in his Sunday clothes and had waved aside the £2,000 for useless flummery and the disguising of himself for what he is not, he would have struck a blow for his class – aye, and for the honour and dignity of the Kirk that is sadly missing in his participation in and acceptance of mediaeval aristocratic follies.'

Brown's response, according to Emrys Hughes, who reported meeting him on a train, was unprintable. 'Tell Johnston from me that he's a dirty beggar,' was the toned-down version Hughes retained for inclusion in the draft form of his own unpublished memoir, *Rebels and Renegades*.

Johnston's account of a garden party at Holyrood Palace a few years later, during the period of the second Labour Government, when he was an Under-Secretary in the Scottish Office and James Brown was again Lord High Commissioner, suggests there was no long-term rift between the two men. Johnston attended the garden party in the company of the Secretary of State for Scotland, William Adamson, a former miner and a great friend of the Lord High Commissioner. The occasion presented Johnston with 'a never-to-be-forgotten spectacle: the busloads of colliers who arrived in honour of Jimmy Brown: some of them in tall hats that had never been out in use since the Disruption, and placidly smoking their clay pipes; and Willie Adamson and Jimmy Brown, two old colliers, representing the King's Majesty at the ancient castle [*sic*]. I would not have missed that sight for much'.

Other MPs with constituencies in Scotland, including the indefatigable Emmanuel Shinwell, who was put in charge of mines, were appointed to junior roles during the life of the first Labour Government. But there was nothing for the free-spirited James Maxton, despite strong support from his friend John Wheatley, or Tom Johnston, the party's leading propagandist. The decision angered and disappointed both men. Johnston had been specialising in colonial affairs and, as the party's regular spokesman on the subject prior to the election, was entitled to expect some reward for his efforts.

Ramsay MacDonald's first government, in which he also kept the Foreign Office for himself, lasted less than nine months. For all its historic significance it is generally remembered as a dispiriting experience. Gordon Brown, a leading member of the modern Labour Party, believes 'Labour's choices were not as limited as they may seem now. Labour might have entered office, introduced a bold socialist programme, and then faced defeat in the Commons and a fresh election.' On economic questions as a whole, the Budget strategy and the relief of unemployment, the measures pursued by the first Labour Government were completely inadequate, according to Brown.

G.D.H. Cole believed the new administration was never likely to do other than 'refrain from any action that would deliberately provoke Parliamentary defeat and would try to make the best it could of such measures as the Liberals could be induced to support'. Within weeks of taking office MacDonald himself explained: 'My great concern at present is the failure of our backbenchers to respond to the new conditions. Some of the disappointed ones maintain a feud and are as hostile as though they were not of us.'

If the Prime Minister believed his old friend, the MP for West Stirlingshire and editor of *Forward*, could be counted among the malcontents, he also knew, just as surely, that Tom Johnston was in a powerful position to disseminate his opinions outside, as well as inside, the House of Commons. *Forward* played an important, and influential, role in the affairs of the Labour movement and, by extension, the nation; a fact which was certainly not lost on MacDonald, far less its editor.

MacDonald had been a regular contributor for many years. On 19 December 1922, in a letter to Johnston, he proposed ending the association. Johnston replied, expressing his 'deepest regret, alike from a journalistic, a party, and a personal point of view'. But there was no sign of any false modesty, in his courteous reminder to MacDonald, about the value of the platform within his gift. 'Your weekly article has helped to steady us in many ways and I think it has been a platform not without its assistance in recreating the party after the war and in making your election to the leadership possible,' Johnston claimed.

His powers of persuasion appeared to work: the future Prime Minister continued to contribute intermittently to *Forward*, appealing directly to its staunch, varied and highly opinionated left-wing readership. By doing so MacDonald no doubt hoped he could fashion the conflicting strands of political opinion which called itself the Labour movement into a powerful and responsible party of government which the electorate could trust.

Johnston hadn't been shown any preferment when MacDonald became Prime Minister for the first time: there was no reason for anyone to expect *Forward* to present a flattering picture of the new administration. Johnston later acknowledged that 'in the heyday of his power, flattered and fawned upon, we took occasion again and again to criticise, in a friendly and temperate way, certain failures and weaknesses and unnecessary concessions to the forces of anti-socialism. We may have been right or wrong but we certainly think that frank criticism was of more service to the real interests of the Labour movement than was the sustained chorus of adulation and hosannas which emanated from some quarters.

As an example, on 26 January 1924, less than a week after Ramsay MacDonald accepted the King's invitation to form a government, a leading article in *Forward* declared: 'When we think of the nation we think of the unemployed in the queue, of the homeless, of the slum dwellers, of the miners at the coalface, the shunters on the railway sidings, of the men and women in the factories, of the downtrodden agricultural labourers on the land, of the teachers in the schools, of all those who with hand and brain render service to the community. To these and these alone Labour is responsible.'

Forward, which could command the attention of a large section of committed Labour voters and opinion formers, offered little comfort to anyone assembling round the Cabinet table who might be nursing notions of compromise. 'A Labour Government must not hesitate to challenge privilege and vested interests whenever they stand in its way,' the newspaper declared. 'It must show quite clearly that it stands for a new social order. It must aim at great things. It must show that it is in earnest. If in attempting to do this it is defeated the people will not blame the Labour Party, they will blame the people who will conspire to destroy it.'

Two issues of the newspaper later Johnston signalled his profound disappointment with at least one important post still to be announced: Lord Advocate. Johnston and the rest of the Scottish Labour MPs wanted Rosslyn Mitchell, a Glasgow solicitor and prominent ILP member, who had been narrowly defeated in Glasgow Central at the recent election, appointed. Ramsay MacDonald appeared unwilling to consider their demands. Worse, he invited the Faculty of Advocates in Edinburgh to express their opinion.

Johnston and his cronies, meeting in Miss Cranston's, were enraged. For it was then, as Johnston interpreted the matter, that the entire Advocates Trade Union began to protest and threaten. 'They will not have dilution,' Johnston exclaimed. 'They refuse to allow a common solicitor to lay his hands upon the patronage and power which the Faculty of Advocates has succeeded in monopolising for generations.'

When the Prime Minister finally decided to appoint Hugh MacMillan KC, an Edinburgh advocate and self-professed Conservative supporter, to the post, Johnston observed coldly: 'Every effort should have been made to fill these important offices by men who were determined to transform the system of judicial spoils and patronage into a Civil Service. But we have failed in our protest and that's an end to it. We do not propose to keep nagging at a Labour Government which, as we are glad to testify, is doing so well in other directions because it didn't see its way to face up to the pretensions of the bewigged corporation at Edinburgh.'

A bravura performance, during the committee stage of Labour's first Budget proposals, earned him the gratitude of his own front bench. Sir Robert Horne, a former Tory Chancellor and MP for Glasgow Hillhead, claimed Labour in power posed a serious threat to the value of sterling which was now worth only $4.30, compared to $4.50 six months earlier. He told the House of Commons on 30 April 1924: 'We have paid millions for the felicity of enjoying a Labour Government.' Tom Johnston responded, with considerable vigour, the following day, demonstrating that the pound suffered its worst losses against the dollar while the Conservatives were still in power. Between 1 November 1923, Johnston explained – 'when the Conservative Party imagined that the flowing tide was with them' – and 16 November 1923 – 'when Parliament was prorogued and a definite Protectionist issue placed before the country' – the value of sterling fell from $4.50 to $4.32. 'There is no case to justify the charge that the Labour Government has cost the country millions of money because of a fall in our national credit,' Johnston added. 'The very reverse is the case.'

He believed 'any Budget which transfers a purchasing power of somewhere about £30 million to the common folk of this country is a favourable Budget, and one which makes for more social peace, for greater contentment in the country and for less unemployment'. After three months of a Labour Government this Budget was 'the first attempt, the beginning, to shift the social burdens in such a way as to bring nearer that co-operative Commonwealth and equality in this country for which we on these Labour benches stand'.

Johnston believed housing was one policy area where a Labour Government couldn't afford to compromise. But he was prepared to support John Wheatley's efforts to try and effect an improvement in the living conditions of the working class, as far as they went.

According to a special report, published in *Forward* on 26 January 1924, Scotland had been short of at least 131,000 houses in 1919. And, despite ever-increasing demand, only 23,000 new dwellings had been added since. 'Every year 10,000 new houses are required to keep pace with the normal wastage and with the normal increase in population,' the writer claimed. 'Simple arithmetic shows that the shortage of working-class houses today is at least 148,000 and that we are worse off for houses now than we were in 1919.'

John Wheatley had been demonstrating pragmatic flair at the Ministry of Health. He believed it would take 100 years to achieve socialism in Britain. But that didn't stop him trying to put more than a cosmetic dent in the dreadful housing statistics highlighted by Johnston in *Forward*. In less than seven months Wheatley steered a new Housing Act through the House of Commons to the Royal Assent. This offered additional subsidies to local authorities who built affordable, standard houses for rent to working-class tenants; and, following much persuasion, enlisted the support of all sides of the building industry in achieving his aims.

Ramsay MacDonald believed Wheatley's Housing Act was probably the biggest piece of constructive industrial organisation ever attempted. Many of his colleagues, including Johnston – and Wheatley himself, despite his success – believed the new legislation didn't go far enough. But with it Wheatley laid the foundations of council house policy, and Government attitudes to local authority housing, for another six decades.

The speedy recognition of the Soviet Union during the short, unhappy life of the first Labour Government also found favour with the editor of *Forward*. Britain's action had been 'frank, unequivocal and couched in a phraseology that carries no suspicion of patronage'. In fact, it was the ramifications of this agreement, including a British loan to the Soviet Union, where the Bolsheviks had been in power for less than seven years, which brought Labour's first period in office to an end and accounted for the party's subsequent defeat at the polls.

Johnston complained, in a speech delivered to a crowded meeting in the new Miners' Welfare Institute at Cowie, Lancashire, on 24 September 1924, that the Tory method of dealing with 'our Russian customers' was to spend £100 million tearing up their railway lines, destroying their harvests and burning their villages. Labour preferred to 'lend £20 million or £30 million worth of engines and ploughs and steel rails to set Russia on her feet again as an effective purchaser of British goods'.

The Government's difficulties started with the publication of an open letter to the forces which appeared in the *Workers' Weekly*, the official organ of the Communist Party, on 25 July 1924. It encouraged serving soldiers not to turn their weapons on fellow workers, 'neither in the class war, nor in a military war'.

The Attorney General, Sir Patrick Hastings, decided there were grounds for prosecution under the Incitement to Mutiny Act. The acting editor, John Ross Campbell, who, unknown to the Attorney General, had been decorated for gallantry during the war, was arrested and charged. As one prominent member of the Government, Emmanuel Shinwell, observed later, although Sir Patrick was one of the most famous barristers of the period, with a great reputation in the courts, he was no politician. Campbell's arrest angered many Labour MPs. When the Attorney General appeared in the House of Commons to answer questions he was told by one member of the Clydeside group, George Buchanan, MP for Gorbals, that the article largely expressed 'the views and feelings of Labour Party Conferences and some of the men who are at present sitting on the front bench'.

Charges against John Ross Campbell were eventually withdrawn after he offered to apologise. Tom Johnston believed the law officers were influenced in their decision when it was learned that the Communists intended to call the Prime Minister to the witness box and examine him about a speech he 'delivered in the House of Commons in 1912 in defence of Mr Tom Mann, when that gentleman had also incited the armed forces to refuse duty in a trade dispute'. It was a charge MacDonald denied vehemently at the time. On 30 September 1924 he assured the House of Commons that he left the whole matter to the discretion of the law officers, 'where that discretion properly rests. I never received any intimation, not even a hint, that I should be asked to give evidence.'

But the Campbell case was far from finished. The Prime Minister had been accused of political interference in a judicial matter. The main opposition party, the Conservatives, proposed a vote of censure: the

Liberals would have been satisfied with an amendment seeking a select committee investigation into the whole affair.

During the censure debate which followed, on 8 October 1924, Tom Johnston suggested there were occasions when 'it would be the duty of any politician to attempt to protect the good name of the Government and of the law from undertaking a very foolish prosecution'. He believed the widest possible latitude should be given for free speech. No harm was done if a man indulged in foolish sentiments which no one believed. 'But if the Government start prosecuting opinions, there is no saying where the prosecutions will end,' Johnston warned.

Ramsay MacDonald was determined to resign as Prime Minister if he was defeated on either the vote of censure or the Liberal amendment. It was an opportunity the Tories were unlikely to miss. The leader of the opposition, Stanley Baldwin, ordered his troops to vote with the Liberals.

Soon allied as it was in the public mind to the appearance of the forged Zinoviev letter in the *Daily Mail*, four days before polling, the Campbell case and Labour's earlier efforts to harmonise relations with the Bolshevik Government in Moscow reduced the 1924 general election to a sterile and malevolent debate about the Red menace infiltrating Britain.

Johnston, writing in *Memories* more than a quarter of a century after the event, offered the view that Labour probably exaggerated the effect of the Zinoviev letter on the result of the 1924 election. By the time the letter appeared, on the Saturday before the election, Johnston believed 'most men and women had their minds or their prejudices already fixed as to how they should vote. Moreover the method of disclosure carried with it all the smell of an election stunt designed to bear upon the central issue of the election: the proposed treaty with and loan to Russia.'

Signed, supposedly, by Grigory Zinoviev, President of the Communist International, and addressed to Arthur MacManus, the British representative on the Comintern Executive, the letter suggested a Labour Government could be used to prepare a military insurrection in Britain. Shortly after it first appeared in the *Daily Mail* on 25 October 1924 – beneath a series of wild headlines, including 'Civil War Plot by

Socialists – Moscow Order to our Reds' – Tom Johnston denounced the letter as 'the most shameful electoral trick ever sought to be played upon the working class of this country – the alleged Russian plot'. According to Johnston, writing in *Forward* on 1 November 1924, three days after the election, the Zinoviev letter was an 'obvious concoction which had "electioneering dodge" written all over it'.

Unfortunately for Labour, in a scattered constituency such as West Stirlingshire, there was insufficient time, between its first appearance in the *Daily Mail* and the Government's dithering response, to save the election. 'In villages where we expected to poll from one-third of the vote upwards we got literally nothing,' Johnston reported, 'and the Tory machines swept the Timid and the Fearful by the thousand into the ballot boxes.' On an 81 per cent turnout, Johnston polled 9,749 votes, 507 more than in 1923. But in a straight fight with the Conservative candidate, G.D. Fanshawe, he failed by 294 votes to hold the seat.

Labour, with candidates in 515 constituencies – a record for the party – suffered a net loss of 40 seats, including eight in Scotland. But the party could at least claim it now provided the main unchallenged opposition in the House of Commons. The election had been a disaster for the Liberals, reduced from 158 seats to 42.

Of course, people like Tom Johnston, who hated the idea of Stanley Baldwin in Downing Street and the Conservatives running Whitehall, viewed the Liberal collapse as justice well served; considering the part they played in forcing Ramsay MacDonald's resignation and the death of the first Labour Government.

Johnston was also heartened by the response of his own supporters following the count in West Stirlingshire. With ill-concealed pride he recorded: 'Thousands of men and women, many of them in tears, swear that they have already begun to prepare for an emphatic reversal next time.'

CHAPTER EIGHT

NOT SURPRISINGLY, in view of his indifferent performance at the head of the first Labour Government, and his muddled response to the crisis created by the Zinoviev letter, some people inside the Labour Party wanted Ramsay MacDonald replaced as leader following the 1924 election. The dissidents included an angry James Maxton, re-elected at Bridgeton. Among those who disagreed was Tom Johnston. He dismissed speculation about the leadership as 'a wanton and unnecessary disruption of the party'.

Johnston also refused to accept talk about a coalition with the Liberals. This was 'simply grotesque nonsense'. According to Johnston, 'Neither Ramsay MacDonald or J.H. Thomas are on friendly terms with the Liberal rump.' He added: 'Indeed these two are the least likely Labour leaders to be nibbled at by the Liberals.'

As his deputy, Emrys Hughes, observed roughly many years later: 'Johnston certainly never dreamt then that the time would come when MacDonald and Thomas would be gobbled up, not nibbled at, by the Tories!'

Johnston wasn't out of Parliament for long following his defeat in the 1924 general election. The death of E.D. Morel several days later left a vacancy in Dundee. At a meeting of Dundee Trades and Labour Council on Wednesday, 19 November 1924, Johnston was adopted as the ILP candidate to succeed Morel.

E.D. Morel enjoyed a five-figure majority at the general election and no one expected Tom Johnston to lose in Dundee. According to Johnston's own account of the campaign the real issue was made clear from the start – socialism versus capitalism. For 20 years, Johnston claimed, he had been using voice and pen to campaign 'for every cause that would raise the standard of life of the common people, and against all forms of monopoly and privilege which exploit and oppress the working class'. His election address included a pledge to fight higher food prices, including an annual £175 million graft which he claimed existed on bread, milk and tea alone. He would also make it his business, once he had been returned to Westminster as one of two MPs representing Dundee, to pursue a national referendum on the prohibition and sale of intoxicating liquors as a beverage. In addition he made plain his belief that 'Scottish Home Rule would enable the Scottish people to deal more speedily and more effectively with the reforms we so urgently require'.

The presence of British troops in Egypt also attracted his attention. Egypt had been a British protectorate between 1914 and 1922. But it was now an independent kingdom under Fuad I. 'We had no more right to rule Egypt than Egypt had to rule us,' Johnston contended, adding that it was time British troops were withdrawn from the desert country.

The former Prime Minister, Ramsay MacDonald, added weight to his campaign. On 15 December 1924, in an open letter to the Dundee electors, he wrote: 'The new Government has been in office but a week or two and already we have only too good evidence that in it all reactionary interests have their champion. It has turned its back upon every good we were pursuing and has already proclaimed to the world that our nation has returned to the old ruts of militarism and the old ways of Tory ascendancy.' Labour's first Prime Minister hoped the electors of Dundee would return Tom Johnston to the House of Commons as 'a proof that the country has recovered from the irrational credulities and fears of the stunt election and is demanding a policy of peace and social reconstruction such as the Labour Party alone can secure'.

A poll scheduled for three days before Christmas was never likely to attract a large turnout anywhere; but least of all in a safe Labour seat, with a cold wind blowing in from the Tay and the electorate rightly convinced the result was a foregone conclusion. On a 42.4 per cent turnout Johnston won handsomely, polling 22,973 votes against 10,234 for his sole opponent, a Liberal, E.D. Simon.

One other outcome of the Dundee by-election no doubt pleased

Tom Johnston: he had been able to re-establish good relations with Ramsay MacDonald. These had been strained as a result of Johnston's exclusion from the first Labour Government and *Forward*'s strictures on its performance. Since then, however, Johnston had been a strong supporter of MacDonald continuing as Labour leader. He also extended an open invitation to the former Prime Minister to resume writing in *Forward* whenever he wished.

Reviewing a collection of essays by MacDonald when they appeared in book form, Johnston almost purred: 'Had Mr Ramsay MacDonald not been a successful politician he might have been the greatest descriptive journalist of his time.' According to Johnston, sounding every inch the wheedling editor, huge audiences gathered round MacDonald's platform 'while he waves the magic of his prose poetry; in a non-offensive but wholly honourable interpretation of the words, he is a great spell-binder'.

The former Prime Minister clearly enjoyed flattery. Before the year was out, as one close witness of these events, Emrys Hughes, testified, he was again 'doing his spell-binding every week in *Forward* and continued writing regularly for us until he was again Prime Minister'.

Johnston was soon perceived as a figure of some importance in Labour ranks at Westminster. On 8 August 1926 *The Observer* claimed he was formidable in debate and on paper and 'one of the few possible national leaders among the Labour rank and file'.

A few days later an article in another publication with its base in the south suggested Johnston was different from the rest of the Clydeside group. What made him different, the *English Review* explained priggishly, was a near absence of wildness and a tendency not to indulge in noise or tumult. According to the *English Review* the MP for Dundee was the intellectual spokesman of extreme Labour in Scotland. Unlike other intellectuals Johnston eschewed abstract discourses in favour of a lawyer-like love of documentation, however. He was a storehouse of facts, a devourer of blue books and of other kinds of forbidding literature. 'The facts which he accumulates with patient labour he marshals with the order and precision of a logician, and out of what in other hands might be a mess of undigested matter, an orderly argument emerges.'

Johnston delivered his speeches in a dry voice and exhibited an unadorned, rather careless style. He owed his success, the magazine continued, almost entirely to the severer qualities of the mind. Sometimes, in his speeches, he achieved a moral fervour which 'diffuses the harder qualities, and lifts him into the higher regions of speech, in which the impression is made, not by argument and knowledge, but by moral appeal'.

It was unfortunate for Johnston, the object of so much unexpected praise, that the *English Review* failed to award him high marks for presentation. 'If his voice and manner were adequate to his mind his power as a debater would give him a commanding place,' it claimed.

During the five years he spent as one of two MPs representing Dundee Johnston carried his crusade against slave labour wages direct to India, the jewel in the Empire's crown. Jute, a major source of employment in Dundee, was a notoriously low-paid industry. Employers in the city blamed competition from Bengal.

Invited by the local Jute and Flaxworkers Union to investigate, Johnston travelled to India in the company of the union secretary, John Sime. At Marseilles, where they boarded the SS *Caledonia* for the longest stage of their journey, by way of the Suez Canal, to Bombay, they found the quay 'filled with sword-swallowers, weight-lifters, fortune-tellers, musicians who played *God Save the King*, and furtive retailers of filthy postcards, the latter being darted after vigorously by the police'.

Their fellow passengers, according to Johnston's own account, included the Maharajah of Patiala who travelled with 15 tons of luggage and 'a suite of some 30 persons, mostly in turbans and whiskers, and a major domo in green-grey uniform, and swaggering a huge gold stick'.

Excesses of a different kind also awaited them on their arrival in Bombay. Of no one in particular, except anyone with influence in the affairs of India, Johnston demanded angrily on his return: 'What pray are we to say about the street of Grant Road in Bombay where, under the British flag, and subject to the control and regulation of British policemen, some 900 women are kept in cages with iron bars for prostitution purposes?

'In some of the cages are as many as six women – women of all nationalities except British and American. Indian women and Japanese women predominate but there are French women, Austrian women, Rumanian women, and women of other European nationalities.

'The usual price of admission to a cage is four annas – roughly fourpence – and nights, particularly Saturday nights, there are queues outside some of these cages waiting their turn. The four annas are passed through the bars of the cage, then a cage door is opened from the inside and a man enters. From the pavement and from the passing trams you can see right into the cages. There are usually two beds or couches, sometimes only one. There is no medical inspection and, outside pimp or procurer hunting, no police interference.'

It is easy to imagine the normally shy and taciturn middle-aged editor seated at his desk, quivering with shock and rage, as he contemplated the lessons of his visit to the Indian subcontinent on behalf of the oppressed jute workers of Dundee. His article on the Grant Road cages, which appeared in *Forward* on 30 January 1926, was accompanied by photographs of the scene. The use of photographs, to support an already sordid story, was unusual then. Johnston forestalled criticism, and charges of sensationalism, by defending himself vigorously in advance. 'How can the Bombay cages for women ever be closed unless first the moral sense of the British people be roused to their brutality, bestiality, and human degradation and to the utilisation of British policemen and British authority for their supervision and continuance?' he demanded. 'And how may the moral sense of the nation be roused unless it be first instructed on the facts.' By publishing photographs, in support of his report, he hoped 'some of the women's societies will take the matter up'.

Two years later another prominent Labour politician, Fenner Brockway, visited Bombay and found Grant Road, and its cages, unchanged.

Johnston wasn't long settled in his hotel room, following his arrival in Bombay, before he was invited to meet the leaders of a local cotton strike. More than 150,000 workers were involved in the struggle against a proposed 20 per cent cut in wages. These, Johnston learned, averaged £2 3s for a 240-hour month.

Immediately sympathetic to the workers' case he cabled London for funds which were soon forthcoming from trade union sources. In the end, the strikers won. 'But the wage rates were not the worst of it,' Johnston wrote, 'not by a long chalk mark.'

Taken to inspect the one-room tenement chawls in which many of the strikers lived, Johnston was nauseated by what he saw. The chawls were 'foul smelling, pitch-black holes, eight feet by six feet, in rows, ashpits and water taps adjacent: the lavatories, little boxes containing a drain for urine and a hole for excrement – the boxes I was told were removed once a day in a basket'.

According to figures published by the Health Department of the Government of Bombay fewer than 200 new-born babies in every 1,000 survived the first year of life in the chawls. However, as Johnston observed many years later, 'it was not the death rate in conditions like that that amazed me, but the living rate'.

The main purpose of his visit to India, to study work practices in the Bengal jute industry, produced other startling indictments of social conditions under the Raj. Between 1915 and 1924, Johnston learned, profits from the jute industry in Bengal totalled £300 million. This considerable sum was achieved by the sweat of between 300,000 and 327,000 workers who each earned, on average, twelve shillings and tenpence a year. Johnston calculated that the average annual profit was eight times the wage bill; giving investors a 90 per cent profit margin each year.

'There are many thousands of shareholders but the identity of large numbers is difficult to establish owing to the practice of the dividends not being remitted to a home address but to a bank,' Johnston reported. He also found that even the poorest workers were compelled to pay an initial bribe to the foreman, or *sardar*, in return for a job in the mills. 'There was no fixed tariff,' Johnston wrote. 'Every *sardar* simply screws what he can out of his applicants.' Weavers, looking for work, had been known to pay 75 rupees, which could be as much as three months wages, in return for a job. Usually, however, the *sardar* settled for ten rupees. 'But that initial capital levy upon future wages was only the first toll,' Johnston revealed. 'There was a regular backsheesh demanded after that, upon pay day every month, of a penny or twopence per employee.' One *sardar* who worked for 22 years on an average wage of 15 rupees per week had 'amassed a fortune amounting to two laks of rupees – about £13,000', Johnston added.

Throughout the whole of his early adult life, as a young councillor, party loyalist and leading propagandist, Tom Johnston responded eagerly to the political aspirations of the Independent Labour Party. Founded in 1893 by Keir Hardie, and older than the Labour Party by several years, its main aim was always the social and political betterment of the working class.

Like many of his contemporaries, Tom Johnston believed the ILP was the mainstay of the entire Labour movement. In 1929, when Dundee Trades and Labour Council decided to disaffiliate from the ILP, he abandoned his safe city seat in return for the nomination at West Stirling – despite his defeat in a straight fight in the same constituency last time!

Robert Keith Middlemas, author of *The Clydesiders,* believed it was a matter of some envy and derision that the ILP was far more literate and literary than its rivals. In its heyday more than 40,000 people had been attracted by its good intentions and eccentric ways; although, after nearly four decades, 16,000 was the official membership figure used to calculate the level of affiliation fees due to its precocious, and demanding, offspring, the Labour Party.

Labour's first Prime Minister, Ramsay MacDonald, had been a member since 1894 and, in the opinion of Tom Johnston, rendered memorable service to social democracy. 'He was one of the main architects of the Labour Party, and for at least a decade and a half no man did more than he to enthuse the common man and inspire and raise his dignity,' Johnston wrote.

MacDonald's departure from Downing Street, following the collapse of the first Labour Government, was marked by months of acrimony and a sourness of spirit inside the Labour Party, which threatened to destroy the entire working-class movement.

Anticipating its arrival, Keir Hardie's son-in-law, Emrys Hughes, detected a sense of high optimism among frontline party activists.

Hughes, who had been imprisoned for refusing to serve in the First World War, later observed that, prior to the 1923 election, many people believed there would never be a need for any other kind of government once the country experienced a Labour Government, and saw what socialism could achieve.

Following his election Ramsay MacDonald's sense of priorities was probably conditioned by a realistic understanding of the ways and mood of the House of Commons. He never expected to achieve much by way of socially improving legislation with a minority government lasting less than nine months and the benches opposite stacked against him.

But the practicalities of government, and the difficult nature of MacDonald's position during most of 1924, mattered little to many of his old comrades in the ILP. People like James Maxton, the fiery-principled MP for Bridgeton, argued in favour of a complete socialist programme under Labour. Maxton believed 'a widespread revolt among the people, determined courage and readiness to sacrifice everything' could be used to encourage the slow-moving machinery of Parliament to act swiftly in favour of socialist ideals. And at the Labour Party conference, held in Liverpool in 1925, no less a figure than Ernest Bevin, representing the Transport and General Workers Union, urged delegates to declare in favour of Labour never again accepting office without a majority in the House of Commons. If he was ever an MP, Bevin argued, he would refuse to accept office unless he could 'speak with the power that rested on the knowledge that I had a majority behind me both inside the House of Commons and outside in the nation'.

Ramsay MacDonald, who was present, put himself in direct opposition to Bevin, arguing, as G.D.H. Cole recorded in his *History of the Labour Party*, 'the unwisdom of the party binding itself not to take office before it could know under what circumstances the question might arise'.

The usually persuasive Bevin failed to carry conference, securing only 512,000 votes – most of them from his own union – against a massive 2,587,000. As G.D.H. Cole noted: 'Even many who were highly critical of MacDonald and of the first Labour Government were not prepared to lay down that Labour should not again take office without a clear majority.'

101

During the troubled life of the first Labour Government when his friend and close political ally, John Wheatley, was Minister of Health with a seat in the Cabinet, James Maxton was inclined to speak encouragingly, in public at least, of Ramsay MacDonald's mould-breaking minority administration. Man for man, he claimed, it was twice as good as any previous administration. However, long before the ramifications of the Campbell affair and aid to Russia forced MacDonald's resignation, Maxton would have been happy to see the man from Lossiemouth consigned to the waste-bin of history.

Maxton, in the words of one biographer, Gordon Brown, 'saw himself as the keeper of the conscience of the Labour Movement with a duty to keep working-class spirits alive and defend the principles upon which the Labour Movement was founded'. Following the 1924 election Maxton tried, through a vote of the Parliamentary group, to remove Ramsay MacDonald from the Labour Party leadership, and failed.

Maxton disagreed hotly with anyone who believed the existence of the Labour Party meant there was no longer a need for the ILP. Labour was becoming increasingly absorbed in the responsibilities of Parliamentary life, he warned. Whether its members provided the official opposition, or the Government, he believed there would be a tendency to concentrate on 'the immediately practicable which always creates the tendency to lose sight of ultimate ideals'.

He never faltered in his belief that Labour would obtain a majority in the House of Commons and achieve political success eventually. 'But political success itself is a poor end unless, behind the Parliamentary majority, there is a determined socialist opinion,' Maxton argued.

In some quarters, as Maxton acknowledged, he was considered an irresponsible extremist. His election, as chairman of the ILP, more than a year after the first Labour Government was forced from office, was bound to cause trouble; especially when Maxton continued to insist, ominously, some thought: 'It will be part of my duty to try to make as far-reaching as possible this feeling which I believe is the feeling of the Labour Party.'

An open alliance with Arthur Cook, controversial secretary of the Miners Federation of Great Britain at the time of the general strike, produced a manifesto in direct opposition to official Labour Party policy. The authors of this highly provocative document believed there had been a serious departure from the principles and policy which animated the founders of the Labour movement. 'We are now being asked to believe that the party is no longer a working-class party, but a party representing all sections of the community,' the two dissidents complained. 'As socialists we feel we cannot represent the views of capitalism. Capitalism and socialism can have nothing in common.'

Ruminating on the principles which united Right and Left in the Labour Party, Tom Johnston decided any difference which existed between members was chimerical. Only the temperament of the individuals concerned set them apart, he claimed. Both sides believed the production of goods for private profit resulted in poverty for the masses and was wrong and foolish. Similarly, they were convinced the social product to which everyone contributed should be equally enjoyed. 'That belief is what makes us socialists,' Johnston declared.

Cook–Maxton believed that 'much of the energy which should be expended in fighting capitalism is now expended in crushing everybody who dares to remain true to the ideals of the movement. We are convinced that this change is responsible for destroying the fighting spirit of the party, and we now come out openly to challenge it.'

G.D.H. Cole thought the programme they proposed was 'a good deal more drastic than the leaders of the Labour Party were prepared willingly to accept'. As Cole explained: 'At the least it called for the immediate adoption of a national minimum wage adequate to meet all needs in all public services and by all employers working on public contracts, supplemented by machinery for the legal enforcement of rising minima on industry as a whole, as well as by expanded social services financed out of taxation on the bigger incomes, and by a nationally financed system of family allowances.'

Tom Johnston's interest was aroused on two fronts: in his world, journalism and politics were often mutually supportive. Before an interview conducted on behalf of *Forward* he described Maxton as someone inspired by the highest and cleanest motives. 'What he signed he believed or he would not have signed it,' Johnston reported.

Maxton assured Johnston that he wasn't about to launch a new socialist party in opposition to the ILP. 'We have not the slightest intention of doing any such thing,' he insisted. 'I am only going, if I can, to keep the party on the road where Keir Hardie set its feet.'

Maxton's close collaboration with Arthur Cook, the miners leader, followed the defeat of organised labour in the general strike two years earlier. The strike was a direct consequence of Britain's return to the gold standard, announced by the Chancellor of the Exchequer, Winston Churchill, in 1925.

Churchill, according to his official biographer, Martin Gilbert, recognised a return to the gold standard 'favoured the special interests of finance at the expense of the interests of production' while no less a financial authority than J.M. Keynes believed it would be 'wiser and simpler and saner to leave the currency to find its own level for some time longer than to force a situation where employers are faced with the alternative of closing down or of lowering wages, cost what the struggle may'.

Faced with the threat of cheap imports, including coal, British manufacturers attempted to impose a reduction in wages and longer hours on the workforce – a threat disguised as a proposal the unions were quick to reject. To them, as G.D.H. Cole explained, it looked like 'an attempt to pass on to the workers the entire burden of meeting an economic crisis that had been deliberately intensified by bad financial policy, accepted by the Government at the dictation of the bankers here and in the United States'.

The strike started on 3 May 1926 and, for everyone except the miners, lasted barely a week. *Forward*, which supported the strike, and missed two editions by not appearing while it lasted, returned with an angry and scornful admission by its founder-editor: 'I never had sixpence worth of faith in the general strike as a method of securing anything very perennial, or very material, to the working class.' Tom Johnston could understand the General Council of the TUC surrendering if and when their armies began to desert. 'But I'm blessed if I can understand what on the face of it looks like a surrender before they were beaten, and while yet their followers were in good heart, and the women and children were being fed.'

It was a view supported by John Wheatley, a hero of the first Labour Government, who observed: 'The workers have sustained a smashing reverse. It was not inflicted by their bosses nor due to their own weakness. It is a most astonishing result to a most magnificent effort. The struggle will surely rate as the greatest and most bungled strike in history.'

Alone among the unions, the Miners Federation of Great Britain, headed by Arthur Cook, refused to accept the employers' terms. The miners remained on strike for another six months. It was a long and bitter struggle which divided the country and threatened the future of the entire Labour movement.

Tom Johnston accused the coal owners of seeking fabulous profits for themselves; while trying to make the miners exist at the cheapest, lowest-possible rate of civilisation. He forecast a permanent settlement couldn't be achieved. 'There cannot be a settlement within a system that reduces a million men to borderline starvation. However, and whenever, it ends, the result can only be a truce,' Johnston warned.

When he abandoned a safe seat in Dundee to concentrate on a difficult and unpredictable return to West Stirlingshire, Tom Johnston demonstrated a strong measure of solidarity with the aims of the ILP. He didn't know then that James Maxton's chairmanship of the party, in which he spent all the years of his early political development, would result 'in first perplexity, then resentment, and finally wholesale resignation'.

Ramsay MacDonald was the most important member of the Parliamentary Labour Party to distance himself from the ILP because of Maxton. Another veteran, Philip Snowden, whose dedication to the cause earned him the chairmanship in 1903, resigned in December 1927, at serious odds with its policies and claiming there was no further need for the ILP.

In his address to the 1928 ILP conference Maxton declared his commitment to making the ILP a socialist party within the Labour Party. Few appreciated the strength of his commitment; far less the destructive nature of his campaigning zeal.

CHAPTER NINE

JOHNSTON APPEARED TO be gambling dangerously with his own future Parliamentary career, at least, when he decided to abandon his safe seat in Dundee in favour of a return to West Stirlingshire in time for the 1929 general election.

There had been some disagreeable local squabbling between the Independent Labour Party and the Trades and Labour Council in Dundee prior to his departure. Both sides allowed the local MP to adopt a position of complete neutrality. However, as the differences between the two sides escalated to all-out war, there was never any real chance Johnston could remain impartial through the election and beyond.

The trouble started when the Trades and Labour Council attempted to organise a boycott of the locally powerful publishers, D.C. Thomson, for using non-union labour and continuing to operate during the general strike. There was never much chance of local newsagents, dependent on the city's highest-selling daily newspaper, the *Dundee Courier*, and other Thomson titles for a large part of their income, supporting a boycott in numbers that mattered. The campaign was doomed from the start.

Hardliners on the Trades and Labour Council weren't inclined to accept defeat gracefully, however. They were particularly angered at the actions of one newsagent, a certain Mrs Carr, who showed no interest in pursuing lost causes; or denying her customers the newspaper of their choice. And this despite the fact she was also the wife of the secretary of the ILP!

Tom Johnston was never really involved in the early stages of the dispute. But it would have been difficult for the once-banned editor of *Forward* to argue against a respectable newspaper's right to be read. The Trades and Labour Council showed less regard for the principles and importance of a free and untrammelled press, however. Disciplinary action was required against Mr Carr for failing to keep his free-thinking spouse under control!

There was clearly a comic dimension to the row. But the ILP was right to resist proceeding along such a dangerous and dubious route. When its officials refused to take any action against the hapless Mr Carr there was a successful putsch inside the Trades and Labour Council to disaffiliate the ILP.

Tom Johnston could no longer avoid taking sides. He had been an ILP-nominated candidate throughout the whole of his Parliamentary career. It was hardly surprising to everyone outside the Trades and Labour Council in Dundee that he sided with the ILP.

But even without the trouble caused in the constituency by the strong-willed Mrs Carr it is likely Johnston would have been looking for a way out of Dundee before long. He was never happy there. Another former Labour MP in the city, George Thomson, now Lord Thomson of Monifieth, explained: 'The Labour Party in Dundee had a long history of quarrelsome, schematic behaviour. He told me once that every time he went up the steps at Tay Bridge station on his return from London there would always be two groups, representing different factions, waiting at the top to give him hassle and tell him their problems. He was extremely relieved to get out and back to West Stirling.'

Short-term at least, events proved Tom Johnston calculated wisely when he supported Ramsay MacDonald for the Labour leadership following the 1924 election defeat and later in the squabble surrounding the collapse of George Buchanan's 1924 Home Rule Bill. His stand on both counts was bound to appeal to the hurt and angry former Prime Minister. As gestures of loyalty they no doubt assisted the editor of *Forward* to a place in the next Labour administration.

Significantly, a month before polling in the 1929 general election, MacDonald wrote to him seeking advice on what he should say on a forthcoming visit to Scotland. 'I have had to book meetings at Oban, Inverness and Glasgow during the election,' MacDonald explained in a letter dated 10 April 1929. 'Could you help me by advising me what I should say at these places – the chief subjects I should deal with and the line I should take? I should be greatly indebted to you for help in this matter.'

Shortly before polling on 10 May 1929 Johnston sent MacDonald a detailed brief on the subject of Scottish housing. This had been specially prepared, at Johnston's request, by a Lanarkshire County Council official, W.E. White. According to Johnston he was the leading authority on housing in Scotland and 'these facts and figures are the latest and most up-to-date stuff'. Conspiratorially, the journalist of long standing in Johnston couldn't help adding, 'No one else has been supplied with them'.

Seeing an opportunity for himself and his paper, his letter also contained a special request. 'After you are finished with them at the end of your Scottish tour I would be greatly obliged if you could let me have them as I should be able, in the future, to make considerable use of much of this material.'

Johnston, who had been the favoured candidate in West Stirlingshire and Clackmannanshire on two previous occasions, found the number of people entitled to vote in the constituency greatly increased since the last general election on account of women being given the vote. Then the electorate totalled 24,420. Five years later 32,383 men and women were registered to vote within its boundaries. And just as the number of people entitled to vote in West Stirlingshire and Clackmannanshire on 10 May 1929 showed a substantial increase from the last general election, so the percentage figures for those who actually voted also improved: 81 per cent in 1924 against 82.7 per cent five years later. Similarly, an exhilarating swing to Labour ended with 15,179 voters declaring in favour of Tom Johnston, rejected last time, against 11,589 who continued to believe G.D. Fanshawe was the superior candidate.

The results of polling on 30 May 1929, combined with the vagaries of the British electoral system, helped to ensure that the party which won most votes finished second. An additional 304,000 voters from the popular register backed the Conservatives to win against Labour. But it wasn't enough. Labour, with 287 seats from 8,360,000 votes, was now the largest single party in the House of Commons.

Supporters of the previous Tory administration who remembered gaining 155 seats in 1924 were left to weep and ponder as their numbers crumbled from an astonishing high of 413 seats last time to 261 on this occasion.

The final results of the 1929 election also revealed 5,300,000 voters who were attracted to the Liberal cause, almost a third of the total combined support enjoyed by the other two parties in the country at large. Translated crudely, in terms of voter share, it suggested the Liberals were due perhaps as many as 150 seats in the House of Commons.

In fact, throughout the short, unhappy life of the second Labour Government, which almost but didn't quite match the short, unhappy life of the first Labour Government, the highest number Lloyd George could muster, from the Liberal ranks, to vote against Ramsay MacDonald, totalled 59. And even this scant reward, in terms of seats, for the number of votes polled was wantonly reduced by the sudden defection of William Jowitt, who accepted an offer from MacDonald to become Attorney General; and the loss of three other MPs, including Sir John Simon, who resigned the Liberal Whip the following year.

Summoned to Buckingham Palace, and invited by King George V to form a Government, Ramsay MacDonald realised it was a task he relished but didn't enjoy. 'Most painful days in one's life,' MacDonald, the diarist, recorded later. 'Not good experience for maintenance of respect for mankind.'

His list of possible Ministers included two names he considered right for Scotland: William Adamson, who had been Secretary of State in the first Labour Government, and a man he felt obliged to overlook last time, Tom Johnston.

According to Johnston's account of the meeting the Prime Minister 'began by distributing some saponaceous lather' before telling them he proposed rewarding Adamson for past services with a seat in the House of Lords, as well as the Cabinet, and the title of Secretary of State. However, he also wanted Adamson, a former miner and a popular figure in Labour circles, to concern himself mainly with ceremonial matters, leaving his Parliamentary Under-Secretary, Tom Johnston, to assume full responsibility for Scottish business in the House of Commons.

MacDonald was probably motivated by misplaced feelings of kindness, or a deep sense of respect for his old comrade, in his treatment of Adamson. Certainly it is hard to imagine this peculiar arrangement affecting the governance of Scotland commanding respect with many people, even then. Judged solely on ability, there was an ample choice of candidates available, for the role of Secretary of State, within the ranks of the Scottish Parliamentary group. In addition to William Adamson, his preferred choice, and Tom Johnston, the man he expected to shoulder most of the real work, the Prime Minister could call on the highly experienced John Wheatley, or even gamble on James Maxton, to run Scotland.

Instead, the Prime Minister, a pronounced Scot, born in humble circumstances in Lossiemouth, appeared to act in haste, allowing Adamson the trappings of power so long as Johnston agreed to lend his support and carry the burden of office in the House of Commons. 'He hoped we would both agree quickly,' Johnston later observed tartly, 'for he was very busy, and time was precious, and he had other appointments.'

Fortunately, for the sake of MacDonald's eccentric scheme, Tom Johnston also harboured a deep affection for the former Fife colliery worker. That and an understandable desire to test himself against the demands of Government office helped him decide in favour of MacDonald's curious proposal. Adamson also agreed, saying he would go to the Lords, and the two men shook hands. Instructed to remain silent about the arrangement until after the official announcement, Adamson looked glum. He wanted to tell his wife and son he was going to the Lords.

'I didn't know you had a son,' MacDonald cried, and immediately abandoned his scheme on the grounds he was against appointing peers with heirs able to inherit. Thus, as Tom Johnston, who was no worse off as a result of MacDonald's change of mind, recalled, with some amusement, years later, 'was blotted out a noble lord, and the Scottish Office had to run with the usual administrative set-up'.

However, the Prime Minister also ordered Adamson to ensure his deputy got plenty of rope; a plea MacDonald cushioned with a warning to Johnston not to hang himself.

MacDonald, who returned to Downing Street on 5 June 1929, was once again obliged to govern without the safety net of an overall majority. He was totally dependent on the loyalty of his own supporters. But this didn't stop him denying office to John Wheatley, an undisputed star of the first Labour Government and leader of the previously influential Clydesiders.

The snub to his friend infuriated James Maxton, similarly ignored by the Prime Minister. His disillusionment with the mechanics of power was complete. Henceforth, he decided, ILP Members of Parliament, including Ministers, would be required to comply with ILP policy; even if this meant forcing them to vote against the Government on key issues. The 1930 annual conference of the ILP, held in Birmingham, made Maxton's mission to control the way MPs voted in the House of Commons official ILP policy. Those who disagreed with Maxton included the new Under-Secretary of State at the Scottish Office, Tom Johnston.

Johnston wrote to John Paton, secretary of the ILP, to complain about the policy. He believed the real issue was the relationship of the various constituent bodies in the Labour Party to the joint organisation. There was 'no escape from the dilemma that if every constituent body in the Labour Party demands similar rights to those now claimed for the ILP, the Labour Party will be smashed to fragments, to the great joy of the anti-socialist interests in the country, and to the serious detriment of the working class', Johnston warned.

A member of the Government couldn't be expected to vote against the Government of which he was a member, Johnston continued, either at the bidding of a group in the party or the NAC, although he could understand 'the ILP declining to affiliate to the Labour Party and declining to allow its members to accept office in the Labour Government'.

What he couldn't understand was the ILP agreeing to affiliate to an organisation 'and at the same time binding its representatives to vote if called upon against the considered decisions of the body to which it has affiliated. The position appears to me to be untenable and indefensible.'

Johnston was unable to accept membership of the ILP group upon the conditions stated. One who did was Emmanuel Shinwell, another from the historic Labour class of 1922, who had been appointed Secretary for Mines in 1930. He had been a member of the ILP since 1903. 'As I do not regard the present mood of the ILP as permanent, I can afford to wait,' Shinwell informed John Paton. 'Meantime, I am not prepared to allow the ILP, in whose principles I still have faith, to be mishandled by a group who have only one idea in common, their hatred of the Labour Government.'

John Paton, in a reply published in *Forward*, maintained the ILP never accepted the view that its affiliation to the Labour Party precluded it from exercising an independent judgment and vote in the House of Commons, although, in over 90 per cent of divisions in the present Parliament, the ILP group voted with the Government. 'The ILP, as an autonomous unit within the federal structure of the Labour Party, will seek to maintain the liberty it has always exercised,' Paton added. 'It asks from its own Members of Parliament the same general support of its party policies and programme that it is prepared to accord, as an organised unit, to the Labour Party.'

It was the beginning of the end of the ILP. The party of Keir Hardie could boast 140 MPs from the 1929 election. But only 18 showed a willingness to accept the authority of their own conference. Until a settlement was reached the Labour Party Executive refused to endorse ILP candidates. Predictably, both sides blamed each other.

As G.D.H. Cole explained in his *History of the Labour Party*: 'The ILP claimed that the Labour Party was seeking to alter a long-established practice under which the ILP representative had been allowed freedom to act up to their socialist principles; the Labour Party Executive maintained that the ILP was the innovator and was attempting to impose pledges which were in conflict with the Labour Party Constitution.'

There was even the threat of an unseemly row over the succession in Shettleston following the sudden death of John Wheatley, from a cerebral haemorrhage, on 12 May 1930. On that occasion, at least, the Labour Party Executive withdrew their objections and an ILP candidate, John McGovern, was selected to succeed the lost leader.

But after another two years of bitter wrangling, the Labour Party Executive refused to accommodate the idea of a fully fledged ILP group within its Parliamentary ranks free to vote as it pleased. Half a century after Keir Hardie launched the Independent Labour Party in Bradford the same sturdy Midlands town witnessed, for all practical purposes, the last act in its self-willed political demise.

By 241 votes to 142, a special ILP conference, convened in July 1932, agreed to disaffiliate from the Labour Party with a view to becoming 'a completely independent force with a programme and policy appealing to all socialists who realise the necessity of a break with the past and a new approach to the future'.

A last-ditch appeal by David Kirkwood went unheeded. Kirkwood was one of the original Clydesiders, a popular and decent man, described by Tom Johnston as an artist who 'could flash into the minds of working-class audiences mosaic pictures of social injustice and inequity in a way that the other more text-booky speakers among us found impossible'. A small band of theorists, who criticised everybody, threatened the whole Labour movement, Kirkwood warned. 'This role of John the Baptist does not appeal to me,' he added pointedly. 'I prefer to work with my comrades in the front trench rather than pray in the wilderness with a chosen few.'

Another veteran of the Glasgow ILP, Patrick Dollan, later knighted for his political services to the city, believed the vote at Bradford was an absurd manifestation of ILP opinion. According to Dollan most of the branches weren't properly represented and calls for a referendum of the membership or, at the very least, a roll call vote of the delegates present at the special conference, were ruled out of order by Maxton's supporters on the Standing Orders Committee.

Dollan also alleged support for disaffiliation was most pronounced in London and the southern counties, East Anglia and the south-western counties. 'Mr Maxton and his friends owe their mandate for disaffiliation to the backward areas,' Dollan went on. 'Perhaps now he and his colleagues will concentrate their campaign for an early revolution in these districts which are more in need of socialist attention and propaganda than say Bridgeton, Gorbals and Shettleston. No one will be more delighted than I if Mr Maxton succeeds in creating such intense feeling in the South of England that the Red Flag will soon be hoisted over the town halls of Bournemouth, Eastbourne, Exeter and Chelsea,' Dollan added. 'It will be a great achievement.'

The secretary of the ILP, John Paton, later defended the Standing Orders Committee against Dollan's attack, claiming it was unscrupulous and unjust. And if the chairman erred at all in his conduct of the conference, Paton claimed, it was in favour of those who wished to remain inside the Labour Party.

Still, for all practical purposes the ILP, which was once the principal driving force of the political aspirations of the British working class, died that July day in 1932, in Bradford, the town of its birth. 'The ILP now runs candidates in opposition to Labour,' one writer observed. 'By-election results and forfeited deposits proclaim that the working class are going to have no part in such wrecking tactics.'

Following the special conference of the ILP, held in Bradford in 1932, Tom Johnston recalled how, when it all started, the trades unions – in so far as they took any part in politics at all – were attached to the Liberal Party. The co-operative societies had no politics and what socialist movement there was had 'neither municipal nor Parliamentary influence, and was engaged, mostly in the cellars of Soho, in subdividing itself like an amoeba, and expelling its minorities over hair-splitting disputes about theories of value and the like'.

It was the ILP that advised the trade unions to form their own political party. As a result the trade unions, the Social Democratic Federation, the Fabians and the ILP had united in 'one gigantic Labour Party which, even amid the scare and terror of the last election – with the whole organised force of the money power, the press, pulpit and rene-gade Labour leaders against them – could poll nearly seven million votes'.

Now the Labour Party, which the ILP could claim a major share of the credit for helping to create, was to be attacked and harassed. 'The energies and subscriptions of the membership of the ILP, instead of being devoted to socialist propaganda, are henceforth to be dissipated in sterile, internecine feuds,' Johnston complained. 'Enthusiasms that might have been directed to municipal houses and banks and works departments, and a national organisation of trade and credit, and to international peace and an international effort to raise the buying power of the peoples of the earth, and to a great world federation of working-class and socialist parties to save the mass of mankind from the domination of fascism and finance – these activities are now, if you please, to be transferred to a fratricidal war on the left flank of the Labour Party.'

Tom Johnston wanted no part in such folly. Sooner than waste the remaining years of his life, he threatened to 'get out of politics and public life altogether'. Others who tried to sunder and disrupt the great army of the working class suffered from the same delusion, Johnston argued: they believed it was possible to achieve socialism without the support of workers organised within the ranks of the trade union movement. However, anyone who favoured the ILP leaving the Labour Party went further, Johnston raged. They believed socialism could be achieved without the support of the organised workers – 'by flouting them, opposing them, and weakening them at the polls'.

Many people blamed James Maxton for the ILP's premature end as a party of influence. Patrick Dollan believed the two parties would have been capable of reaching agreement without Maxton. It was Maxton who made agreement impossible, Dollan insisted, adding waspishly, 'Thanks to the admiration of enthusiastic admirers he would rather be the leader of a small party in Parliament than a co-operator in the Labour Party.'

His most recent biographer, Gordon Brown, acknowledged his subject, and what remained of the ILP, were 'distanced from power, and diverted from political campaigning by factional strife, just at the time when social and economic conditions of the people they sought to represent were at their worst and demanded a united left-wing voice of power and influence'.

Tom Johnston later decided the emotional qualities which endeared Maxton to public audiences were 'not at all suited to the administrative hazards and encounters in a great organisation like the ILP'. But he never abandoned his admiration for Maxton personally. And he never allowed himself to forget the memorable part Maxton played 'in changing a public opinion which was complacent and acquiescent in face of needless suffering in the midst of plenty, to one that was resolutely determined upon fairer shares for all. I am thankful to have known him,' Johnston declared.

CHAPTER TEN

LABOUR WOULD NEED to behave – or else!

That warning from Lloyd George, the Liberal leader, barely a fortnight after the polls closed and the count revealed a seriously divided House of Commons, characterised the difficulties Ramsay MacDonald faced throughout the life of the second Labour Government. 'The mandate of the Government ends when it fails to pursue a Liberal policy,' Lloyd George, addressing a crowded chamber on 13 June 1929, announced solemnly. 'The very hour the Ministry decides to become a Socialist administration its career ends.'

By combining with the Tories the Liberal leader could, on paper certainly, end the life of the Government at any time. At the very least, as *Forward* noted, the Liberals could be expected to throw their 'weight against any attempt by a Labour Government to carry out a programme of nationalisation or any big measure of social reconstruction which might be characterised as an attempt to overthrow capitalism'.

At the opening session of Parliament on 2 July 1929 MPs were told that Ministers would be concentrating their 'foremost endeavour' on finding a cure for the country's worsening unemployment problem. In addition, however, the Prime Minister and his team would be working to improve transport services, stimulate overseas trade, improve the condition of agriculture and encourage the fishing industry.

As outlined in the King's Speech, its agenda also suggested changes could be made in the organisation of the coal industry to include a shorter working week and the ownership of minerals. Iron, steel and cotton had been targeted for aid, slum clearance would be encouraged and legislation to make life easier for widows, orphans and pensioners would be forthcoming, His Majesty announced. Considering the

116

Government's minority status it was a not unambitious programme for change. There was even a promise to appoint a Commission on Electoral Reform representing all the major parties. In fact, as Gilbert McAllister observed in his biography of James Maxton, a constant and usually ferocious critic of his own side, the King's Speech at the start of MacDonald's second term as Prime Minister covered at least six, and possibly seven, of the nine promises Maxton made to the electors of Bridgeton prior to the election. 'The three points not covered were the granting of a maintenance wage for children kept at school beyond the leaving age, an amendment to the Compensation Act providing that every person injured at work would receive full wages while disabled, and the proposal to establish a minimum wage for all workers.'

Tom Johnston, a member of the Government with important responsibilities for the first time, believed long-term benefits could be derived from intelligent disbursement of national resources in aid of the greater good. Together with another Scot, the scientist and nutritionist, John Boyd Orr, later Director-General of the United Nations Food and Agriculture Organisation and a future winner of the Nobel Peace Prize, he'd already attempted to secure 'something on the lines of a national dividend from increased production and the bounties of nature'.

As part of a controlled experiment John Boyd Orr arranged for surplus milk, previously wasted, to be given to children at a number of schools in Glasgow and Belfast. 'One group of children was given from a half to a pint of milk every day at school, some receiving whole milk and others separated milk which contained the proteins, vitamins and minerals of whole milk,' Boyd Orr explained. 'The test ran for seven months and showed a marked improvement in the health of the children,' he went on, 'the improvement being most marked in the children of the poorest families.'

A similar study of mothers and children in Lanarkshire, conducted during Tom Johnston's time as Under-Secretary of State at the Scottish Office, enabled Boyd Orr and his team to confirm their earlier findings – increased milk consumption produced beneficial results.

Boyd Orr's report led directly to a House of Commons-approved scheme permitting local authorities to provide cheap or even free school milk in Scotland; followed by England and Wales. In an earlier report on the progress of the scheme the Under-Secretary of State for Scotland told the House of Commons: 'It is my firm conviction that we can prove we have actually saved more money in public health by this milk supply method than we have expended on the milk.'

Further studies by the Aberdeenshire-based scientist 'showed that one-third of the population of this country, including all the unemployed, were unable, after paying rent, to purchase sufficient of the more expensive health foods to give them an adequate diet'. The scheme which allowed local authorities to dispense free milk in schools saved 'the milk producers from ruin, the children from ill-health, and the public purse from much expenditure upon hospitals!' his associate, the Under-Secretary of State for Scotland, Tom Johnston, claimed later.

Still, any such interference with the natural laws of supply and demand also aroused great and foolish opposition, Johnston recalled. People who supported the idea were forced 'to bow before a united opposition of those on the one hand who thought we would wreck the commercial system of profit-taking, and those on the other hand who thought we would shore it up and perpetuate it'.

On 22 May 1930, as an example of the difficulties he faced, Johnston recounted, for the benefit of the House of Commons, what happened when the Scottish Office tried to assist egg producers in Skye. Following a glut the price of eggs on the island had been reduced to sixpence – less than two and a half new pence – a dozen. Johnston authorised his officials to prepare a scheme for the coming year whereby the Government purchased the island's entire output of eggs at the previous year's wholesale price. In addition, Johnston explained, if the egg producers on Skye agreed to participate in the scheme, he proposed the eggs should be graded and stored for as long as any glut lasted, at no cost to the producers. 'At the end of the glut period,' Johnston went on, 'when the price had again risen, we offered to dispose of the eggs, saying that whatever surplus was over after the administrative expenses of the experiment had been met would accrue to the growers.'

Johnston believed his offer 'would be joyfully and enthusiastically accepted by every poultry breeder in Skye. It was costing them nothing, and they were getting their co-operative started without any risk or cost to themselves,' he observed. Instead, he had been amazed to learn that the suppliers in question preferred to continue as before: dealing direct with the same local merchants.

It wasn't easy to break down engrained prejudices and habits and customs of generations, Johnston noted in his speech to the House of Commons. 'Many poor people who are in debt to merchants cannot very easily break away from the old system of merchanting their eggs and take up a co-operative system.'

Despite his early bluster, without Conservative support, Lloyd George couldn't prevent the Government continuing. So long as the main opposition parties didn't combine and turn against him in a serious and organised fashion, MacDonald was safe – apart from the dangers he faced from inside his own party.

MacDonald's position as leader of the Labour Party was probably helped by John Wheatley's death on 12 May 1930, a week short of becoming 61 and less than a year after Labour achieved power for only the second time in history. As Robert Keith Middlemas observed in his history of the Clydesiders: 'It is only speculation to say that Wheatley would have led the Labour Party, but many political commentators believed it at the time.'

John Wheatley, denied office at any level, was the obvious casualty-in-chief of Ramsay MacDonald's careful soundings and tortured deliberations following the 1929 election. Wheatley had been a member of MacDonald's first Cabinet and was often tipped as a future leader of the Labour Party. His 1924 Housing Bill had been hailed as a major Parliamentary achievement. Some people believed he was capable of becoming Prime Minister in succession to MacDonald himself whenever the need arose.

Wheatley, along with his close friend, James Maxton, had been a constant irritant and relentless critic of MacDonald while in opposition. When the Cook-Maxton manifesto first appeared the political weight provided by Wheatley, more than Maxton's passion and brilliant oratory, presented a massive challenge to Ramsay MacDonald. The manifesto included plans for a series of mass rallies aimed at focusing ILP opinion on the need for socialist policies, untainted by any hint of electoral pragmatism, which enraged the Labour leader.

But the threatened rebellion against his authority, inspired by the Cook–Maxton manifesto and orchestrated by John Wheatley, barely materialised and didn't last long. Bitter at the outcome, Wheatley blamed an uncharacteristically poor speech by his friend Maxton, at a heavily promoted rally in St Andrew's Hall, Glasgow, on 8 July 1928 for initiating its collapse.

But the man who so impressed the House of Commons and the country in the only previous Labour Government now found himself fatally isolated, on the extreme left wing of the party, from the leadership he once served; just as MacDonald prepared to resume power. Once in Downing Street again, as Wheatley soon learned, the Labour leader wasn't inclined to forgive – or forget!

In a letter to Wheatley, following the 1929 election, the Prime Minister expressed his regret 'that you did not see your way to continue with us. It would have been a great pleasure to me had you done so.'

Some of his senior colleagues questioned the wisdom of MacDonald's decision to overlook Wheatley. They believed the acknowledged leader of the Clydesiders might be less trouble inside the Cabinet than outside. MacDonald shrugged whatever danger existed aside. Embarking on his second minority administration, and writing to Wheatley to explain his omission, MacDonald hoped 'the work to which we are to put our hands will receive the support of all our members. Our position will be tight and strenuous.'

MacDonald was right to worry about his former Health Minister's future conduct. Wheatley's appetite for political mischief-making was demonstrated clearly enough when he virtually accused Tom Johnston of intentionally misleading the electors of West Stirlingshire during the general election campaign. Emrys Hughes later observed; 'Wheatley knew how to get under Tom Johnston's skin by reminding him of what he had said when in opposition and asking him what he intended to do about it.'

On 20 December 1929, from a position behind the Government

front bench in the House of Commons, the MP for Shettleston rose to inquire: 'I should like to know what happened to the mid-Scotland canal? I remember that during the election some of my honourable friends, one of whom is now a prominent member of the Government, had a cut and dried scheme which they put before the electorate for the making of that canal. I have not heard anything about it since. Has that canal served its purpose, or is the scheme to fructify, and are we to benefit from it, just as the honourable gentleman benefited when he appealed to the electors?'

Tom Johnston listened carefully as his old friend from Miss Cranston's turned against him. 'I want to know,' John Wheatley continued, 'when the committee on this canal is likely to report, because we are told that considerable employment would be given to the labouring classes of Scotland in the making of such a canal.'

Johnston believed Wheatley's open antagonism, both to himself and the second Labour Government, deserved a wider audience. As a member of the Government he had been obliged to assign the editorship of *Forward* to his deputy, Emrys Hughes. But this didn't mean he couldn't appeal directly to Hughes to print *Hansard*'s account of Wheatley's challenge – which he considered 'a rather wicked misrepresentation' – alongside his own disclaimer. Hughes later noted: 'He was obviously hurt and angry and his reply showed that his sense of humour had temporarily disappeared. Wheatley had touched on some sensitive areas.'

But the one-time hero of the first Labour Government was now the man under attack. Johnston accused Wheatley of inventing his story about the mid-Scotland canal for the purpose of having a slap at the Government. There was never a cut and dried scheme for such a canal, Johnston insisted. 'No one ever said they had such a scheme. All they asked for in their speeches and writings was for an inquiry – a geo-physical enquiry – without which no estimate of cost could be made.' This committee had been appointed within a fortnight of the Government taking office and was now sitting, taking evidence, Johnston added.

His response failed to silence Wheatley, however. In a letter to *Forward*, published on 4 January 1930, he continued to maintain the proposal for a mid-Scotland ship canal, which Johnston had been keen to pursue during the election campaign, 'figured largely in his speeches and was one of the main issues between himself and his Tory opponent'. The project wasn't 'held up to the public as something that might merely be inquired into. They were promised a canal, not a committee,' wrote Wheatley. Such a scheme had been examined, advocated and opposed by experts for about 20 years, Wheatley continued. Johnston's committee had 'all the facts and evidence in the pigeon-holes. They had only to decide if and when the work was to begin.'

Wheatley also wanted to know what Johnston proposed doing about unemployment, now he was a Minister and partly responsible for dealing with the problem. The position was now worse than when he took office, Wheatley complained. 'We are entitled to ask Mr Johnston what has become of the employment proposals he submitted to the public in the early part of the year, and if they were to be regarded as only for election purposes.'

It would have been impossible for anyone to write critically of Tom Johnston in the pages of *Forward* without him hearing about it first; long before the offending words reached the printers, in fact. Emrys Hughes was still, nominally at least, only acting editor.

Excerpts from newspaper reports, and *Hansard*, were quickly assembled to support the founding-editor's version of events. In a letter printed alongside Wheatley's bitter attack, Johnston countered angrily: 'I do not mind criticism. I give it and I am prepared to take it. But I will not tamely suffer misrepresentation.'

Wheatley's claims concerning the proposed mid-Scotland ship canal were untrue and without the shadow of justification, Johnston claimed. 'It is typical of the methods Mr Wheatley has been recently adopting. I nowhere and at no time did other than urge a geo-physical inquiry, as without such an inquiry the probate costs could not be ascertained.'

John Wheatley wasn't alone in wanting to find work for the unemployed, the Under-Secretary of State for Scotland added loftily. 'But if Mr Wheatley imagines that by his reckless, controversial methods he is impressing the Labour and Socialist movement with the sincerity of his wish to find work for the unemployed, he is very much mistaken.'

Readers of *Forward*, Emrys Hughes later observed, were 'perplexed and bewildered and hurt' to discover two such prominent socialist propagandists had fallen out; and at the 'venom and bad blood' which the dispute over details of the proposed mid-Scotland canal revealed.

Hughes, not surprisingly, sympathised with his not-quite-absent chief. 'Johnston was not a Cabinet Minister, only the Under-Secretary of State for Scotland,' he wrote. No one could blame Tom Johnston 'if some of the measures he proposed when in opposition didn't instantaneously become the legislative programme of the minority Labour Government'. And in his view nobody knew that better than John Wheatley who had been a member of a minority Labour Government in 1924. Hughes, in his unpublished memoir, *Rebels and Renegades*, also insisted: 'Johnston, who had tremendous energy, was doing what he could at the Scottish Office and was largely responsible for giving Scotland a new Slum Clearance Act which was, in its way, as progressive as Wheatley's Housing Act.'

Johnston was playing politics in print, of course. His poor opinion of John Wheatley's influence on Labour attitudes was probably optimistic and overstated. It certainly wasn't universally shared.

On 30 January 1930 *The Observer* forecast: 'The day will probably come when the Prime Minister will bitterly regret his decision to exclude Mr Wheatley from his administration. The Clydeside leader is not a popular figure but he commands the support of one who is – Mr Maxton – and the loyalty of a group which holds the key to the present Parliamentary situation. It is no exaggeration to say that the fate of the Government depends more upon Mr Wheatley than Mr Lloyd George. When the final crisis comes, his will be the hand that will strike Mr MacDonald and his colleagues from power. It is not a hand that will flinch from the task.'

His appointment to the Scottish Office meant Tom Johnston had been obliged to remove himself from any formal involvement with *Forward*. Emrys Hughes, who took possession of the editor's chair, was entitled to hope, for a variety of reasons, personal and political, that the paper's founding editor would be preoccupied with other matters for a good long time. However, Johnston himself envisaged a day when he might return. 'If the need were to arise I should drop the other duties without hesitation and return, uncontrolled and untrammelled to its service,' he warned.

On 4 January 1930 *Forward* reminded its for the most part committed socialist readership that Labour didn't enjoy a mandate for socialism. *Forward*, like a majority of its readers, found this state of affairs unsatisfactory. But unlike some who paid two pence weekly to digest the trenchant political outpourings of Emrys Hughes and his team, *Forward* believed the Labour Party had been right to take office, despite the difficulties it faced with a minority administration. In office Labour could 'seek to justify itself by attempting to carry into effect as much of its social and international policy as circumstances permit, in the belief that this would result in still further convincing the country that it should be entrusted with full power to proceed with a bigger and bolder programme'.

Its achievements so far included formal diplomatic recognition of the Bolshevik regime then in power in post-revolutionary Russia. There were also proposals for ending the arms race with the United States, a new policy for India and plans to strengthen the League of Nations. In addition, on the domestic front, half a million widows had been introduced to the pensions roll, housing subsidy had been restored and legislation was pending which would 'save the miners a further cut in wages, lead to a reduction in hours and a drastic reorganisation of the coal industry'.

It was a brave enough defence of the Government's record. But it left unstated any criticism of Labour's failure to grapple effectively with the country's principal concern – rising unemployment.

Lloyd George, J.M. Keynes, Sidney Webb, Sir Alfred Mond and Lord Beaverbrook all believed they knew how the problem could be tackled and made proposals for schemes which duly failed. Lord Inchcape thought the simple solution was to despatch the unemployed abroad. Others, like Sir Arthur Steel Maitland, Minister of Labour in Stanley Baldwin's 1927 administration, went further. He assured Tom Johnston there was no solution to the problem: unemployment was an act of God.

While still in opposition Labour proposed a select committee 'to consider schemes of work of national benefit designed to provide employment and report at intervals not exceeding one month during the sittings of this House'. Lloyd George and the Liberals supported Labour. But the motion failed – at the end of what Johnston described as a partisan division – by more than 100 votes.

Given the prominent Tory view that the Government faced opposition of a celestial nature in its attempts to reduce unemployment, this was hardly surprising. Similarly, two years later, when Ramsay MacDonald invited the opposition to submit representations on unemployment, there was no response.

Long before he became a Minister Tom Johnston believed relief works, to aid the unemployed, should be 'lifted entirely out of the arena of partisan political strife'.

By his own account he set out to persuade first the Labour Party and then the House of Commons that 'water supplies were equally necessary to Socialist, Tory and Liberal consumers: that land drainage, afforestation, Empire Marketing Boards, and dozens of other projects for adding to the national wealth and providing rational employment for our people could surely be discussed on their merits without our first being lined up into groups whose settled policy was to frustrate any other group from doing anything'.

In May 1930, as Under-Secretary of State for Scotland, he explained his belief to the House of Commons that relief work was too big for any one party, harassed by strong opposition, to undertake. 'Until we can get unemployment and its emergencies regarded as an all-party question in this House, treated as questions were treated in the emergency of the war; obstructions swept away; the pettifogging delays which take place in this House over legislative proposals abolished; an all-party committee responsible to Parliament, making recommendations to Parliament – unless the House can rise to such a conception of its duties,' Johnston declared, 'I do not believe it is possible, quickly, to expand the area and the scope of relief works in this country.'

Between the armistice in 1918 and 1933, he later noted, Britain spent £380 million on relief and unemployment insurance benefit and 'got in return for that expenditure not one brick laid upon another, not an extra blade of grass: nothing'.

Some English and Welsh counties suffered 42 per cent and 45 per cent unemployment: over all Scotland, 35 per cent of the male workers were unemployed. But at least 'no longer did anyone declare that involuntary idleness was due to the victim's double dose of original sin, his drunkenness, his slothfulness, shiftlessness, or improvidence', Johnston recalled.

'Men in all classes now saw that productive capacity, inventiveness, labour-saving devices, were steadily outrunning permitted consumption of goods. Improved techniques were increasing year by year the actual and potential wealth of the world. The problem now was the problem of the glutted market, the electric navvy, the combined harvester; it was one of how to distribute the greatly increased wealth that was pouring from the machines.'

That was the month John Wheatley died. For most of the previous year he had been suffering from failing health and private business worries, as well as a growing sense of political frustration. Shortly before his death, at his home in Shettleston, on 12 May 1930, Wheatley complained to the social historian, Beatrice Webb, that working people were without a will of their own. She claimed only pious belief in the Roman Catholic Church prevented the former Health Minister in the first Labour Government becoming a communist.

'In these later days,' Emrys Hughes admitted, in a tribute to Wheatley published in *Forward*, 'many of us disagreed vigorously and emphatically with his views on policy and tactics. But the positive things that he did will live. His Housing Bill was the most substantial achievement of the first Labour Government.'

Tom Johnston thought his old friend and latter-day political antagonist was 'a born administrator and a man of great force of intellect and reasoning power; one of the most convincing advocates of socialism I have ever known; a great personality who has left an indelible imprint upon his day and generation'. Johnston remembered how Wheatley 'was always inordinately proud and bitter over his boyhood days in a

Lanarkshire slum'. He was proud, Johnston explained, 'that he had come from the working class, and had done something to inspire it with rebellion against the sordid poverty of his earliest days, and bitter against those in high places, ecclesiastical, legal, political, or financial, who sought to maintain the system of hunger and want, fear and servility, so rampant among the working class'.

CHAPTER ELEVEN

FROM THE HIGH cliffs around Hirta, far out in the Atlantic, more than 100 miles from the Scottish mainland, a million seabirds cacked and called. Dead dogs floated in the bay. In each abandoned house a peat fire burned. Smoke drifted slowly in the wind.

The inhabitants of the loneliest place in Britain huddled together near the stern of the fishery protection vessel HMS *Harebell* as it turned and headed for the mainland. George Henderson, an official from the Department of Health at the Scottish Office, headed for the ship's radio-room. He knew the Under-Secretary of State was waiting to hear from him.

The cable Henderson despatched to a private address in Kirkintilloch lacked detail. But it told Tom Johnston, at home in Monteviot, all he wanted to know about the last stages of an operation which some people considered a waste, and others a crime against humanity: 'Evacuation successfully carried out this morning. Left St Kilda eight a.m.'

In 1764 a rare visitor to the remote island group of St Kilda, which is located in the Atlantic 50 miles due west of Harris, suggested the hardy inhabitants 'may be ranked among the greatest curiosities of the moral world'. The Rev. Kenneth Macaulay, from Ardnamurchan, also concluded that if all things were fairly weighed in the balance of unprejudiced reason, 'the St Kildans possess as great a share of true substantial happiness as any equal number of men elsewhere'.

An earlier visitor, the historian Martin Martin, who arrived in Village Bay in 1697, reported a total population of 180. But an outbreak of smallpox in 1740 accounted for most of the people he encountered. By 1758, when the Rev. Kenneth Macaulay first landed on Hirta, the main island, only 38 males and 50 females survived. And by the summer of 1930, when the entire adult population decided living conditions on the island were now so dire they wanted the Secretary of State for Scotland, William Adamson, to evacuate the island, the total number of people living there had been reduced to less than half that number; too few to support life in the fearful conditions which often prevailed in the Atlantic.

Written by Dugald Munro, the missionary, on paper issued by the School Board of Harris, and signed by all the adults, who numbered 12 men and eight women, the appeal was dated 10 May 1930. It stated: 'We the undersigned, the natives of St Kilda, hereby respectfully pray and petition HM Government to assist us all to leave the island this year and find homes and occupations for us on the mainland.'

Several able-bodied men were determined to leave St Kilda in the weeks ahead, to seek employment on the mainland, regardless. But already there were barely enough men left on the island to carry on the necessary work and the latest departures would cause a crisis. 'These men are the mainstay of the island at present, as they tend the sheep, do the weaving, and look after the general welfare of the widows,' the desperate St Kildans informed St Andrew's House. 'Should they leave conditions for the rest of the community would be such that it would be impossible for us to remain on the island another winter.'

William Adamson despatched his deputy, Tom Johnston, to the island on 10 June 1930. Johnston visited every family separately and found all of them suffering great poverty and hardship. Reporting to the House of Commons he later confirmed: 'I was assured in every case that it was their earnest desire not to spend another winter on the island.' The islanders couldn't afford syrup, treacle, margarine or butter and sea spray destroyed the potato crop. Everyone had been without milk for three months. Children suffered severe stomach pains from a constant diet of fulmar and mutton. One family of ten survived on an annual income of £30.

In the House of Commons the Under-Secretary of State for Scotland later paid tribute to the service and devotion of Nurse Williamina Barclay who spent two winters on the island as the official representative of the Department of Health. 'Heaven only knows what tragedies would have occurred without her,' he said.

Johnston, on his short visit, found the islanders 'a lovable, simple, uncorrupted and healthy people'. However, as he also attested in an interview with the *Glasgow Herald* on his return, 'The villagers in that bleak, barren, rocky outpost in the Atlantic are unanimous in their desire to remove.'

His visit to St Kilda lasted six hours. Johnston visited every house in the village to meet the various family groups and see for himself the conditions they were forced to endure. Some of the talk was in Gaelic, translated by an interpreter. Before leaving he went to the little schoolhouse and addressed a meeting of all the adults. Once the Government decided on a course of action, news of the decision would be relayed to the island with all possible speed, Johnston promised.

On hearing his report the Secretary of State 'could refuse to do anything in furtherance of the appeal, saying the Government had no precedence in the matter', Johnston explained later, 'or he could make a precedent and ask a development of the duty of all to care for each'. Either way he recognised the Government could be in difficulty. If they refused to assist in the evacuation of the island and famine brought the community at St Kilda to a calamitous end the following winter, the Secretary of State and everyone else involved in the decision would be held responsible for the tragedy. Similarly, if they assisted in the evacuation they were sure to be denounced as the lineal successors of the men responsible for the Highland clearances.

Johnston, musing on the latter possibility, was bound to find the association, even in his own mind, disagreeable. Twenty years earlier, in *Our Noble Families*, he reminded the world of a 'peasantry that had been a country's pride hunted, ragged and homeless, to a barren coast'.

The island's owner, Sir Reginald MacLeod of MacLeod, told the *Glasgow Herald* he was sorry to lose a population that had been tenants of his family for a thousand years. 'But they themselves have elected to go and I cannot blame them. The life is one of hardship and inconvenience,' Sir Reginald observed.

The editor of the *Oban Times* believed it was a mistake to proceed with the 'complete clearance of an island which has nurtured people in bad times and good times for centuries. A Government's duty would have been fulfilled by establishing and maintaining some kind of reasonable communication between the island and the mainland,' he argued.

The Scotsman also noted that much had been done for the St Kildans except the one thing that might have been most helpful – the deliberate organisation of their economic life. 'There is sadness in the thought that an island so long held by man should not [sic] be abandoned, and to the individuals concerned the breach with the past and the desertion of familiar scenes must be matter at least for sentimental regret.'

One such worrying expression of regret, written by Compton Mackenzie, reached the editor of the Oban Times shortly after Tom Johnston presented his report on the islanders' desperate plight to the House of Commons. Mackenzie had been present on St Kilda, in the company of the man who was technically responsible for St Kilda's social and political welfare, the Liberal MP for the Western Isles, T.W.B. Ramsay, when the official Scottish Office party arrived on the island.

Johnston's mind was obscured by seasickness and he was in no condition to appreciate the real state of affairs on the island, the world-famous author, who defeated Johnston and two other candidates for the Lord Rectorship of Glasgow University the same year, alleged dangerously. Nor, it seemed, had he ever read 'a more pusillanimous admission by the member of any Government that his party was incompetent to deal with the problems of modern Scotland than Mr Johnston's statement in the House of Commons on the subject of St Kilda', Mackenzie continued.

It didn't help then that Compton Mackenzie retracted his criticism a decade later, saying Johnston had been right to evacuate St Kilda. Johnston, who had been put in charge of the operation, was impatient with people who believed the islanders should be encouraged to remain on St Kilda. But he was especially critical of 'literary poseurs' who found poverty picturesque so long as it was someone else who suffered.

A report prepared by George Henderson of the Department of Health dismissed any future economic development of St Kilda as unpracticable. Henderson saw no reason, apart from sentiment, for persevering with a population of any size there. 'I do not think it could be seriously contended that even the greatest possible development of its natural resources could give it any real economic value to the nation,' Henderson added.

Johnston had been sympathetic and considerate in his approach to the islanders ever since they first contacted St Andrew's House about their plight. He was optimistic jobs could be found for all the able-bodied men, with houses for everyone. But he was just as determined, throughout various discussions, statements in the House of Commons and considerable correspondence with an assortment of organisations and individuals, to stress the limits of the Government's commitment to the St Kildans. He acknowledged readily enough that some of them might require poor relief, but it was never his intention to exempt the islanders from rent or otherwise 'induce them to look upon themselves as a specially and permanently subsidised class'.

Sir Reginald MacLeod, chief of the Clan MacLeod, who owned the island, wanted an assurance from the Scottish Office that the St Kildans would be obliged to renounce their rights under the Crofters Holding Act before any large-scale evacuation was effected. 'Without formal renunciation it is possible some may attempt to re-establish themselves and thus defeat the whole purpose of the serious enterprise you have undertaken,' Sir Reginald warned.

Johnston was never committed to achieving a single colony settlement, which some observers considered desirable for the dispossessed islanders, anywhere on the mainland. Following his visit to St Kilda in June he told the *Glasgow Herald*: 'Each family must be dealt with separately.' In fact, family considerations apart, in their petition to the Government, the islanders did not ask to be settled on the mainland as a separate community. All they wanted was 'assistance and transference elsewhere where there would be a better opportunity of securing our livelihood'.

A leading article in *The Times*, on the day of the evacuation, suggested people might easily understand them not wishing to continue living together as a community; though their reasons might offend sentiment. Just as the islanders were tired of the hard life they endured on their oceanic peak, 'they have begun to have enough of each other's undiluted company'.

The cost involved in evacuating and settling the islanders was higher than some people expected. No one could claim the impoverished islanders misled them. Their petition made plain they were 'without the means to pay for the costs of removing ourselves and our furniture'. Officials calculated it would cost about £500 to evacuate the island. Johnston told the House of Commons he hoped 'to sell the sheep and apply the proceeds to the cost of the evacuation and the balance to the future subsistence of the islanders'. He later heard from the Treasury: 'We have been prepared from the start to deal with the situation as sympathetically as possible in the confidence that while everything necessary would be done to secure finality in resettlement of the inhabitants on the mainland you would not incur expenditure other than on a reasonable scale.'

An attempt to obtain financial assistance from the independently administered Highlands and Islands Fund was hardly encouraging. Johnston was told that, after the most careful consideration, the trustees felt unable to provide a block grant but would 'most sympathetically consider any individual cases of distress arising out of the evacuation upon receiving the usual forms of application'. The Highland and Agricultural Society of Scotland likewise considered it inappropriate to use money from its St Kilda Fund to buy furniture for the people in whose name the money was held in trust. Indeed, the directors of the society appeared surprised by the request: they understood the entire cost of the evacuation was a charge which should be met from public funds.

Before the day of the evacuation the islanders, assisted by two shepherds and a pair of sheepdogs provided by the Department of Agriculture, had been able to corral 573 sheep belonging to the Hirta flock. Another 200 animals, thought to be running wild on Boreray, were abandoned.

The business of transferring the sheep in a small boat, a dozen at a time, from the Hirta jetty to the hold of SS *Dunara Castle*, anchored in Village Bay, proved exhausting work. In addition 13 head of cattle were required to be tied to the stern of the island's only craft and wrestled and dragged, half-swimming and bellowing fearfully, to the side of the waiting cargo vessel where the few able-bodied men capable of tackling the work struggled for hours to haul them on board.

On the afternoon and evening of the day prior to the evacuation 'some hundreds of sheep were placed in small boats and towed out to the *Dunara Castle* as she lay at anchor in the village bay', *The Times* reported. 'Owing to difficulty in working with the sheep, which are semi-wild, operations had to be suspended about midnight, and the natives began to transport their belongings by the light from a couple of lanterns. The goods consisted mainly of wooden kists containing clothes and personal effects, spinning wheels, querns and pieces of furniture, many of which have been bought by tourists who visited the island in the SS *Hebrides* some days ago.'

Dogs outnumbered people on St Kilda. Small, lean beasts of collie extraction, Tom Steel noted in *The Life and Death of St Kilda*, 'they appeared to the outsider to be owned by no one in particular'. Steel also observed: 'At an early age, each dog had his teeth either broken or filed down so that he would not tear the flesh of the sheep as he ran them to the ground. When they were not being used, a rope was tied round each animal's neck and one foreleg passed through the noose so that they could not escape from the village area and worry the sheep and the nesting birds.'

However, as *The Scotsman* warned its readers at the time of the evacuation, many of the dogs on St Kilda were 'in diseased condition and only a few are fit for removal'. A heavy stone tied round the neck of each dog, followed by a short walk to the end of the jetty, settled their fate. 'Weeks later,' wrote Tom Steel in *The Life and Death of St Kilda*, 'when the SS *Hebrides* paid a visit to the island, the bay was still full of dead dogs.'

Unusually, perhaps, considering his own highly developed instincts as a journalist, and his frequently professed interest in the bleak nature of Scottish history, the Under-Secretary of State for Scotland refused to allow any newsreel coverage or any press photographs of the remote colony's final hours. Alasdair Alpin MacGregor, who reported the evacuation for *The Times*, claimed officials were under strict orders to carry out the evacuation with as little publicity as possible out of consideration for the feelings of the St Kildans themselves. MacGregor was also informed: 'The Admiralty are naturally hostile to the idea of publicity and Mr Johnston himself is strongly of the opinion that the utmost effort should be made to avoid the miseries of the poor people being turned into a show.'

Before they embarked on the 17-hour voyage to the mainland of Scotland, and a strange new life in unknown territory where they were bound to be viewed with suspicion by some of the inhabitants, the islanders left an open bible in every house, some oats and a welcoming fire. Aboard the fishery protection vessel HMS *Harebell* they turned for one last look at their remote island home. Few among them expected to see it ever again.

Life on the mainland proved difficult for the last native inhabitants of St Kilda. Tom Johnston obtained jobs – most of them with the Forestry Commission – for all the able-bodied men and houses for the various families. Most of them were located in the Morvern area around Lochaline, as promised. One of the islanders, Neil Ferguson, son of the postmaster, wrote to the Scottish Office in September to say, 'We can never forget your kindness to us since all this great change started for our good, I believe.' But in the months and years that followed there were some who wished themselves back on St Kilda. Their aspirations, as Tom Steel chronicled, were probably beyond anything the islanders were entitled to expect. Unemployment was high in Scotland and the civil servants couldn't lavish too great a benefit on the St Kildans; or offer them more than they were used to on Hirta. 'After all,' wrote Steel, 'it was the St Kildans, not the Government, who had asked for the evacuation, and there were many people watching to see whether the then Labour Government would pay too much or too little heed to the needs of a people who themselves had begged for help.'

In fact, the man chiefly responsible for organising the evacuation, Tom Johnston, was entitled to believe his talent for organisation had been well used on behalf of the men, women and children of St Kilda – at a final cost to the British taxpayer of around £1,000 and no lasting embarrassment to the Labour Government.

Johnston also believed the business of assisting the unhappy islanders

135

established a useful precedent; as he was quick to note in a speech delivered at a sale of St Kilda sheep in Oban, a week after the evacuation. By agreeing to help the St Kildans the Government demonstrated it was prepared to shoulder the responsibility for finding economic employment and opportunities for those in need.

It was a principle Tom Johnston intended to extend – and exploit – in the years ahead.

CHAPTER TWELVE

RAMSAY MACDONALD, on becoming Prime Minister for the second time, addressed the problem of unemployment by appointing a four-man committee – J.H. Thomas, Lord Privy Seal, George Lansbury, Commissioner for Works, Sir Oswald Mosley, Chancellor of the Duchy of Lancaster, and Tom Johnston, Under-Secretary of State for Scotland – to produce schemes and recommend ways of dealing with the problem.

Johnston, who later suggested the committee was an ingenious scheme devised by the Prime Minister in order to keep some of his potential troublemakers quiet, also claimed he couldn't imagine a more ill-assorted team. 'Looking back upon it,' he commented gleefully, more than 20 years after the excitement of MacDonald's sorry initiative, 'I can well understand the sardonic glee with which its appointment was received. It was openly asserted that the committee was set up so that the critics would confound each other: dogs were to be kept busy eating dogs.'

The committee was given an office at the Treasury and the services of a department official to act as full-time secretary. But it showed a determined laxity of purpose and, by Johnston's evidence, met only twice in six months; although, as Johnston also noted, the opposition 'remained in blissful ignorance' of this damaging statistic.

Sir Oswald Mosley, in his account of the quartet's desultory activities, claimed George Lansbury and Tom Johnstone [*sic*] were 'usually too occupied with their own departments even to attend our weekly meetings at the Treasury. They appeared to realise quickly that with Thomas we should get nowhere at all, but they always gave me loyal support in my efforts; particularly Lansbury, who was the less busy of the two.'

Mosley's contempt for the committee chairman, J.H. Thomas, a former railwaymen's union official, didn't stretch to dislike. 'It was impossible to dislike Jimmy, as he required all the world to call him, for he had many endearing qualities,' the future leader of Britain's fascists observed grandly. 'Every week he and I used to meet the heads of all departments in the Civil Service to review progress with the unemployment problem,' Mosley went on. 'These admirable people listened with patience to the trivial absurdities with which J.H. Thomas sought to mask his complete failure to understand the real subject.'

Mosley's efforts produced a document more than 25 pages long. The policy he advocated 'resembled at many points the Socialism Now programme of the ILP, with which indeed he was actively associated at the time,' G.D.H. Cole observed. 'It was, however, different in emphasis,' Cole added, 'being put forward not as a general socialist programme, but as a set of measures designed to cope with unemployment.'

Cole considered it an ambitious plan. Mosley 'wanted control of imports, either by tariffs or by direct limitation, bulk purchase agreements with overseas suppliers, especially in the Dominions and Colonies, and active development of home agriculture in order to reduce dependence on imports'.He also 'proposed the use of a liberal credit policy, to be ensured by public control of banking, a development of the social services and a more generous policy of pensions on retirement and of benefits and allowances, and a rationalisation of industry under public control in order both to increase exports and to make more goods available in the home market'. Mosley was intent on introducing a series of emergency measures designed to improve Britain's unemployment figures by at least 700,000. He believed this figure could be achieved by employing as many as 300,000 men on a much-needed programme of public works. In addition, Mosley suggested, an emergency pensions scheme could be used to remove another 280,000 people from the unemployment register. A statutory increase in the school leaving age would facilitate the rest.

The three main schemes he proposed to provide work for 700,000 to 800,000 people were not entirely original, Mosley conceded. However, he maintained, in *My Life*, first published in 1968, 'the method and machinery for doing this was in those days not only novel, but a direct challenge to current thought, for it was to be done by loans'. Mosley also claimed: 'The making of a short-term programme to meet the emergency of unemployment was essentially an administrative matter, and could only be achieved by a Minister in contact with all departments, who could get the facts and put them together into a whole of practical executive action.'

He had been given 'a task rare to the point of being unique in Government administration, having direct access to all the main departments of state and the right personally to consult with civil servants on any subject. From this experience I derived a lasting benefit,' Mosley added.

His colleagues on the unemployment committee, George Lansbury and Tom Johnston, were invited to approve the Mosley Memorandum before it reached the Cabinet. In general they agreed with most of it, Johnston reported. But he and Lansbury could see Mosley 'had contrived to widen his front of attack and bring in monetary policy and long-term planning of permanent economic reconstruction.' In addition, according to Johnston, 'there were already indications that he was preparing his ammunition for a breakaway movement, and that, as we both told him, would get the unemployed nowhere'.

In fact, there was never any hope of Mosley's radical proposals becoming official Government policy while Philip Snowden remained at the Treasury. During the difficult period of the memorandum's brief existence, before the Cabinet, headed by Ramsay MacDonald, finally decreed its fate, he told Mosley: 'All those things to which you refer, such as the rationalisation of industry and the displacement of man's labour by machinery, have been going on for long past. They were met in the past by a gradual raising of wages which increased the power to consume, and by a gradual shortening of hours which reduced the power to produce. Above all, in due time fresh markets opened overseas to absorb our surplus production.'

Snowden, according to G.D.H. Cole, 'believed as fanatically in free trade as in the gold standard, and would agree to nothing that would interfere with either. In these circumstances,' he went on, 'it was utterly impossible to check the rise in unemployment, which followed partly on export dumping in the British home and export markets and partly on the necessity of internal deflation in order to maintain the rates of exchange in face of falling world prices.'

Snowden's formal response to the Mosley Memorandum, by way of an official report to the Cabinet, was bleak. 'However much we may be criticised,' his Treasury report observed coldly, 'we must not be rushed into shovelling out public money merely for the purpose of taking what must inevitably be a comparatively small number of people off the unemployed register to do work which is no more remunerative and much more expensive even than unemployment.'

Treasury 'arguments against Mosley's proposals were restatements of classic objections to state intervention in the economy', historian Robert Skidelsky complained. They were the arguments of Labour's opponents, Skidelsky, in his biography of Mosley, continued sharply. 'Mosley did not feel the need in the memorandum to make a philosophic case for the state intervention. He took it for granted that all its readers accepted the case,' Skidelsky explained.

When, finally, the Cabinet rejected his proposals, Mosley resigned from the Government and, later, the Labour Party. Tom Johnston, who believed there was merit in his proposals for dealing with unemployment, was sorry to see him go. Johnston believed, during the political blood-letting which followed the appearance of the Mosley Memorandum, that its author had been 'trampled on; his talents ignored'. And years later, after Mosley left the Labour Party to form the New Party, which later became the precursor of the British Union of Fascists, his former colleague on Ramsay MacDonald's unemployment committee mused on the futility of speculating 'upon when and under what impulse Mosley began his political decensus Averno, shouting anti-Semitic slogans, wearing black shirts, and parading about as a miniature Musso-Hitler, indeed parading himself into detention as a menace to his country during the war'.

According to Johnston, there was a time in Mosley's life when there was no sign of these aberrations; despite the views of some *post facto* commentators. Johnston defended Mosley, at the time of his resignation, on the grounds he could be used. And he continued to believe the leader of Britain's pre-war fascists might have been of great service to his generation. 'No doubt he was ambitious,' Johnston observed, a touch philosophically, 'but he was not too wisely handled, and he grew up and shot out the wrong way.'

Johnston's close involvement in the fight against unemployment, as a member of Ramsay MacDonald's second Labour Government, didn't end with the Mosley Memorandum, however. On 23 March 1931 an unexpected letter, from the Prime Minister in Downing Street to the King in Buckingham Palace, took him to the Cabinet for the first time. 'Mr MacDonald, with his humble duty to the King,' the Prime Minister wrote, 'has the honour to recommend for Your Majesty's most gracious approval that Thomas Johnston Esquire, MP, Parliamentary Under-Secretary of State for Scotland, be appointed Lord Privy Seal in succession to the Right Honourable Vernon Hartshorn, OBE, deceased.'

Johnston had been happy at the Scottish Office, where he was succeeded as Under-Secretary of State by Joseph Westwood, and resisted leaving. But when he was summoned to appear before the Prime Minister to discuss becoming Lord Privy Seal, following the sudden death of Vernon Hartshorn, the previous incumbent of that ancient and curious office, MacDonald 'turned on the heavy appeal. He was in difficulties: needed help: needed somebody to put up real unemployment relief schemes. I was the man, and so on. Reluctantly, I yielded,' Johnston remembered.

His new post, which carried no specific departmental responsibilities, paid £2,000 a year, which was £800 more than Johnston received as Under-Secretary of State for Scotland. It also entitled him to membership of the Privy Council. 'He has proved himself an able lieutenant to Mr William Adamson in all phases of Scottish administration,' the *Glasgow Herald*, which appeared to welcome his appointment, commented. 'His chief asset is that he is a man of action. The expeditious manner in which the evacuation of St Kilda was decided upon and effected is a striking case in illustration of his driving force,' the *Herald* added.

Johnston, speaking perhaps with an inverted sense of pride at his own achievement, evidently believed the post was no longer 'a mere ceremonial relic, a dignity without duty'. Addressing a town hall gathering in Kirkintilloch he observed ruefully: 'Today, alas, it deals, or seeks to deal, with unemployment policy, at least so far as great and world-shaking cataclysms permit of any policy being organised on a national basis. And it is a post of such political difficulty and wear and tear that the insurance brokers at Lloyds would not readily assess it to any one holder for more than a few months.

Before sending for Tom Johnston to strengthen his Cabinet team, the Labour leader, Ramsay MacDonald, had been trying to impress on the country his new-found belief that public works should be referred to as such, and not relief works, which suggested they were of no long-term value to the country. On 12 February 1931 he warned the House of Commons that Britain was undergoing nothing less than an industrial revolution. Between 2,500,000 and 2,750,000 people were out of work on account of the reconditioning of the economic world. As a result of increased international competition 'the standard of living enjoyed by our competitors in the foreign markets is having a more and more direct bearing upon our social problems here', MacDonald explained.

MacDonald appealed for a great national effort aimed at providing an increased programme of public works and for people to see that Britain's prospects were good, so long as everyone involved could be mobilised to carry out the Government's programme with energy and resource. If that happened, the Labour leader insisted, the unemployment problem would be solved and a new source of power and wealth would be created. He and his new Lord Privy Seal were unlikely to quarrel greatly on that score!

On 16 April 1930 Johnston demonstrated his support for the Prime Minister's view that the world was changing. All the major industrial and agricultural countries showed a marked increase in capacity, he warned in a speech to the House of Commons. In his opinion, rationalisation couldn't be stopped. 'We must have efficiency,' Johnston declared, 'we must develop our economic resources.' As a socialist he did not 'desire to inherit derelict factories or obsolete machinery,' Johnston went on. 'I do not want to fall heir to a graveyard.'

The latest unemployment figures, cited by Johnston in his speech to the House of Commons, were devastating. If anyone needed proof they showed clearly enough the range and depth of the slump affecting British industry. Of the major industries which had been affected, shipbuilding and ship-repairing was worst hit with a life-diminishing 49 per cent of the workforce unemployed. In the cotton industry the figure was 41 per cent, while mining, an industry dear to the hearts of Labour supporters everywhere, suffered a 22 per cent jobless rate.

Earlier, in a speech to a constituency meeting at Fallin in Stirlingshire, the Lord Privy Seal warned his listeners that the capitalist system was employing an ever-decreasing number of human producers to provide the world's goods. For example, he noted, a 40 per cent increase in coal output in the United States between 1919 and 1929 had been achieved despite a seven per cent reduction, during the same period, in the number of workers regularly employed in the industry.

Johnston believed industrial rationalisation was inevitable and necessary to combat unemployment in all the developed countries. But he also adopted the somewhat optimistic, and largely unrealistic, view that the nations of the world would 'very speedily see that only by international regulation, and diminution of the hours of labour to keep pace with the increase in production, can the problem be successfully tackled'.

He appealed to Britain's iron and steel interests to combine to remove obsolete plant and inefficient marketing from their operations. An iron and steel cartel had been established in Europe and was already regulating its members' output, Johnston claimed.

The Government couldn't compel national ownership, Johnston went on. But it was steadily encouraging and assisting the country's basic industries to reorganise themselves into large-scale units. 'It is doing its utmost to wipe out the chaos and anarchy which has hitherto existed both on the productive and the marketing sides of these basic industries,' Johnston announced.

A letter from Ben Turner, former chairman of the General Council of the TUC, appointed Secretary for Mines in 1929, congratulated the Prime Minister on his choice of Johnston as Lord Privy Seal: 'Tom

Johnston is a first-class promotion,' wrote Turner. 'He has vision and character.'

People familiar with his career knew Johnston was a man of robust opinions – often plainly, and sometimes wildly, expressed. As yet undeveloped, perhaps, after less than two years as a member of the Government and only a few weeks' membership of the Cabinet, was a sense of ministerial propriety.

On 12 May 1931 he was the target of a serious reprimand from the Prime Minister following an unauthorised speech, delivered at various venues in Scotland, the previous day. In this he fiercely condemned attempts by the British iron and steel industry to obtain Government-imposed tariffs on European steel. He also canvassed openly for early nationalisation of these industries. Instead of squealing for tariffs to prevent low-price steel reaching Britain from the continent, Johnston suggested, the leaders of Britain's iron and steel industries should form themselves into a public utility corporation and wipe out inefficiency.

A tariff on imported steel would allow British manufacturers to raise prices. 'But if that happens the shipbuilding industry in this country which depends for its existence on cheap raw materials, will suffer,' he warned. Johnston wanted the leaders of the iron and steel industries to recognise they were responsible for a public service. 'Let them amalgamate, wipe out inefficiency, become a public corporation, agree to limit dividends, limit prices, stop competition among themselves, wipe out all waste and pay a reasonable wage level,' Johnston thundered.

Once that happened they could apply to the Government for assistance in the matter of cheap loans and cheap money. 'But if they can't run their works efficiently, on a co-operative basis as a public service, they should clear out and leave things to the nation. The nation is vitally interested in this matter and it will ensure that they are run efficiently,' Johnston declared.

A report in the *Daily Herald* was the first the Prime Minister knew of it. 'I am almost certain to be bombarded with questions which will be exceedingly awkward to answer,' MacDonald complained. His letter to Johnston was surprisingly frank. It had been written, the Prime Minister explained, with all possible speed, and without waiting for any explanations, because 'I want this letter to be in before protests reach me from any of your colleagues'.

This candid admission was probably the desperate response of a crisis-threatened Prime Minister approaching the end of his tether. MacDonald seemed set on distancing himself from unrewarding trouble. And the imposition of tariffs was a highly sensitive subject which divided the country as well as the Labour Party.

Although a journalist himself, there was little journalistic camaraderie on offer to the toiling scribes on Labour's own newspaper where it appeared from his letter he'd first read reports of Johnston's speech. It was possible, the Prime Minister suggested, that Johnston had been misquoted or quoted out of context. But, if not, he advised the Lord Privy Seal to issue some fresh statement designed to limit whatever damage might be caused by his remarks.

Johnston was a newcomer to government at the highest level. But he was left in little doubt about the scope of the Prime Minister's anger. Awkward questions from fellow Cabinet Ministers, including, presumably, the Chancellor of the Exchequer and the President of the Board of Trade, wasn't the worst of the repercussions he could anticipate as a result of Johnston's ill-timed remarks, about tariffs, especially. 'You will remember at the last meeting of the Cabinet it was decided that the Chancellor, the President of the Board of Trade and myself should see the Governor of the Bank and discuss the whole situation with him, and that pending this we should hold our hand,' MacDonald continued. 'I am afraid your statement will upset things.'

He reminded Johnston that Ministers were required to be awfully careful not to announce Government policy without his knowledge. 'There are so many things going on at the same time which may make an inopportune pronouncement most awkward, inconvenient and embarrassing,' he wrote.

CHAPTER THIRTEEN

JOHNSTON, ON BECOMING Lord Privy Seal, was expected to persevere with a series of consultations aimed at securing the support of the Liberals, which his predecessor had been pursuing at the Prime Minister's behest. MacDonald, who was especially keen on his own survival, wanted a regular weekly meeting with the Liberal leader, Lloyd George. Such an arrangement, MacDonald suggested, in a letter to Lloyd George dated 20 March 1931, 'would enable me to see how things are going generally from your point of view'. It would also help him concentrate his attention upon the various points of weakness,' MacDonald argued.

In his biography of Ramsay MacDonald, David Marquand thought it reasonable to assume MacDonald 'wanted a coalition if he could get one: that Lloyd George wanted one as well: and that both believed that they were more likely than not to have their way'. Marquand also noted that when he became Lord Privy Seal 'the policies that emanated from Johnston's office were indistinguishable from Lloyd George's'.

However, according to G.D.H. Cole, there was a serious downside: '. . . talks with the Liberals overlapped both the Government's own discussions and the work of the Economic Advisory Council. All the proceedings were secret and no committee knew what the others were doing. The handling of the problem, which was growing more serious every day, went from bad to worse.'

As late as 13 June 1931 the Lord Privy Seal was offering generous odds against an early general election. However, as he informed a meeting in Denny, Dunbartonshire, on that date, if an election proved necessary, he believed it would be fought on the Government's record on unemployment.

Johnston had been studying how other countries dealt with the problems of the great trade depression 'which has smitten the world. And I can say, without fear of contradiction,' he maintained, 'that in no other country has there been anything approaching the humanity and spirit of Christian brotherhood in which the problem has been treated as in Great Britain.'

It was a view supported by Gilbert McAllister in his biography of James Maxton. He noted that work schemes introduced during the life of the second Labour Government provided employment for a quarter of a million men. 'The full significance of that achievement can only be realised when the Labour Government's expenditure of £183 million on work schemes in two years is contrasted with the £6.8 million spent by the Baldwin administration in four and a half years of office,' McAllister wrote. 'The fact that Labour's assumption of office coincided with the general slump in world trade, which caused unemployment figures to mount rapidly both here and in America, clouded the achievement in the public eye but does not detract from the reality of the work done by the three successive Lords Privy Seal, Thomas, Hartshorn and Johnston,' he added.

G.D.H. Cole, who served on the 1929 Government's Economic Advisory Council, believed 'it was utterly impossible to check the rise in unemployment, which followed partly on export dumping in the British home and export markets and partly on the necessity of internal deflation in order to maintain the rates of exchange in face of falling world prices. Either going off the gold standard or a drastic policy of restrictions on imports might have made some contribution to dealing with the problem, though neither could have prevented Great Britain from feeling some of the effects of the developing world crisis.'

However, contrary to what Tom Johnston believed, when the financial crisis of 1931 brought the Government to its knees Labour's acknowledged concern for the unemployed was easily overshadowed by its failure to protect the pound in the world's money markets.

According to the former Lord Privy Seal the financial crisis which ended the life of the second Labour Government 'developed to catastrophe with all the inevitability of a Greek tragedy'. It began in

Austria, swiftly engulfed Germany, and then spread outwards, through Europe, to the rest of the world.

Johnston dismissed loose talk about a Bankers' Plot to destroy the Labour Government. He claimed it was the Money Traders' press which raised impudent clamours and mesmerised the public into the belief that it was the Government, and not the Money Traders, which was responsible for the crisis.

As the crisis unfolded the wrong prisoner was accused, and subsequently found guilty, Johnston complained. 'Only by blind partisan folly could the British Labour Government be blamed in any way for the crisis!'

Between 15 July and 29 July the nation's gold reserve fell from £164 million to £132 million. 'Trade languished,' Johnston wrote. 'Commercial houses failed; unemployment increased; the sources of public revenue diminished; in a world of plenty, poverty multiplied and intensified.' For as long as the crisis lasted, and while the Government survived, day-to-day policy had to be 'trimmed, curtailed, and amended, because of decisions taken in the City by groups of the Government's bitter political enemies'.

Johnston didn't like the City's beggar-my-neighbour system of international lending of other people's money by private groups. He also disapproved the practice of leaving 'our tickets for the exchange of goods and services in the control of some thirty non-elected gentlemen who run a company which is not required by law to file accounts'.

In early August, when the money crisis was at its height, and the Bank of France was accused in British newspapers of speculating against sterling and organising the run on London's gold reserves, Tom Johnston was despatched to Paris to determine the truth. According to Johnston the French Prime Minister, Pierre Laval, and his chancellor, P.E. Flandin, both assured him 'that they had offered to lend money to London in order to save the £ sterling, and that upon at least two occasions when the Bank of France had bought gold, it had done so at the direct request of the Bank of England which had made the request for purely regulatory and administrative reasons'.

However, as Johnston also noted in his published account of the crisis, 'it was not easy at the time even for members of the Government to get at the facts. We never saw the Governor of the Bank of England. He was, we were informed, away somewhere in the wilds of Quebec taking a cure for his health, and was far beyond the reach of a telephone. Nor did he return until after the Government was broken, and evicted from office.'

On 7 August 1931 the Prime Minister, resting at Lossiemouth, received a letter from Philip Snowden, the Chancellor of the Exchequer, warning him that 'the Bank is still losing gold and foreign exchange very heavily. At the present rate the point of exhaustion will come very soon with disastrous consequences.'

According to Snowden the root cause of the crisis was a belief among foreign investors that the Government's budgetary position was unsound. Until that view was remedied, or until there was evidence that the Government was taking drastic steps to set it right, this uneasiness abroad would continue, Snowden warned. 'Three millions of unemployed is certain in the near future and four millions next year is not out of the question,' the Chancellor went on. 'We are getting very near exhausting our borrowing powers for unemployment, and the only course will be to try to raise money for the unemployed grants by a public loan for the purpose which, I am sure, would be a failure, and in that event would be an admission of national bankruptcy.'

The advice on offer to the Prime Minister was further complicated by a letter from J.M. Keynes. Keynes had been previously opposed to devaluation and in favour of maintaining the gold standard as the means of solving sterling's problems. Now, in a letter dated 5 August 1931, he urged the Prime Minister to abandon the gold standard in favour of seeking agreement on a common Empire currency.

Keynes believed the new currency could be extended to include countries outside the Empire in South America, Asia and Central Europe. He also envisaged Italy and Spain eventually adhering to the new currency which 'might be a gold unit obtained by devaluing existing units by not less than 25 per cent'. Devaluation on this scale was vital, Keynes believed. But once a realistic exchange rate had been achieved 'we should then proceed to organise activity and prosperity at home and abroad along the boldest possible lines'.

In his account of the 1931 financial crisis which destroyed the second Labour Government Tom Johnston later recalled: 'During the summer of 1931, while this great and moving drama was being played out, the Money Traders were scared stiff with fright. The abler men among them well knew that the financial earthquake that had shaken Austria and Australia, Germany and South America, was not caused by the British Government, but was due to some breakdown in a money system, with which the democracies of Europe and their elected representatives had been repeatedly warned not to interfere. Yet such was the hysteria of the times,' Johnston complained, 'that the poor unemployed, and not the system of private enterprise gambling with other people's money, got blamed in the press for the crisis in our national affairs.'

Writing in 1934, three years after the second Labour Government suddenly sagged at its knees and fell dead, as he described the events of that momentous year, Johnston could also claim it was 'clear that no democratic Government can function freely if its projects are to be at the mercy of its political enemies in the City. And as an essential preliminary to any change towards democracy in finance,' Johnston continued, 'we must first shatter the delusion that the oracles of the present financial dispensation are to be obeyed with awe and reverence. What advice they have tendered successive governments in the recent past has been proved to be wildly and ludicrously wrong.

'They were wrong about reparations from Germany and its effects,' Johnston claimed. 'They were wrong when they advised Mr Churchill about the gold standard, and wrong when they pled in 1931 that the resuspension of that standard would knock the bottom out of civilisation.'

When he began his attack on Britain's growing deficit, and dwindling fortunes, the Chancellor of the Exchequer, Philip Snowden, proposed, in addition to an increase in taxation, cuts in Government expenditure totalling £99 million. This included a massive £67 million reduction in unemployment benefit; which Snowden wished to pursue knowing several of his Cabinet colleagues, including the Foreign Secretary, Arthur Henderson, and the Lord Privy Seal, Tom Johnston, were opposed in principle to cuts affecting the unemployed.

As the former Lord Privy Seal recalled: 'The poor, it appeared, had been eating far more than was consistent with compound interest, and as it was considered to be of the first importance that there should be no cut in the rate of annual tribute upon war loan – not even, as in Australia, a voluntary reduction in the rate of interest! – the Government was strongly pressed to balance its budget by a reduction of the sustenance given to the unemployed.'

According to Johnston 'a majority in the Government strove in desperation against such a solution of the country's difficulties'. In its place they were prepared to impose a revenue tariff on imports of manufactured goods; although, as Johnston noted, this was a revolutionary and hazardous change for most of them. A majority of the Cabinet 'declared themselves open to consider further reductions in armaments, and to make whatever other restrictions in expenditure might be adjudged necessary to balance the Budget,' Johnston revealed.

The Prime Minister, Ramsay MacDonald, returned to London, on the night train from Inverness, on Monday, 10 August 1931, to find the financial crisis deepening. A letter sent from Downing Street to Sandringham, for the attention of the King, described his first day back in the capital. 'The situation in the City was bad and the press were making all sorts of speculations, some of them with a party sting which in fact could only be detrimental to the national credit.'

A fortnight of hectic political and financial activity involving Downing Street and the Bank of England followed MacDonald's return to London. On Wednesday, 12 August, the Prime Minister chaired a three-hour meeting of the Cabinet Economics Committee. The following day he consulted the main opposition leaders, Stanley Baldwin and Neville Chamberlain, on their reaction to the Government's proposals for saving the pound. Lobby correspondents from the Press Association, Reuters, Central News and the Exchange Telegraph were also briefed on the seriousness of the crisis; and fervently availed of the Prime Minister's earnest wish that, for the good of the country, they would demonstrate responsibility and moderation in their reports.

On Sunday, 16 August, MacDonald made the long overnight

journey to Inverness and Lossiemouth, returning to London three days later. In a message to the King at Sandringham he advised the monarch to continue with his holiday arrangements and proceed to Balmoral as planned.

The inquiry from Sandringham reached Downing Street an hour before midnight on Wednesday, 19 August, shortly after an almost continuous meeting of the Cabinet, which began 12 hours earlier, ended. At that meeting a committee, chaired by the Minister of Labour, Margaret Bondfield, was given 24 hours to find savings in Government expenditure amounting to £20 million. Their recommendations included 'a needs test to be applied by the Ministry of Labour through such local machinery as may be devised to persons not entitled to ordinary benefit'.

The same committee, which included the Lord Privy Seal, Tom Johnston, also suggested deducting an additional twopence a week in national insurance contributions from all insured persons in work; bringing national insurance contributions for people with jobs to one shilling a week. As a means of raising money through direct taxation without, at the same time, imposing any additional burden on the employer or the state, this proposal was bound to cause future embarrassment to Johnston and other members of the Cabinet who, critically, as the crisis unfolded, refused to sanction a further ten per cent cut in unemployment benefit.

For the moment, however, all Margaret Bondfield and her committee, meeting in haste, could achieve were savings amounting to £9 million. Of this amount £5 million was expected to accrue from the needs test and the rest from an increase in national insurance contributions.

After three weeks of hard bargaining, and much restlessness inside and outside the Cabinet, the Chancellor of the Exchequer, Philip Snowden, had been able to achieve agreement on economies totalling £56 million. This sum was a long way short of the £99 million target Snowden hoped to attain. But there was now general agreement on the need for a reduction in unemployment benefit amounting to £22 million. This occurred despite the misgivings of at least half the Cabinet and provided some cheer to MacDonald and his hard-pressed Chancellor.

Unfortunately, for the future well-being of the second Labour Government, the world's money lenders were unimpressed with these results. A further £20 million in savings, to include £12.5 million in unemployment benefit, was required before they would agree to support the pound. An end to the Government's troubles was nowhere in sight.

MacDonald knew it was hopeless to expect unanimous Cabinet support for another huge cut in unemployment benefit. Several Ministers, notably Arthur Henderson, the Foreign Secretary, and Tom Johnston, the Lord Privy Seal, were bound to resign. However, as MacDonald made clear at a meeting of the Cabinet on 23 August 1931, if there were 'any important resignations, the Government as a whole must resign'.

In addition to the Prime Minister, who occupied a place at the centre of the long Cabinet room table, 19 Ministers were entitled to vote. The narrowest of majorities kept them apart. Ten supported MacDonald. They were Philip Snowden, Herbert Morrison, Thomas Shaw, W. Wedgwood Benn, Lord Amulree, Lord Sankey, Margaret Bondfield, Lord Passfield (formerly Sydney Webb), H.B. Lees Smith and J.H. Thomas. Arthur Henderson, William Graham, William Adamson, George Lansbury, A.V. Alexander, Christopher Addison, Tom Johnston, Arthur Greenwood and J.R. Clynes all voted against imposing an additional ten per cent cut in unemployment benefit.

At noon the following day Ramsay MacDonald sat at the head of a Labour Cabinet for the last time. Two hours earlier he had been driven to Buckingham Palace to deliver his resignation to the King. Letters of resignation, which the Prime Minister requested from all his Cabinet colleagues at their meeting the previous evening, went with him; ready for acceptance by His Majesty.

All morning huge crowds gathered in Downing Street, pressing close to the door of No 10 to await an official announcement concerning the Government's future. The crowd thought it knew what to expect. It was common gossip: too many senior Ministers were ready to resign rather than accept the moneymen's terms for MacDonald and his divided followers to survive.

Inside the Cabinet room Ministers listened in silence as the Prime Minister told them of his meeting with the King. His Majesty was prepared to accept the Government's resignation, MacDonald announced, to no one's great surprise. What startled most of the Ministers present was the disclosure that MacDonald himself had been asked to continue in office as Prime Minister, at the head of a National Government embracing the Conservatives and the Liberal.

Others, MacDonald went on, surveying the room, would be invited to participate in the new Government, not according to party affiliation, but as individuals. The number of people invited to serve in the Cabinet would be kept to a minimum, MacDonald added.

MacDonald expected to be denounced and ostracised for his actions. However, on that fateful day in August 1931, when he appeared to turn against the party he helped create and fashion, the last Labour Cabinet for more than a decade recorded 'their warm appreciation of the great kindness, consideration and courtesy invariably shown by the Prime Minister when presiding over their meetings'.

For the Labour Party as a whole, when the second Labour Government collapsed there was nothing that could be rescued from the bitterness of the occasion, or the awful finality of the crisis. G.D.H. Cole offered a bleak assessment of its fortunes. 'Caught in entanglements with the other parties, which were in a position at any moment to turn it out, led by a Prime Minister who was set on retaining office at any price and by a Chancellor of the Exchequer who was utterly determined to resist the only measures which could have enabled it to confront the crisis without surrendering its principles, and consisting mainly of men who had no understanding of the nature of the crisis or of the forces that were arrayed to defeat them, the second Labour Government floundered from mistake to mistake.'

Added Cole: 'It is a sorry story; and there is nothing to be gained by attempting to make it out as better than it actually was.'

CHAPTER FOURTEEN

THE NATIONAL GOVERNMENT had been formed at the request of the King to deal specifically with the financial crisis which threatened the country. Ramsay MacDonald headed a ten-man Cabinet which included four Conservatives and two Liberals. Their prime concern was to maintain the gold standard and defend the pound.

On 10 September 1931 the Chancellor of the Exchequer, Philip Snowden, introduced an emergency budget detailing the Government's proposed economies. Measures, such as tariff reform, which would have been unacceptable to some members of the coalition, including Snowden, were avoided. Instead, the Chancellor presented a package of economies totalling £70 million which included increased duties on beer and spirits, petrol and entertainments, higher rates of income tax and surtax, together with a £13 million cut in unemployment benefit.

It was claimed, damagingly, that a similar package had been accepted by the last Labour Cabinet. But during the debate which followed Tom Johnston said he didn't propose to go into controversial matters about what the last Cabinet decided and didn't decide. He claimed that it was common knowledge that he and his colleagues agreed to balance the Budget. Unfortunately, the men who controlled the money markets of the world 'insisted, and their political parties insisted, upon balancing the Budget in a particular way'. Unless people in Britain were very careful, Johnston warned, 'we shall see the beginning of a system in which foreign finance will dictate to the Government of this country exactly how they shall run their affairs'.

He believed the vital decision in the struggle over cuts took place upon the rate of benefit to be paid to the unemployed. If unemployment rates could be lowered the men who controlled the nation's finances would ensure wages would be next. The reduction in unemployment benefit was a 'cruel and unnecessary attack upon British standards of civilisation'. But the rate of employment benefit was 'the barrier that Wall Street set to break', he claimed. 'It was the barrier that the city of London set to break, and I regret to say that in breaking that barrier they succeeded in breaking the Government of this country.'

In his speech to the House of Commons the former Lord Privy Seal also insisted that 'the sums of money which are being allocated and voted for the maintenance of the unemployed in this country are insufficient to maintain body and soul together'. Under the new rates a single unemployed man would receive 15s 3d a week; women 13s 6d; a man, his wife and two children 27s 3d.

If the single man paid one shilling a night for his lodging he would be left with 1s 2d on which to live, Johnston calculated. Assuming the family rent amounted to 12s 6d a week, there would be 'a balance of 14s 9d to feed and clothe and provide light and heat for four persons for a week — 3s 8d per head — sixpence-halfpenny per day for them to live'.

According to the former Lord Privy Seal the country was faced with the spectacle, not of a National Government, but of a Wall Street Government. 'We deny absolutely the right of any outside influences, financial or otherwise, to dictate, to dragoon, to coerce us,' Johnston warned.

Reviled by many of his old colleagues the Prime Minister reacted bitterly. In his view he had been deserted by colleagues who 'simply ran away and left everything unprotected'. This illogical response, written on 1 September 1931, seriously distorts the events of the previous week when MacDonald virtually forced his Cabinet to resign. The same entry in his diary also offers the opinion: 'If this is the best Labour can do, then it is not fit to govern except in the calmest of good weather.'

Tom Johnston numbered among those who reacted angrily to a suggestion, widespread at the time, that members of the previous Cabinet abandoned their responsibilities at the bidding of the TUC. 'Neither Mr MacDonald nor Mr Snowden nor Mr Thomas has been guilty of repeating this jibe,' Johnston noted in a speech delivered in Paisley a few weeks after the collapse of the second Labour Government.

'But it is to their everlasting discredit that they sit silent while their new friends and their half-witted followers keep chanting it.'

Among the Prime Minister's new friends at least one man with his eye on Downing Street believed no one could 'withhold a meed of admiration for the courage of Mr MacDonald, Mr Snowden and Mr Thomas. They stood by their conviction in the face of their own failure,' Neville Chamberlain explained in a speech delivered at Dumfries on 11 September 1931. 'Indeed,' said the future man of Munich, 'the moral courage that was required to take that action was something far greater than has been called for from any of us Liberals or Conservatives.' But as a party Chamberlain also believed 'the Unionists have shown patriotism and a sense of duty to the State that has never been surpassed in history and of which those who come after us will be proud'.

Both as an opinion and a view of recent events Chamberlain's words were guaranteed to infuriate members of the previous Cabinet who believed the crisis could have been solved differently. Speaking at an open-air demonstration held at Commonhead, Airdrie, on 14 September 1931, Tom Johnston, with steady determination, continued to blame 'the great financial institutions that ruled the world' for the depreciation in sterling. 'I resent their attempt to dictate to the Government of this country how to balance its Budget and, in particular, insisting that confidence in the financial world can only be restored by taking ten per cent off the standard rate of unemployment benefit in Britain.' He believed it was 'the nearest thing to slavery if a group of financiers in New York or in Paris or anywhere else is going to dictate, secretly and privately, to the Government of Great Britain how many loaves of bread the unemployed men and women of the country are allowed to eat'. Before social services and the unemployed were hit 'surely we can ask the holders of the public debt, who draw nearly 40 per cent of the total revenue in interest, to convert at a lower rate of interest and save the country £50 million, even £100 million, a year, and so obviate the necessity of attacking the poorest of the poor', Johnston suggested.

A week later, at a meeting in Kilsyth, the former Lord Privy Seal claimed the country would be treated to a struggle between 'protective profiteers' and the 'formentors of revolution' in the Labour Party 'before the unemployed and the teachers and the workers generally were made aware of the financial slavery into which the nation is being sold'.

On 15 September 1931 a mutiny over pay cuts among ratings serving with the British Atlantic Fleet at Invergordon sparked a fresh run on funds. A statement issued from 10 Downing Street five days later announced Britain's withdrawal from the gold standard. Since the middle of July, it explained, funds amounting to more than £200 million had been withdrawn from the London market. These withdrawals had been met partly from gold and foreign currency held by the Bank of England, and partly from the proceeds of various foreign credits. 'During the last few days the withdrawals of foreign balances have accelerated so sharply that His Majesty's Government have felt bound to take the decision mentioned above,' said the statement.

Earlier, a letter received in Downing Street from the Governors of the Bank of England revealed the true nature of the crisis threatening Britain. Huge credits, totalling $325 million, together with nearly a billion francs, which had been arranged in New York and Paris, were virtually exhausted. 'The heavy demands for exchange in Paris and New York continue,' wrote an official. 'In addition, the Bank are being subjected to a drain of gold for Holland.'

Once the New York and Paris exchanges withdrew support for sterling it would be impossible for the Bank of England to honour its existing commitments, and allow for any contingencies which might arise. MacDonald and his Cabinet, having digested the stark reality of their position, agreed it would be expedient to release the Bank of England from its obligation, under the 1925 Gold Standard Act, to sell gold in the form of bars to any person demanding it.

Details of the ruinous flood of funds from London were given to the House of Commons by the Chancellor of the Exchequer, Philip Snowden, on 21 September 1931: 'In the last few days the withdrawals accelerated very sharply,' Snowden reported. 'On Wednesday it was £5 million; on Thursday £10 million; on Friday nearly £18 million; and on Saturday, a half day, over £10 million.'

Credits could do little more than disguise the symptoms of the present trouble, but could do nothing to remedy the disease, Snowden claimed. The man who hadn't previously wavered in his devotion to orthodox finance was also forced to admit: 'There is, in sober truth, a world-wide panic on the part of the investment markets. The whole world seems to be bent upon selling securities for cash and denying the possibility of the existence of credit.'

And such a course could not be pursued for very long, Snowden warned, without, inevitably, causing the breakdown of the whole world system of credit. 'In the face of such a panic as that,' Snowden declared, 'we must protect ourselves.'

More than 100 Labour MPs voted against the emergency legislation suspending the gold standard. Tom Johnston abstained.

Abandoning the gold standard solved the balance of payments crisis: the work of the National Government appeared complete.

Most newspapers favoured an early poll. A majority of Conservatives in the House of Commons were easily convinced it would be against their own best interests to delay. Tories who pressed their leader, Stanley Baldwin, to demand the dissolution of Parliament expected to emerge from an early election, in which tariffs would be the main issue, as either the strongest party in a fresh coalition, headed by MacDonald, or as Conservatives in their own right.

In a speech delivered in Paisley on 2 October 1931 Tom Johnston complained about the speed with which the electors were being forced to decide the nation's future. 'Why is there to be no time given to the people of the country to acquaint themselves with the facts and figures which are essential if they are to formulate a considered judgment?' he demanded. 'All the wealth and power in the land is being rallied to the National Government at the present moment,' the former Lord Privy Seal continued, 'and yet the supporters of that Government are running about the lobbies of the House of Commons like scared rabbits, entreating, pleading, bullying and threatening in a desperate attempt to have a general election over before the British public can be made aware of the extent and nature of the terrible rush which is being imposed upon them.'

Johnston continued to believe the mainspring of the present

'despicable agitation against the poor of the country' could be found in the City of London. Not until people wanted a 'change from the present system will it be possible for anyone to stand on a public platform and prophesy prosperity and happiness'.

Ramsay MacDonald, who had been expelled from the Labour Party over his recent activities, hoped to avoid an early poll. But he also wanted to continue as Prime Minister. And he was obliged to acknowledge the nature of the forces ranged against him.

On 5 October 1931, according to the official minutes of the occasion, the Cabinet decided to 'go to the country on the general policy on which it was unanimous, leaving discretion to the various parties to deal with control of imports and tariffs on their own lines'.

According to at least one distinguished Parliamentarian, Lloyd George, it was the most unpatriotic election in history. The Government didn't require a new mandate to deal with the currency situation, Lloyd George insisted. He had been absent from the House of Commons, due to illness, when the National Government was structured. Now, in a letter to his constituents, the Liberal leader claimed: 'The Tory leaders have deliberately provoked dissension because they saw a distinct party advantage in fighting an election now.' And he warned: 'This tricky attempt to utilise the national emergency to smash the political influence of organised labour may achieve a temporary triumph, but in the long run it will do nothing but provoke exasperation and accumulate mischief. I sincerely trust that the nation will mark their resentment at this unworthy and reckless manoeuvre by withholding its support from candidates who are seeking to profit from the intrigue.'

It was a hard and bitter campaign: ugly scenes, and disagreements, many of them involving old comrades, disfigured the hustings. G.D.H. Cole recalled: 'The Labour Party was represented as a squandermaniac party bent not only on ruining the country, but also on confiscating the savings of the poor, on using the deposits in the Post Office Savings Bank to meet the Budget deficit, and on leading the country by way of economic collapse into revolution.'

In a highly controversial radio broadcast ten days before polling the Chancellor of the Exchequer, Philip Snowden, who was no longer a

Tom Johnston looked and acted and talked the part of a modern-day Scottish hero. One admirer called him 'a man of destiny and all the bigger because he decided to do the job at his own door'.

FORWARD, SATURDAY, OCTOBER 13, 1906.

COME AND HEAR
THE WOMEN SUFFRAGISTS
Who went to Prison for their Principles.
MRS. PANKHURST.
MISS PANKHURST

most of the Councillor
SHAREHOLDERS I
Naturally, the agitati
its quietus. There
found why the Gaswo
chased, but no excuse
that the profits of the
going into the pockets

Forward appeared for the first time in 1906. 'We betake ourselves with a light heart to our business,' Johnston wrote. In its heyday the paper sold 30,000 copies a week and, during the First World War, was banned for stirring up friction among munition workers.

Johnston's work as a journalist and politician over more than half a century was appreciated in many quarters. But he never forgot his roots in Kirkintilloch, where he became the first freeman in the history of the town.

Johnston believed in planning but he was suspicious of planners based in Whitehall. He wanted Scotland's future decided by Scots living in Scotland.

He hated having to make the long rail journey between Glasgow and London but, with so much Scottish business centred on London, he had little choice.

OPPOSITE (MAIN PICTURE):
HM Queen Elizabeth leaves Loch Sloy accompanied by Johnston.

OPPOSITE (INSET):
HM Queen Elizabeth opens Loch Sloy, the first of 38 different major projects commissioned by the North of Scotland Hydro-Electric Board during Johnston's 13 years as chairman.

TOP RIGHT:
Johnston fought hard to achieve his dream of a hydro-board in Scotland, similar to the Tennessee Valley Authority in the United States, which 'converted a wilderness, a desolation, and a despair, into a land of thriving prosperity'.

RIGHT:
Johnston didn't want any of the honours usually available to a senior politician if it meant using a title. As a Companion of Honour, pressed on him by Churchill, he could remain plain Mr Johnston!

Personal and Confidential

10, Downing Street,
Whitehall.

May 2, 1953.

My dear Johnston,

When we lunched together in Glasgow I asked you whether you would allow me to submit your name to The Queen for a C.H. I hope very much that you will allow me to do this. I can think of no more suitable holder of this distinction and I feel sure that all the Scots will be delighted. It might even make them forget the Scone Stone. I have received The Queen's informal permission to make the offer to you and needless to say she was delighted by the idea. I hope so much that you have overcome any doubts you may have had.

Yours sincerely,
Winston S. Churchill

The Rt. Hon. Thomas Johnston.

ABOVE: *A number of important landowners organised fierce opposition to Johnston's plans for the North of Scotland Hydro-Electric Board. Here he discusses the future of the Highlands with Lord Lovat and Sir Donald Cameron of Lochiel. According to one historian, Johnston demonstrated 'a consummate ability to achieve his objectives'.*

MIDDLE: *Emmanuel Shinwell, Minister of Fuel and Power in the first Attlee government, supported Johnston in his fight to maintain the hydro-board's independence from London.*

BOTTOM: *Looking left! Johnston with Herbert Morrison, Lord President of the Council, and Joseph Westwood, his successor as Secretary of State for Scotland, checking work in progress at Loch Sloy.*

Johnston was Chancellor of Aberdeen University for 14 years. Before accepting the role in 1951 he took advice 'as to his fitness in the public eye for such an academic post'.

Johnston was a keen angler when time and duties allowed. Dougie, the wire-haired fox terrier on the look-out for ripples, was a favourite companion.

A portrait of Tom Johnston, fashioned in bronze by Evelyn Barron for the North of Scotland Hydro-Electric Board, occupies a place of honour in the foyer of Scottish Hydro-Electric plc at Perth. The privatisation of hydro power, under a Tory government, would have been the final blow to his ambitions for the Highlands.

candidate for the House of Commons, described Labour's election programme as 'the most fantastic and impracticable document ever put before the electorate'. Snowden was a former chairman of the ILP, first elected to Parliament as a socialist in 1906. But now, after more than a quarter of a century campaigning on behalf of the Labour movement, he appeared set on destroying it. 'Every day,' Snowden later admitted, 'from the first day of the election campaign to the eve of poll, I launched attacks upon my late Labour colleagues.'

G.D.H. Cole complained, in his account of the second Labour Government, that when Snowden agreed to the 1931 election he allowed his venom for Labour to override his free trade principles. 'Snowden, indeed, pursued his recent colleagues with neurotic fury, losing no chance of discrediting them or of making the most of their past yielding to his demands.'

The former Chancellor's behaviour during the election horrified Tom Johnston. Snowden had been one of the great pioneers of socialism in Britain. Yet, to Johnston's astonishment, he 'walked off the stage uttering venomous and atrabilious gibes at the men with whom he had worked for a third of a century'. Added Johnston: 'A medical friend of mine explains this strange perversion by the nature of Mr Snowden's recent physical trouble at the prostate gland. If that be so, the occasion is not one for blame but for commiseration.'

Probably the most effective, and damaging, of Snowden's onslaughts on his old comrades was the radio broadcast he delivered by way of the BBC on 17 October 1931. His use of the medium was, by all accounts, masterly. If Labour was elected, Snowden explained: 'All the derelict industries are to be taken over by the State and the taxpayer is to shoulder the losses. The banks and financial houses are to be placed under the national ownership and control, which means, I suppose, that they are to be run by a joint committee of the Labour Party and the Trade Union Council.

'Your investments are to be ordered by some board,' Snowden went on, 'and your foreign investments are to be mobilised to finance this madcap policy. This is not socialism. It is bolshevism run mad.'

Two days later, in a fighting speech delivered at Causewayhead, his former Cabinet colleague, Tom Johnston, recalled how, in a book entitled *Labour and the New World*, published in 1921, the same Philip Snowden insisted: 'No scheme of national financial reform can be carried through without the nationalisation of the banking institutions.' Snowden also claimed: 'Nationalisation of the banking system would effect economy of administration. It would give greater security to depositors. It would secure for the state enormous profits now made by the joint-stock banks, and it would give to the state more effective control over the regulation of prices.'

Said Johnston: 'With these views I find myself in wholehearted agreement even although Mr Snowden has changed his views and chooses to describe his own proposals as bolshevism gone mad. If he chooses to play apostate to the principles for which he has stood for over 30 years that is certainly no reason why I am going to change mine.'

Returning to the frequently repeated suggestion that former members of MacDonald's Labour Cabinet had been guilty of running away from their responsibilities to the nation Johnston demanded to know: 'Who ran away from their honour? Who ran away from their principles? Who deserted the policy and the programme upon which they were elected? Who deserted the policy and the programme about which they had written books and made countless speeches?' Johnston claimed he didn't intend to attack any man's motives. 'I merely say this, that I hold still to the beliefs which I have preached and argued since I was at college.'

According to the *Glasgow Herald* the former Lord Privy Seal continued to deny Labour was responsible for the financial crisis. It also attributed to Johnston a claim that it would have been a simple matter for the Government to raise a loan of £100 million at three per cent.

After listening to Johnston address an election meeting at Cambusbarron a certain Mr Harold Monteith, a colliery agent from Stirling, wrote to the Chancellor of the Exchequer, at his Downing Street address, to inform him: 'I asked him why, as a highly paid and responsible official in office at the time, he had not put this suggestion forward then. He replied that he did so in the Cabinet and on being asked by me what the Cabinet's decision was he said that he was not allowed to divulge Cabinet decisions. I therefore said that I would assume that the majority of the Cabinet were against his suggestion and this he admitted.

'His reticence about what happened in Cabinet does not seem to be shared with others in the same Cabinet who, to mention Mr Graham only, are making statements very far from the truth, and which you have immediately had to controvert. I think that it is highly desirable in national interests that if Mr Johnston's statement is incorrect it should also be controverted.'

Snowden, who was more than happy to controvert his old colleague, obliged with some alacrity. From Downing Street, on 23 October 1931, he wrote to Mr Monteith: 'If Tom Johnston has stated that he could have borrowed £100 million at three per cent it is the most fantastic invention of this election. There is not an atom of foundation for the statement. I will make this firm offer to him. If he can find me £100 million at three per cent, or even at four per cent, I will accept the loan today.' In a postscript Snowden authorised Mr Monteith to publish his reply if he so wished; which the colliery agent from Stirling did, as did the editor of the *Glasgow Herald*.

Johnston responded, in a speech delivered at Gargunnock on 24 October 1931, that every lender was entitled to 'attach his own conditions to a loan. But when we discovered that America would only lend money on condition that our social services and our unemployed were cut most – most of us said no.'

Some members of the Cabinet 'believed there were other methods of raising the money', Johnston went on. 'We suggested and pressed these other methods but they were not accepted. We proposed, for example, that the British public should be told the whole truth, and that we should ask the British public for an immediate loan, to assist the Bank of England in its difficulties, of anything up to £100 million at three per cent. We believed we could get the money if the British public were told the whole truth.'

According to the former Lord Privy Seal a majority in the Cabinet was against telling the public the whole story on the grounds it would undermine confidence in the Government and probably cause a panic.

They were advised, instead, to borrow abroad quietly and privately. 'We declined to agree to the terms offered by Wall Street,' Johnston added. 'We resigned and we think we acted properly and honestly in so doing.'

Unfortunately for Johnston, and Labour generally, there was no rush to bestow a halo of unselfish pride and justification on the previous Cabinet. His highly emotional appeal failed to achieve much in the way of lasting appreciation from the mass of the electorate: the 1931 election was a triumph for the national coalition. For the Labour Party as a whole, the election was a rout; an unallayed disaster in terms of seats.

In more than 400 contests coalition candidates, representing Conservative, Liberal and hard-core supporters of MacDonald, calling themselves National Labour, avoided each other; forcing official Labour candidates to compete against everyone else for votes.

Labour had been the largest single party in the House of Commons, with 287 seats, following the 1929 election. Two years later, after a summer of political and financial turmoil in Britain, the party was reduced to 46 MPs, excluding five who were loyal to the ILP and colonel J.C. Wedgwood, a Cabinet Minister in 1924, who campaigned as an Independent seven years later.

Against this largely impotent Parliamentary rump could be measured an unassailable coalition with 556 seats under its command. Of these 471 were Conservatives and 72 were Liberals. In addition 13 MPs, who responded to the description National Labour, joined Ramsay MacDonald in the House of Commons.

Casualties from the last Labour Cabinet included Arthur Henderson, Foreign Secretary, Emmanuel Shinwell, Secretary of State for Mines, Margaret Bondfield, Minister for Labour and the first woman to achieve Cabinet rank in Britain, William Adamson, Secretary of State for Scotland, and his former deputy, later Lord Privy Seal, Tom Johnston.

G.D.H. Cole blamed Snowden for the immensity of the Labour defeat: Labour losses were everywhere severe. The party was left without a single seat in the south, outside greater London, and with only one MP – Sir Stafford Cripps – in the West. Thirty-nine seats were lost in Lancashire and Cheshire, 45 in Greater London and 33 in Yorkshire. Wales and Monmouthshire narrowly missed achieving single figure losses with a total of ten seats gone, and was the least worst-hit area in a disastrous campaign. That sorry distinction went to the Midlands where Labour lost 44 seats, reducing its representation in the House of Commons from England's industrial heartland to three. 'In Scotland,' wrote Cole, 'its representation fell from 37 in 1929 to three, not counting four belonging to the ILP group.'

Tom Johnston's supporters in West Stirlingshire and Clackmannanshire hoped their candidate enjoyed sufficient personal support to avoid following the national trend. However, as in 1924 when Labour was similarly discredited at the polls, the mixed central Scotland constituency failed to rally behind their outspoken MP.

Johnston considered himself a champion of the poor and the unemployed. But in a straight fight with a Conservative coalition candidate, J.C. Ker, his vote crumbled from 15,179 in 1929 to 12,952 this time; 1,819 fewer than his opponent. An increased turnout in a constituency where the number of voters also rose slightly reflected the acute nature of the unpopularity which had been attached to all Labour candidates by the coalition's well-organised campaign.

Johnston blamed his defeat on 'the daily blast of fear and frenzy in the press and over the wireless about the dire possibilities to the value of the pound, and to the safety and security of the deposits in the Post Office Savings Bank. We were certainly gaining during the last week of the contest but the scaremongering was too well done, especially in our great rural hinterland, for us to win this time.'

Johnston never despaired that the electoral tide would one day turn in Labour's favour. Many people were already sick and sorry at the way they had been tricked 'now that they see the capitalist press frankly admitting the great deception'.

In fact, the catastrophic results of the 1931 election, in terms of seats won and lost in the House of Commons, concealed a solid base of support for Labour in the country at large. Research conducted by G.D.H. Cole for his *History of the Labour Party* showed that candidates representing Labour in the 1931 election actually succeeded in achieving nearly a third of the popular vote: 6.6 million. By contrast, various strands of the Liberal Party, who won 72 seats in the new Parliament, due largely to their participation in the coalition, could only accumulate 2.3 million votes.

'Under these circumstances,' claimed Cole, 'the Liberals were over-represented, and not under-represented as they had been in 1929, when they had fought almost everywhere as a third party. With hardly more than one-third of the Labour votes, the Liberals had 20 more seats than Labour and Independent Labour combined.'

Those who succeeded in reaching the House of Commons under a Labour banner against the general tide of public opinion in the winter of 1931 immediately found themselves leaderless. The previous chairman of the Parliamentary group, Arthur Henderson, had been defeated and was no longer an MP. An election to find his successor was won by George Lansbury, the only man with previous Cabinet experience still an MP. Clement Attlee, who had been Postmaster General in the last Labour Government, was elected deputy leader.

It was unlikely that either man, faced with opposition properly representative of the party outside the House of Commons, would have been successful, in a leadership election. Attlee biographer, Kenneth Harris, believed any one of a dozen candidates from the previous Parliament, including Tom Johnston, would have defeated Lansbury and Attlee for the leadership. The 1931 election, Harris suggested, was an ill wind for Labour which blew Attlee nothing but good.

CHAPTER FIFTEEN

IN ALL HIS MANY parliamentary campaigns between 1918 and 1935 Tom Johnston included Home Rule for Scotland as an important part of his personal manifesto. He did so from a belief that the 'Imperial Parliament was so increasingly being choked with world affairs that it had little time for attention to Scots domestic problems'.

Johnston had been a member of the Scottish Home Rule Association, founded by his old friend and business associate, R.E. Muirhead, since 1918. He spoke in favour of two Home Rule Bills which foundered in the House of Commons, in 1924 and 1927, and, almost a decade after the second debacle, he launched the London Scots Self-Government Committee with the aim of converting the Labour Party to outright support of a Parliament in Edinburgh.

As a historian, with pride in his roots, he never forgot that it was only in Scotland that 'the onrush of the Roman legions was stopped, and that here they had to build defensive walls for themselves against the Caledonians'. Readers of his autobiography were also reminded that the armies of Bruce and James IV defied not only the English enemy, but the dread curse of papal excommunication.

Similarly, it pleased him to recall how, in the days before the Union, 'when an English lawyer called Attwood published a book wherein he maintained that England had direct superiority over Scotland, our Parliament in Edinburgh ordered copies of his book to be burned by the common hangman'. Not that Johnston could be counted much of an admirer of the Auld Scots Parliament which continued to meet in Scotland's capital city until 1707 – unless his claim that it was venal, corrupt, despicable, servile to the Crown and tyrannical to the people is ever allowed to serve as an endorsement for anything.

The country never lost a national Parliament in 1707, Johnston claimed: its departure to London simply rid the people of Scotland of a feudal oligarchy. And, Johnston argued waspishly in his *History of the Scottish Working Classes*, whatever some publicists, intent upon propagating the idea of Scottish Home Rule insisted, its absorption, to form a British national Parliament at Westminster, was certainly not a calamity for Scotland.

As perceived by Johnston, this was no benign national institution sitting in Edinburgh's Parliament Hall. Following the Reformation, and prior to 1610, Parliament was controlled by an executive, called the Lords of the Articles, who were chosen thus: 'the nobles chose eight bishops, who in turn chose eight nobles, and the 16 thus chosen selected eight barons and eight burgesses'. Once the Lords of the Articles had been elected at the start of each session members of Parliament were free to return home. But in 1610 the power of the nobles, the bishops, the barons and the burgesses to elect the Lords of the Articles was withdrawn and replaced with a system of 33 Parliamentary representatives nominated by the sovereign. It was this nominated caucus, Johnston explained, which was bribed out of existence 100 years later, in as 'dirty a cloud of fraud, corruption, and scoundrelism as the history of the world can find parallel'.

But he wasted no sympathy on the distressed Scots capitalists rescued by King William in London following the collapse of the Darien Scheme which was expected to bring 'shower storms of gold far beyond the dreams of avarice, into the coffers of the bailies and the barons, the magistrates and the merchants who were fortunate enough to secure shares'.

William, who was fearful of Stuart plots, had been trying for years 'to abolish the Scots Parliament and bring all the legislators to London where he could have them under his effective control. William knew the men he had to deal with,' Johnston, a future King's Minister, contended, 'and his method was not coercion and threat, but cash down.'

When the Darien Scheme failed, and a swarm of ruined speculators blamed the cursed greed of the thrice accursed English, the response from the King in London was simple, Johnston asserted: 'He bribed them to his will.' In exchange for £398,085 10s in cash, to be used in refunding the speculators their capital with interest and in discharging arrears of Government pay, King William proposed a Union of Parliaments. 'Capitalist Scotland rejoiced,' Johnston observed, 'swore eternal loyalty to William, suffered the Scots Parliament to snuff itself out, and awaited the "Equivalent" which ultimately came guarded by Dragoons who were stoned on the streets of Edinburgh by a non-investing working-class mob, roused to anger by this flaunting of the cash nexus.'

Scotland was allowed 45 commoners and 16 peers in the composition of the new Parliament. First-time members were selected by the existing Scots Parliament and weren't required to seek the approval of constituencies. All heritable offices, superiorities, heritable jurisdiction, offices for life and jurisdictions for life were also retained by the owners. 'And that,' Johnston added glumly, 'was the origin, the history, and the end of the auld sang!'

An ambitious Scotland Day pageant and rally, organised by the Scottish Home Rule Association, which attracted 35,000 people to Glasgow Green on Saturday, 25 August 1923, appeared to worry Johnston as much as it pleased everyone else who was present. A common resolution, proposed from six separate platforms, committed everyone in the huge crowd, individually and collectively, 'to work steadily for national self-government until the Scottish people regain full control of their own affairs'.

There was much cheering, despite the rain, when James Maxton, a much-loved figure with normally critical Scottish audiences, suggested people were witnessing the beginning of a movement for Scottish self-determination. Previously, according to Maxton, there had been no real movement for Scottish independence. The majority of Scottish people, together with their public representatives, accepted domination by England. He himself hadn't been convinced of the need for a Scottish Parliament until he found himself a member of an English one. 'From a short experience of the mental calibre, and moral outlook, of the majority of MPs, and from a short experience of the deadening influence of the city of London as a place from which our affairs should be managed,' Maxton continued, 'I am now absolutely persuaded of the necessity of making a strenuous effort to get a Scottish Parliament absolutely free and independent of the English people.'

A week later, in a signed article in *Forward*, Tom Johnston sounded doubtful about the lasting benefits of the day's events. He was especially concerned that the pageantry and the great demonstration witnessed on Glasgow Green were indications 'not of a narrow, sterile, wha's like us pride, but of a resurgence of that national feeling which seeks to cherish the distinctive quality and genius which is ours by birth, by tradition, by social custom, and which, if cherished and strengthened, may be to the glory and profit of all mankind.'

Johnston believed the closer government was to the governed the better. But in his view the political development of the English people was different from the political development of the Scots. Scotland supported 'the Christian doctrine that hungry children be fed, that homes be built, that the sporting estates be broken up, that the mines, the railways, the banks be nationally owned, and that the purchasing power of the people be not decreased but increased, that poverty in the midst of plenty be abolished . . . We in Scotland are ready for great advances in the war against poverty and I know of no reason why we should remain in destitution until our English neighbours desire to march in step with us,' Johnston continued. 'And indeed, rightly considered, Home Rule for Scotland would be to the great advantage of the English people since great advances in the warfare against poverty north of the Tweed would have tremendous repercussions south of it.'

He also believed that perverted nationalism was a curse on the world. But Scots were Scots before they were Britons; and Britons before they were citizens of the world. 'Without first the national the international is meaningless,' Johnston warned. 'We want to preserve our tongue, our native speech, our songs and our traditions for only in so far as we understand the past can we explain the present or guide the future.'

It was a familiar theme. Similarly, there were echoes of old hatreds unresolved in his criticism of various attempts to depict the nation's historical development during the Scotland Day celebrations. He confessed to a feeling of regret that the tableaux on view largely represented the history of the schoolbooks: some of it fiction and some of it sheer aristocratic falsehood. More of the tableaux should have dealt with the life, labour, sacrifice and heroism of the commonfolk. In reality, they were the nation.

'If we are to have Scotland's national days occasions for the remainder of our nationhood, and pledges for the future preservation of the distinctive qualities which we can offer as our gifts to the comity of nations, let us remember,' Johnston suggested, 'that the Scottish national history is not the pageantry of kings and queens and robber barons, and such like useless parasitic trash, but the struggles and development and sufferings and chivalries of the common folk.'

He didn't urge Home Rule for Scotland 'because of our Iberian blood or because our far-off ancestors were Dalriada Celts. I do not urge it because of old forgotten, far-off fights or battles long ago, but because the genius and initiative of our people is cribbed, cabined and confined by an English dominance, and because with Home Rule I believe we can save our rural peasantry from extinction and our city population from poverty and squalor, and because a free development of our native culture and genius would be something valuable we could offer to the world.'

The following year, with a minority Labour Government in power, a private member's Bill aimed at achieving some degree of Home Rule for Scotland was introduced in the House of Commons by George Buchanan, MP for Gorbals. He proposed a single-chamber Parliament, consisting of 148 MPs, elected from 74 Scottish constituencies, to be concerned mainly with old-age pensions, National Insurance and Labour Exchanges in Scotland.

Crucially, however, Buchanan also proposed empowering the new Parliament to vary Imperial taxes in accordance with its members' view of Scotland's needs; although Customs and Excise, like the Post Office, remained a Westminster responsibility. In addition, Buchanan wanted part of the proceeds from Scottish taxation returned to the Scottish Exchequer to be used at the discretion of the new administration. Any differences which might arise between London and Edinburgh would be settled by a joint exchequer board.

The authority of the House of Lords would be trimmed by making the Judiciary Committee of the Privy Council the final Court of Appeal; the same tribunal would also decide constitutional questions. An Executive Committee, appointed by the new Scots Parliament, would advise the King. It was, by Buchanan's own reckoning, 'a comparatively mild proposal'.

Addressing the House of Commons on 9 May 1924 he didn't doubt there was a real demand for self-government in Scotland. It might not be a characteristic of the Scottish race to make their demands in the same way as the Irish people, Buchanan explained, but while their methods might differ and their steps might alter, 'the Scottish people are as sincere, and for the most part as anxious, for this measure as even our friends in Ireland were for their own form of government', he continued.

Tom Johnston, who seconded the proposal, told MPs that in the last 35 years Home Rule for Scotland had been the subject of a Commons debate on 19 different occasions. It had been put to the vote nine times since 1894 and was never once defeated. In June 1919, when the issue was last debated, only one Scottish MP voted against the motion.

In addition, said Johnston, 'we have had what was called a Speaker's Conference on Devolution. Unanimity was not secured upon one issue put before that conference. Upon all other points a very considerable unanimity was secured.' In fact, as Johnston explained, agreement had been reached on the conflicting claims of Central Government and the subordinate legislatures on finance, the judiciary and what powers should be granted to the new Parliament.

The one point on which the Speaker's Conference on Devolution failed to agree was what to do about Scottish representation at Westminster following Home Rule. The latest proposals made no provision for a reduction in the level of Scottish MPs at Westminster; although, as the London Correspondence column of the *Glasgow Herald* reported on 11 April 1924, 'English unionists humorously suggest that if the Bill abolishes Scottish representation at Westminster – which it does not – they will treat it as an agreed measure and assist its progress to the Statute Book'.

Joke or not, as George Buchanan explained to the House of Commons, the English members could rid themselves of Scottish representation as soon as they cared. For his Bill included the provision 'that whenever there is a scheme of devolution agreed on, to apply to England, Scotland and Wales, the Scottish members will cease to take any part or interest in the affairs in which the English Parliament ought to take part'.

Tom Johnston expected the question of Scottish representation in the House of Commons to be the subject of renewed controversy and dispute. It was a matter 'upon which there has been discussion in the past and disputation, and upon which we are quite prepared for controversy and further disputation today', he said. He suggested the matter could be considered again after a general federal scheme had been evolved for the whole of the British Empire. In the meantime Johnston argued strongly in favour of retaining the existing number of Scottish MPs at Westminster. 'If we do not ask to come here to deal with Imperial affairs, and take our share in them, we should be accused, and rightly, of attempting a policy of separation, and we should lay ourselves open to the charge of disintegrating the British Empire,' Johnston declared.

One-third of the people of the world, of all colours and in all climes, lived under the British flag, Johnston added: whatever view people took of it, the British Empire was a big thing in the world. But it would fall, Johnston warned, 'as other great Empires of the past fell, unless you give to each component part of that Empire the right to express its own individuality in its own way and not dragoon them by a central bureaucracy sitting many miles away'.

Westminster couldn't cope with the great and grave social problems confronting Scotland. 'Here we have two days per annum allotted to us to discuss Scottish matters, and we cannot do justice to them in that time,' Johnston maintained. MPs spent much of their time considering all sorts of little parochial questions 'whilst our own nation is bleeding to death and our rural population is being decimated'.

Ramsay MacDonald, the Prime Minister, who previously supported the idea of self-government for Scotland, was expected to vote in favour of Buchanan's Bill at the second reading; at the very least, out of loyalty to his Scottish supporters. MacDonald's presence, especially, was needed to add weight to an occasion the Clydeside group considered vital to the future well-being of the nation. But he and other senior members of the first Labour Cabinet failed to appear.

MacDonald's absence was later denounced by David Kirkwood, forthright MP for Dumbarton Burghs, as an insult to Scotland. But the Prime Minister's action also demonstrated, for all to see, the differences which had been allowed to fester within the fractious Labour group at Westminster during the first few months of the short, unhappy life of the first Labour Government.

William Adamson, Secretary of State for Scotland, appeared and spoke briefly. Instinctively a cautious man, Adamson was a former Fife collier with a reputation for deliberating long and hard before making any decision. In the closing moments of the debate he told MPs that if they cared to examine the matter they would find the demand for self-government in Scotland wasn't new. 'The overwhelming majority of the Scottish people are in favour of it,' Adamson conceded. According to Adamson's account of the view from Downing Street the Government supported the general principles contained in Buchanan's Bill. But it also recognised 'the Bill raises a large and vital issue which is as important to England and Wales as it is to Scotland'. Adamson hoped the Bill could obtain a second reading. If that happened, he promised, the Government would appoint a committee to examine the whole question of Home Rule for Scotland and how this would affect the rest of the United Kingdom.

But as the Secretary of State for Scotland resumed his seat beside the despatch box he could see, clearly enough, that time was running out for Buchanan's Bill. The clock above the Speaker's chair was approaching four o'clock, the deadline set for consideration of the latest Home Rule proposals. Without the formality of a vote on the second reading Buchanan's Bill would perish. And another opportunity to change the way Scotland was governed would have been lost – perhaps forever!

'At this point,' the *Glasgow Herald* reported, 'most of the Clyde members were standing gesticulating wildly towards the Chair and assailing Mr Speaker with epithets which were indistinguishable amid the roar and confusion and general cries of Order and Obey the Chair.'

The bewigged figure who occupied the Speaker's chair was a former

Liberal MP, the Right Honourable John Whitley. He had been MP for Halifax, in his native Yorkshire, since 1900, and Speaker of the House of Commons for the past three years. Confronted with noisy and irregular Parliamentary behaviour he simply ordered a Clerk to proceed as normal and pronounce upcoming business.

The angry, and unmistakable, voice of David Kirkwood, a former shop steward in a Glasgow foundry, could be heard shouting above the din: 'There will be no Order of the Day! We have got to have the closure and I move the closure now!'

But amid the clamour the Speaker persisted. No vote was allowed. Another ten minutes of general disorder followed before he adjourned the House. Kirkwood's cries followed him out. 'It is only the beginning of the end of your Parliament,' he shouted.

Inevitably, accusations of betrayal accompanied the Government's refusal to find additional Parliamentary time for a fresh debate on the Home Rule question. This punishing reversal was delivered by the Prime Minister himself, on 14 May 1924, in reply to a question from George Buchanan.

His followers' rowdy performance on the day of the debate infuriated MacDonald. Buchanan was addressed in a cold, angry voice. But at least one prominent backbencher, Tom Johnston, accepted the Government's view that 'owing to the then state of public business they could not find time for a resumed discussion that session'.

Years later he and R.E. Muirhead, prominent nationalist, old friend and business associate, quarrelled publicly over the issue. 'To argue that the Government did all it could to enable the measure to pass doesn't hold water,' Muirhead fumed in a letter to *Forward* published on 16 June 1928. Emrys Hughes considered Muirhead 'the incarnation of sincerity and honesty and kindliness. He devoted his life to the cause of Home Rule for Scotland and never did any cause have such a determined, persistent and single-minded crusader.'

He was also a director of *Forward*, which probably added salt to the dispute. This began with Johnston reminding his readers how, four years earlier, Labour had been outnumbered in the House of Commons. As a result important debates were generally protracted. Parliamentary business during May, June and July that year included an Unemployment Insurance Bill, a Housing Bill, an Agricultural Wages Bill, the Budget and the Finance Bill. August and September were occupied with holidays. And by the second week in October the Government had been defeated and the country faced an election. 'I submit,' wrote Johnston, 'that it is unjust and unreasonable to accuse the Labour Government of being indifferent to Scottish Home Rule because it didn't drop one of its major measures.'

Muirhead disagreed. He believed Buchanan's Bill was different from other legislation in at least one important respect. As a Home Rule Bill it was clearly a key measure which, once on the statute book, would have enabled Scotland to tackle its own unemployment, housing, land and other problems in a direct and commonsense way; as well as helping to relieve the London Parliament of some congestion.

He could quite understand a Tory Government delaying the advent of a Parliament in Scotland. 'But a Labour Government has a different outlook and surely could have stretched a point to give Scotland self-government,' Muirhead complained. It would have been possible, simply by curtailing its Parliamentary programme, or reducing the autumn holiday by a single day, for the Government to find time for further discussion on Buchanan's Bill. Once that happened, wrote Muirhead, MPs could have been asked to vote on the second reading. Evidently, however, Home Rule for Scotland wasn't considered important enough to justify such action, Muirhead added.

Johnston, clearly irritated by his old friend's apparent intransigence, countered in print by asking which part of the government's programme Muirhead was prepared to sacrifice. Possible, but hardly acceptable, contenders for oblivion, suggested by the man who seconded the Bill under discussion, included the Budget, the Finance Bill, the Unemployment Insurance Bill, Mr Wheatley's Housing Bill and the Agricultural Wages Bill. To drop any one of these Bills would have killed more than the Bill that was dropped, Johnston believed: 'It would have raised a working-class resentment that would have been tactically ruinous for Scottish Home Rule.'

A week later Muirhead, founder of the Scottish Home Rule

Association, responded. Rather than accept Johnston's apocalyptic view of the options available, he chose as his main battleground the several days the House of Commons devoted to a debate on the London Traffic Bill. One of these would have been enough to enable the Home Rule for Scotland legislation to obtain a second reading, Muirhead suggested. Otherwise, MPs could have been asked to settle for 51 days holiday in the autumn instead of 52. If they'd chosen to adjourn on Friday, 10 August, instead of Thursday, 9 August, Muirhead added caustically, there would have been enough time, for anyone who wished, 'to arrive on the Scottish grouse moors in time for the twelfth'.

The dispute involving Johnston and his old friend R.E. Muirhead spilled across the columns of *Forward* at a crucial time for the Home Rule movement. The previous year the number of times the House of Commons debated self-government for Scotland achieved a majority of sorts: 21.

When the Bill proposed by George Buchanan, MP for Gorbals, failed to achieve a second reading on 9 May 1924 there had been 19 earlier attempts at persuading the English voting majority in the House of Commons to loosen the Parliamentary strings which bound their northern neighbour to Westminster.

On 13 May 1927 the Rev. James Barr, MP for Motherwell and a minister of the United Free Church of Scotland, brought that number to a discouraging 21 – in the space of less than four decades. But this time, on the troublesome question of just how many MPs from Scotland would be permitted to attend at Westminster following self-government, there were no vulnerable hostages to fortune on offer. A memorandum on the Bill, published more than a month before it was due to be debated in the House of Commons, stated unequivocally: 'The representation of Scotland in the Commons House of the Imperial Parliament will cease at the date when the Scots Parliament is constituted. The members of the Imperial Parliament who represent Scottish constituencies shall then retire from that Parliament and no others shall thereafter be elected.'

Barr's supporters included two former Cabinet Ministers, John Wheatley and William Adamson, as well as George Buchanan, Tom Johnston and James Maxton. Unlike the 'comparatively mild proposal'

177

tabled by Buchanan three years earlier this latest attempt to obtain Home Rule for Scotland included a demand that all taxes raised in Scotland, including Customs and Excise which escaped last time, should be the responsibility of the Scottish Parliament; with a Scottish Treasury acting on its behalf.

Apart from his views on taxation and his willingness to sanction the complete withdrawal of Scottish MPs from Westminster, Barr's other proposals went a good deal further than Buchanan. Barr wanted old-age pensions, national health and unemployment insurance transferred to the new Parliament; powers sought by Buchanan. In addition, however, the Motherwell MP saw no reason to exclude any of the main public utilities, including the Post Office, from Scots control. The Royal Navy, the Army, the Royal Air Force and the Foreign Office were designated joint services and would function as a shared responsibility of the two Parliaments.

However, there was a provision for any or all of the designated joint services to be run separately 'on the demand of either the Scots or the Imperial Parliaments, or when the Parliaments fail to agree on the proportion of the cost of the joint services to be borne by each or the administration of the joint services'.

Executive authority would continue to be vested in the King who would be represented in Scotland by a Lord High Commissioner 'who shall be appointed in like manner as the Governor-General of Canada and in accordance with the practice observed in the making of such appointments'.

Day-to-day administration of Scotland would be undertaken by the Lord High Commissioner advised by an Executive Committee of a Scottish Privy Council. A Supreme Court of Scotland would replace the House of Lords as the final Court of Appeal. All constitutional questions would be decided by this new tribunal 'subject to the right of any person to petition His Majesty for leave to appeal to His Majesty'.

In addition, 'a constitutional council, to be called the Joint Council, would be established for the purpose of ascertaining and declaring the rights of the two countries in any matters of common interest where there is any disagreement between the two governments'.

It was never likely to succeed. Tom Johnston agreed to second the Rev James Barr's motion, although he was never entirely happy with the decision to withdraw Scottish MPs from Westminster.

On the day of the debate, and the by-now-expected ritual talking out, Johnston confronted those MPs who bothered to attend and listen with the reminder that they were unable to give enough time 'to discussion of Imperial affairs because of the consideration which must be given to petty affairs in Scotland, England and Wales'. He also thought it ridiculous that one man, the Secretary of State for Scotland, controlled 16 departments. It was impossible, Johnston insisted, for any human being to control 16 departments. And for anyone to try didn't make for the better government of the British Empire. 'I submit,' said Johnston, 'that the time has come when this pooh-bah business, this conglomeration of 16 offices in the person of one individual, is an insult to a proud nation.'

But colourful rhetoric didn't help. Scottish MPs wouldn't be ordered to leave Westminster, willingly or unwillingly, yet awhile! There would be no ceremonial return to the splendid old chamber beside St Giles in the Royal Mile where the last Scots Parliament met to agree an end to statehood almost two and a quarter centuries earlier: there would be no constitutional council, to be called the Joint Council, settling whatever differences might arise between the Parliament of Scotland and that representing its vexed neighbour to the south: or any distinguished individual invited to become Lord High Commissioner of Scotland, appointed in like manner as the Governor-General of Canada and given a fine home in Edinburgh to match his splendid, and esteemed, position.

Instead, supporters of self-government for Scotland, on both sides of the House of Commons, as well as in the public galleries overhead, could only watch and listen, in angry bafflement and despair, as an indifferent majority of MPs refused to succour their dreams.

CHAPTER SIXTEEN

FOR THE SECOND TIME in three years far-reaching proposals of great importance to Scotland had been rejected with casual indifference by the collective will of the House of Commons. Labour MPs had been unable to obtain even a second reading for measures which a majority of the membership in Scotland favoured. To staunch supporters of Home Rule it was a dispiriting and disappointing experience which required some form of remedial action.

Within a year several famous names had been persuaded to bury their differences under a single banner: the National Party for Scotland. Its main aim, the *Glasgow Herald* reported on 15 May 1928, was to achieve such powers of self-government 'as will ensure Scotland independent national status within the British group of nations.

'It is expressly stipulated that the party will contest Parliamentary and local government elections and will not lend its support to candidates other than those put forward under its own auspices,' the report continued. 'The party's candidates will be required to pledge themselves to support the object, policy and governing directions of the party, and, if elected, to accept no position from the Government. Withdrawal from Westminster will take place when a majority of Scottish members belonging to the party has been elected.'

The new party had been formed following discussions involving the Scottish Home Rule Association, the Scots National League, the Scottish National Movement and Glasgow University Students National Association. Founder members included R.E. Muirhead, R.B. Cunninghame Graham, Compton Mackenzie and C.M. Grieve.

But not everyone sympathetic to the idea of self-government for Scotland agreed with the new party's simplistic approach to the nation's problems. Tom Johnston reacted witheringly to its aims. A party which threatened to run candidates for Parliament on a programme of 'Scots Home Rule first, and nothing else matters until we get it' represented a policy of despair, Johnston asserted.

In an article published in *Forward* on 2 June 1928 he acknowledged the new party contained men of unimpeachable sincerity and great ability. But he also believed they would be compelled, sooner or later, to take sides upon the great economic issues of the day. 'They will require either to side with the poor or side against them,' Johnston declared, 'for landlord monopoly or against it, for usury or against it.' And once that happened, Johnston argued, 'they will become either Socialist or Tory or Liberal Home Rulers. And that is just where all Home Rule candidates are today.'

He didn't disagree with people who claimed Scotland suffered greater poverty per thousand of the population than England. 'It is the Scottish MPs mostly who have dragged the facts to light,' claimed Johnston. His own catalogue of complaints against the central government, on behalf of Scotland, included transport anachronisms, like the steamer service to the Western Isles which would not be tolerated on the English coast: public taxation raised in Scotland and spent, increasingly, in England on such projects as the naval dockyards, the armed forces and the great civil service headquarters at Whitehall.

He also alleged indefensible, but unspecified, discriminations against Scottish banks, and the financial facilities given to Scottish trade. 'It is equally true,' Johnston thundered, 'that the barring of our mountains to tourists, and the scandal of our deer forests, would not persist for a year under a Scots Parliament.' Nevertheless, he opposed the idea of a new party which ran 'forlorn-hope candidates' before a Labour Government could empower a Scottish Parliament to deal with purely Scottish questions. However unfairly, that party would be regarded as a dummy capitalist agency, designed to secure votes from Labour, Johnston contended.

With a sideways glance at its founder, his old friend, R.E. Muirhead, perhaps, Johnston also warned that 'one immediate effect will be an exodus of Labour men from the ranks of the Scottish Home Rule

Association, if it be a consenting party to candidatures against Labour nominees'.

At least 29 Labour MPs, from all sections of the party, as well as prominent trade unionists, were active in the ranks of the Scottish Home Rule Association throughout the 1920s. Corporate membership included over 100 trade union branches and more than 60 Co-operative societies. Labour Party branches were prohibited from affiliating under the terms of their own constitution. However, according to G.D.H. Cole, no fewer than 50 'political organisations' with Labour sympathies were members of the association around that time.

Tom Johnston, a self-declared, and dedicated, propagandist on behalf of the Labour Party, was finally scathing about the actions of his old chief, Ramsay MacDonald, and how he deserted the Labour Party.

But in 1928, when the National Party for Scotland appeared, no one could foretell the circumstances of 1929, which returned the second Labour Government to Westminster; far less the manner of its bleak, sad end two years later; or the ferocious animosities this bred in the ranks of the Labour movement.

When he offered his strident opinions on the value of a party which was wholly devoted to achieving self-government for Scotland with, it appeared, no regard for all the other considerations which affected people's lives, Johnston also wanted to know: 'Should the National Party candidates, as is likely, poll miserably, what effect is that going to have upon governments in the immediate future? Is it not likely to convince them that there is virtually no demand for Scottish Home Rule?'

Johnston wasn't prepared to waver in his belief that Labour was the party most likely to deliver Home Rule for Scotland. 'Had the Labour Party been given a chance, and had it failed Scotland, then the creation of a new party would be a different matter altogether,' Johnston declared.

Three years later he complained bitterly, when an official national candidate contested a by-election in St Rollox, Glasgow, that the hard-pressed Labour Government needed to win to maintain its already precarious position in the House of Commons. Labour was never sure, from one night to the next, of winning a vote in the House of

Commons, Johnston, by this time Lord Privy Seal and a member of the Cabinet, told an audience in the Woodside Hall, Glasgow.

Government and Opposition were running neck and neck in the division lobbies. And there was a heavy death rate among older MPs because the Whips were compelled to remove sick and ailing supporters 'almost out of their death beds' in order to save the Government from defeat. What the country needed in St Rollox, a grim-faced Johnston contended, was a straight fight between Labour and a representative of 'the vested interests which are already entrenched in every place of power and privilege in the land'. He believed the economic imbalance which existed between Scotland and England could never be repaired so long as the Tories were allowed to gain seats in the House of Commons.

The by-election had been caused by the death of James Stewart, MP for St Rollox since 1922, when Labour enjoyed its first triumphant sweep of Scottish seats. Two municipal wards, Cowcaddens and Woodside, combined to form St Rollox. James Stewart, a former leader of the Labour group on Glasgow Town Council and chairman of the Glasgow Labour Housing Association, was a popular man. A barber by trade, he took a special interest in establishing municipal workshops for the blind. His majority at the last election exceeded 8,000 and until his death St Rollox qualified easily as a Labour stronghold.

What worried Johnston, and other members of Labour's West of Scotland power élite, was the inclusion on the ballot of a certain Miss Emily Campbell, a schoolteacher, representing the nationalists. During the campaign Miss Campbell was rebuked by Johnston for daring to suggest that Scotland's slums, unemployment and industry were in a worse state than in England because of neglect by the House of Commons. 'It is absurd for any political organisation at this time of day to ascribe the poverty of Scotland to the fact that Scotland hasn't got a square deal from the majority in the House of Commons,' Johnston insisted.

A leaflet issued by the National Party of Scotland, which claimed Scotland's slums were the worst in Europe, also attracted Johnston's fury – although a description of the constituency, published in *Forward* shortly before polling, appeared to substantiate the nationalists' claim.

Cowcaddens, according to *Forward*, was notorious throughout the country for its vile housing conditions. The death rate among children aged under a year was a shocking 115 per thousand born. In adjoining Woodside this figure improved marginally to 95 per thousand. But a short tram ride away, along Great Western Road, in fashionable Kelvinside, the mortality rate showed 27 infants died per thousand born.

Kelvinside was a leafy district of handsome terraced houses, peopled by prosperous businessmen and the professional middle class. Woodside, by contrast, as described by Thomas Blake, writing in *Forward* early in 1931, and repeated on 11 April the same year with a by-election pending, was 'a depressing monster'. Wrote Blake: 'Tenement follows tenement, grim and gaunt, forming endless frontages of dull, drab stone, blackened by age and a city's smoke – high walls, unrelieved, except by the rectangular holes for windows. There is no relief in Woodside – Calton at its worst has a character and individuality of its own. Not so Woodside. Judged by an adequate housing standard, most of the Woodside tenements should be razed to the ground.'

Tom Johnston argued a different case in response to nationalist criticisms of Labour's record. 'It is absolutely and definitely untrue to say there are no slums in England. There is a slum problem in Manchester, in the Black Country and in London,' he declared. Since 1918, Johnston continued, nearly £96 million had been spent on housing in England and Wales compared to £12.5 million in Scotland. He acknowledged this was less than Scotland's proper share. But the shortfall wasn't due to 'the fact there is a national Parliament at Westminster, nor that a majority of the members in the present House of Commons were born in England or Wales, with only a minority of them born in Scotland'.

Scotland, according to the Lord Privy Seal, could blame itself for lack of action on the housing front. The 1930 Housing Act, which Labour succeeded in steering through the House of Commons despite its difficulties, actually allowed Scotland more money than England for slum clearance. But local authorities in Scotland – manned and controlled by capitalist representatives, Johnston fumed – simply refused to take advantage of the money on offer. He'd spent much of his time at the Scottish Office, when he was Under-Secretary of State, pleading with local authorities to take advantage of money which was currently available for slum clearance, Johnston claimed. 'There are 20,000 unemployed building workers in Scotland and the Government is offering local authorities money to employ them. The people who are keeping back progress are not the English, nor the foreigners, but the reactionary capitalist exploiters back home.'

His replies failed to satisfy the nationalists. They also wanted to know why unemployment figures in Scotland were 16 per cent higher than in England as a whole – and 150 per cent higher if the comparison was restricted to the south-east area of the country, including London.

Forward, no doubt acting on behalf of its founder, now a prominent member of the Government, with special responsibilities for unemployment, countered angrily. Unemployment in Scotland was lower than similar figures for north-east and north-west England, Wales and Northern Ireland, it declared; adding piously: 'It is a very poor case that requires the cock-eyed use of selective statistics as the Nationalist leaflet uses them.'

It was no part of the paper's business to decry the patriotic sentiments of anyone connected with the National Party of Scotland, a prominent front-page article continued breathlessly. 'But when they begin on economics, and bread and butter politics, and seek to mislead the working classes on matters of vital importance, it is time somebody got after them.'

That somebody, it seemed, was no less a personage then the Lord Privy Seal, Tom Johnston. Addressing his mainly working-class audience in the Woodside Hall he was in no mood to take prisoners. All the authority of his past reputation, together with the prestige of a Cabinet post, combined to impress his listeners. 'All around the cities of Glasgow, London, Manchester and Edinburgh,' the Lord Privy Seal declared fervently, 'millions of pounds have been privately appropriated which were publicly created. A message from you that publicly created values must be publicly owned will do more to encourage the Labour Party, and to scare the reactionaries, than anything else I know.'

Labour kept St Rollox. But support for the party since the last general election, and the death of James Stewart, was seriously diminished. Only 1,382 votes separated the Labour candidate, Bailie William Leonard, from his Tory opponent, a former city councillor, John A. Kennedy. The nationalist candidate, Miss Emily Campbell, finished third, and bottom of the poll. Close observers of the result could see there was a dangerous respectability about her performance, however. The 3,521 votes polled by Miss Campbell was by far the highest number ever achieved by a third party candidate in St Rollox. Johnston had been right to worry.

In March 1932 a vacancy for a High Court judge in Allahabad was the unexpected, and unlikely, cause of a by-election in Dunbartonshire. Three other candidates, including a nationalist and a communist, joined Tom Johnston in seeking to succeed the departing sahib, and man of declared wisdom, J.G. Thom.

Johnston had been reluctant to accept the Labour Party nomination at first, pleading journalistic commitments were commanding most of his time. Just as likely, he probably saw little merit in joining the existing Labour rump in the Conservative-dominated House of Commons. He was also entitled to believe that a few years living under the MacDonald-Baldwin axis would be enough for a majority of the electorate. At the next election Johnston hoped to regain West Stirlingshire for Labour. In the meantime, he was content to concentrate on his writing and business affairs, even travel.

However, as someone who had been born in Dunbartonshire, and continued to live in the constituency, a former Cabinet Minister with a distinguished record of speaking out on behalf of Britain's poor and unemployed, Tom Johnston was an ideal candidate in a by-election which could have been judged unnecessary; except for the distant needs of Empire.

To the voters of Dunbartonshire he offered a stirring manifesto: 'I believe in Socialism, in all for each and in each for all,' Johnston declared. 'I believe in the Labour Party method of approaching it, securing it, maintaining it. I believe in aiding and encouraging the existing organisations and in inspiring them with the Socialist ideal. I believe in persuasion; not violence.'

Adult male unemployment in the constituency averaged 49 per cent, reaching 69 per cent at one exchange. Johnston observed fervently: 'If you took the unemployed and their dependants and placed them round the coast of Britain, three to a yard, you could encircle the coast with a living wall of hunger and misery.'

He hoped the electors of Dunbartonshire would use their votes and their influence 'to aid in the transformation of the existing system of poverty for the many, a harassment and worry for most, into a system where the land and the industrial capital of the country, and the national credit, shall be regarded as a common heritage and used for the benefit of all'.

In this by-election, Johnston continued, he wanted people to use their vote against 'Toryism and the iron heel upon the poor. I ask you to use your vote not to buttress usury and militarism. I ask you not to use your vote to perpetuate a social system which condemns millions to poverty in the midst of plenty.'

John M. MacCormick later revealed, in *The Flag in the Wind*, that the nationalists hesitated before nominating a candidate in the 1932 by-election in Dunbartonshire. 'Tom Johnston had already proved himself to be one of the most sincere Home Rulers in the Labour Party and nobody could have any doubt about his patriotism,' MacCormick explained. 'But we had pledged ourselves to oppose, wherever possible, all candidates sponsored by the English controlled parties and we felt constrained to stand by that pledge.'

Five months earlier a majority of Dunbartonshire electors had been persuaded to vote for J.G. Thom, a coalition candidate, representing the Conservatives. In addition to whatever clarity of mind the former MP was about to demonstrate as a judge on the turbulent subcontinent, as an officer with the Gordon Highlanders during the First World War his courage was rewarded with a DSO and an MC and he was four times mentioned in despatches. The man chosen to repeat his success with the voters of Dunbartonshire was another former military person, retired naval commander, the Hon. A.D. Cochrane.

In a letter to Commander Cochrane, published on 12 March 1932, the Prime Minister, Ramsay MacDonald, demonstrated, for all to see, the distance which now existed between himself and his old comrades in the Labour Party. None of the other candidates – Robert Gray, for the Nationalists, or Councillor Hugh McIntyre who represented the Communist Party – was mentioned by name and no one was singled out for direct attack by MacDonald. But his support for the Conservative candidate, like his betrayal of his former editor, Parliamentary supporter, Cabinet colleague and friend, Tom Johnston, was absolute. 'I have no hesitation,' the first man to head a Labour Government informed the Conservative candidate, 'in begging the electors of Dunbarton to return you to support the National Government in the House of Commons.'

According to MacDonald a return 'to partisan politics would shatter the foundations of confidence at home and abroad upon which all national services must rest'. A government which enjoyed the co-operation of representatives of all parties had to face many difficulties peculiar to itself,' MacDonald added. He acknowledged there had been 'sacrifices upon many people who can ill bear them. But the electors may be assured that no sacrifices were imposed which the serious state of the country did not make necessary, and their restoration will continue to be the anxious study and concern of those whose misfortune it was to be compelled by circumstances to ask for them.'

At every point where stability and confidence were necessary the work and influence of the Government was plainly evident in the improving national prospects, MacDonald claimed. It would be a mistake to weaken the hands of those now in charge of state affairs. By electing Commander Cochrane the electors of Dumbarton [sic] would demonstrate that they were 'allied with the great national effort to restore and maintain the influence of this country and to secure the foundations in healthy trade upon which that influence must be built'.

That same weekend Tom Johnston claimed he didn't want to comment on the letter. Pressed by reporters, no doubt seeking a headline-making display of anger, he recalled some of the Prime Minister's previous activities. To anyone familiar with MacDonald's record, and his affiliations to the Labour movement, Johnston suggested, it would appear as little short of a tragedy that, in the evening of his days, he 'should be reduced to sending letters of commendation to Tory candidates who were standing for the taxation of the food of the people, and for the several items of the Conservative Party programme which Mr MacDonald has spent his life attacking'.

He also reminded his audience that on the occasion of the St Rollox by-election less than a year ago MacDonald had written to the Labour candidate saying: 'All the cures for our industrial ills which the Conservative Party recommend have been tried and have failed, either here or in other industrial countries. They stand for the old system of unregulated, self-seeking, private enterprise which has produced the present collapse in world trade.'

All that had changed since then, Johnston claimed, were Mr MacDonald's affiliations. Doubtless it was part of the heavy price he had to pay for his Premiership. But the former Labour leader was now a 'mere fugleman for the vested interests of the Conservative Party'.

Another prominent Labour politician, Herbert Morrison, speaking in Helensburgh on Johnston's behalf, described MacDonald's letter as an extraordinary and humiliating communication. Commander Cochrane stood 'for everything against which the Labour Party had fought during the whole of its existence', Morrison claimed. 'He stood against the welfare of the people, against the organisation of industry, and against the betterment of conditions of life for the working people of this country.'

Still, the former naval commander won comfortably. A majority of the votes polled were spread amongst the other three candidates. And of these 35.6 per cent went to Tom Johnston. But it wasn't enough. Johnston finished second with 13,704 votes; 3,045 behind the Prime Minister's declared favourite. His nationalist opponent, Robert Gray, with 5,178 votes, probably cost Johnston the seat. The Communist candidate, Hugh McIntyre, attracted 2,870 votes, lost his deposit, and was never a threat.

Johnston blamed his downfall on Liberal sympathisers supporting the nationalist candidate. He believed Liberals disliked Labour, not for its socialism but for its trade union affiliations.

The result, according to John M. MacCormick, altered the course of history. In the circumstances of 1932, with the Labour Party decimated in the House of Commons by the results of the 1931 election,

MacCormick argued, Tom Johnston would have been the elected leader of the Labour Party in succession to George Lansbury instead of the little-known Clement Attlee.

Asked to comment finally on Ramsay MacDonald's intervention on behalf of the Conservative candidate in the Dunbartonshire by-election Tom Johnston maintained: 'I prefer to think of the MacDonald of the wartime, and of the years when he placed his pen, his brain, his platform presence and his ability at the service of the poor.'

CHAPTER SEVENTEEN

OUT OF PARLIAMENT for four years, between 1931 and 1935, Johnston busied himself chiefly with *Forward*, writing an account of the financial crisis which destroyed the second Labour Government, and becoming head of a life assurance company, the City of Glasgow Friendly Society.

The aims and interests of the City of Glasgow Friendly Society suited Johnston admirably. As he himself once inquired: 'What could be more friendly than the decision of the Board of Management during the great miners' strikes of the 1920s that no miner's policy should be lapsed through inability to pay the premiums?'

It had been formed in 1862, as a breakaway movement of the Royal Liver Friendly Society, by a handful of working men, led by an enterprising and far-seeing agent, operating from a single-roomed office in a Glasgow back street. Then, wrote Johnston, 'the great fear among working people was of a pauper's funeral. In hundreds of thousands of homes up and down the country people clubbed together to pay their pennies voluntarily into a fund which would ensure decent burial and widows' weeds.'

Johnston brought his usual heady mix of great commitment, direct involvement, simple analysis, sound administration and outrageous flair to the life assurance business. It was, by his reckoning, an industry in desperate need of fresh organisation.

Years earlier, while serving as an MP for Dundee, he found there were 217 approved life assurance societies with members in the city. Ninety-nine of the societies had less than ten members and 52 only one member each. 'A system like that,' Johnston told a meeting of the Glasgow and West of Scotland Faculty of Insurance, 'calls for drastic treatment.'

He proposed an all-in social insurance scheme covering unemployment, health and pensions, and argued against the folly of excluding people with incomes over £250 a year from the benefits of National Health Insurance. 'In these days,' Johnston claimed, 'there is in suburbia misery such as exists in slums. Is it not a tragedy that such people are outside old age and widows' pensions?'

Teeth and spectacles were on offer to customers of the City of Glasgow Friendly Society long before similar benefits were available on the NHS. Johnston's scheme involved the services of a Glasgow optician and Glasgow Dental College. With wry good humour he later observed: 'The spectacles were a success, but the teeth weren't!'

The centenary history of the City of Glasgow Friendly Society, written by Jack House, claims staff conditions were greatly improved during the period of Johnston's managership. 'This society was the first of its group to give the staff alternative Saturdays off,' wrote House. 'There was also a special system of bonuses for the staff.'

On several occasions, during his early years with the society, when he also served as an MP, Johnston refused to accept any increase in his own salary as general manager. In March 1938 he was offered an extra £500 a year for his services. Knowing there would have to be economies among the lower members of the staff Johnston refused the increase.

On a visit to the Soviet Union in 1934 Johnston tried to avoid going on the kind of conducted tour 'which was frequently arranged for easily acquiescent and readily assimilative tourists. I was a journalist by profession, accustomed to weighing evidence; I did not want to go in blinkers; I wanted to see the rough as well as the smooth.' An official he encountered in Moscow had 'piloted Mr H.G. Wells about just before I arrived, and he quite appreciated the fact that I wanted to see below stairs, and not merely front shop window stuff', Johnston continued.

He was shown new tenement flats where nine square metres had been allocated to each person and two or three families were expected to share three rooms. 'Occasionally, but not often, I found two families to one room,' Johnston recalled. 'On the walls outside the tenement there were placarded particulars of the winning room for cleanliness and tidiness, and by contrast particulars of the worst kept room. On one tenement of which I took particulars, out of 486 apartments 57 in one week were classed as dirty, and the occupants had been fined by the Comradely Court or the Hygiene Commission.'

Six tenants, men and women, were selected to adjudicate on behalf of the Comradely Courts. Offenders charged with hygiene delinquency could be fined up to 50 roubles. Johnston questioned whether the publicity had any shaming effect upon some of the worst sinners he saw appearing. Many thousands of new tenement dwellers had been dragged, suddenly and without any preparation, from villages where sanitary arrangements were primitive, Johnston, the sympathetic eye-witness, explained. They were only a year or two from complete illiteracy and were possessed of the craziest kind of belief in devils and witches and wizards. And, even in the new tenements, they were expected to share the use of a water closet with other families. 'Maybe given the same origins and conditions few of us would have behaved any better than these new industrial Soviet citizens,' Johnston suggested.

Infant mortality, like housing, was a constant passion with Johnston. Figures uncovered in Leningrad showed a 16 per cent death rate among infants the previous year. 'Note the per cent, not per thousand,' he emphasised. Officials blamed interventions and blockades by other governments for these appalling statistics. He believed 'there was no doubt but that the main causes were the unduly high proportion of production that went to capital goods and armaments; the habits of the people; the conditions under which they were housed; and the war on the Kulaks, who had retaliated by killing much of the livestock, and so created the milk and meat scarcities'.

But he appeared to marvel at the free and easy approach to marriage and divorce existing in the Soviet Union. He saw two marriage ceremonies performed in the course of his visit. 'They were most casual and off-hand affairs,' Johnston recounted.

At the office of the Bureau of Registration of Civil Acts the registrar was a young woman, wearing a red bandanna, who sold marriages with the same disinterest and insouciance as if she were a railway clerk selling tickets. 'The registration room itself looks like a rural railway station waiting-room in urgent need of repairs,' Johnston added. Couples, with no compulsory witness in attendance, arrived, were asked to provide their names, addresses, employment, age, and to state whether or not they had been married before. That done, they were told to 'please sign on the dotted line' and informed the fee would be seven roubles; four of which went to the committee in charge of homeless children and three to the Government. Then, as Johnston described the system: 'Out the couple walk, man and wife!'

Divorce, in his experience, was even easier: four minutes! Only one of the parties involved in a divorce action was required to appear before the Bureau of Registration of Civil Acts. And no previous notice was required. 'The first intimation a woman may hear of her divorce is when she gets the formal notice served upon her that she is no longer a married woman. You discard the partner of your joys and sorrows, your bed and board, with the same sangfroid as you discard your old coat or your holey socks.'

In country districts, on visits to collective farms, he found 'the roads were awful, and the furniture in the houses, and the living conditions, betrayed a standard of living far below anything our agricultural labourers have had to put up with. On the other hand I was assured on all hands,' Johnston added, 'that no peasant left the collective farm of his own accord.'

Once he visited a church where 'the priest came round for a collection and distributed blessings as he steered himself, and some following appellants with trays, through the crowd. I gave him what must have been a munificent donation, for they are brave men, these priests, whatever we may think of some of their dogmas. When he saw what was now on the tray he gave me a startled look and his eyes shone with sudden tears.'

Even at the height of the depression Tom Johnston discounted the chances of a communist-led revolution occurring in Scotland. This he credited to the country's sectarian tendencies. Priest and presbyter kept their flocks carefully apart from communist influences, Johnston claimed. 'If you doubt it,' he suggested, 'pay a visit to Glasgow on 12 July when one-third of the proletarian population goes out with its ikons – usually William Prince of Orange on a white horse – and drums and fifes, while another third of the proletarians wave green flags tauntingly, and throw empty beer bottles at the drums.'

Nobody knew how many real communists there were on Clydeside, added Johnston. The figures were secret. However, it was believed that membership of the Communist Party in Glasgow had been in decline since its best days under John Maclean, 'a courageous, desperately sincere and widely respected man'. Its numerical strength in Glasgow was probably under 200. However, according to Johnston, this included 'agents on the payroll of the secret police and delegates from the intelligence departments of the Army, the Navy and the Air Force'.

Writing with his usual sense of droll mischief in the right-wing *Spectator* in February 1934, and keen as always to shock anyone suffering from the plague of Home Counties complacency, he also offered the opinion that there was a greater likelihood of a communist revolution happening in the Isle of Wight, Oxford and Cheltenham than on Clydeside. 'The Communist Party has failed. There is no communist menace on the Clyde. Not enough of it to excite a fascist reaction. The culture of a united proletariat thrives ill on sectarian middens.'

Johnston was no longer editor of *Forward*. On 1 April 1933 a front-page box announced he had resigned to write a book on democracy and finance. Emrys Hughes, assistant editor for ten years, and in complete charge whenever Johnston was away, had been appointed in his place. Johnston would continue as chairman of the *Forward* publishing company and also contribute the main front-page socialist commentary each week. The new arrangement involved no change whatever in the policy of the paper, the statement added.

A year earlier Johnston had been writing in secret to the editor of the *Daily Herald*, W.H. Stevenson, to inquire if his 'paper might be open to consider some deal, either of complete or of partial acquisition'. An arrangement between the two papers would have meant *Forward* operating from a sounder financial footing and the *Daily Herald* widening its intellectual base within the Labour movement. W.H. Stevenson was interested in the idea. But he also wanted his editorial director, John Dunbar, present at any talks.

Arranging a meeting of everyone concerned proved difficult. Barely six days after he contacted Stevenson with his original proposal, Johnston wrote again, on 24 August 1932, to say it was an awkward time to be absent from Glasgow – 'there is political skin and hair flying about all over the place up here these days', Johnston observed.

A take-over by the *Daily Herald*, partial or otherwise, didn't proceed. Three years later, in the midst of a libel wrangle with Beaverbrook Newspapers, ownership of *Forward* passed to a company headed by Johnston's old friend, Rosslyn Mitchell, the Glasgow lawyer who caused a political sensation by defeating Henry Asquith in Paisley in the 1924 general election; and another stir when he resigned the seat before the next election.

On 16 February 1935, with Emrys Hughes in charge, *Forward* announced it was taking the fight for socialism to London. In a front-page proclamation it declared: 'Labour has now a majority on the LCC and is being subjected to a bitter and unscrupulous barrage of criticism and misrepresentation from the capitalist press. In our London edition we will reply to these critics and carry the war into the enemy's camp.'

There was every likelihood it could become a costly campaign. The previous month an attack on the *Daily Express*, and one of its freelance contributors, ended with a writ for libel arriving at the offices of the Civic Press. The case against *Forward* was brought by a part-time author and traveller, Bosworth Goldman. The new year was less than a week old when he found himself inadvertently caught in the middle of a dangerous shooting war between the undisputed champions of left and right in British journalism; the tiny Civic Press, publishers of *Forward*, and the mighty Beaverbrook empire, owners of the *Daily Express*.

The trouble started on the last day of 1934 when the *Daily Express* published a report which claimed two prominent members of the Soviet leadership élite, Zinoviev and Kamenev, had been exiled in an Arctic island prison camp. Goldman had written a book, *Red Road Through Asia*, and claimed to have visited the Arctic camps. When the *Daily Express* story first appeared he contacted the BBC and offered to provide a comment on the prisoners' plight. An editor expressed some interest in airing his views but later the BBC abandoned the story on the grounds it hadn't been confirmed by any of the major news agencies on which it relied.

On 2 January 1935 the *Daily Express* published an account of the BBC's action, accompanied by an announcement that the far-travelled correspondent's views would appear there. Three days later Emrys Hughes commented in *Forward*: 'Why the BBC ever arranged for any of the *Daily Express* Russian correspondents to broadcast outside the Children's Hour is rather a mystery for they must be the joke of Fleet Street.'

Two weeks later he aimed another contemptuous, rough-tongued blast at his Fleet Street rival. 'We have noted,' wrote Hughes, 'that the BBC refused to allow the *Daily Express* correspondent to broadcast until his news had been confirmed by a reputable news agency, but as this particular piece of news was not confirmed, and has not been confirmed yet, the BBC evidently sized up the matter correctly.'

The case against *Forward* was heard before Mr Justice Swift and a jury in the King's Bench Division of the London courts on 13 November 1935. *Forward*'s defence included a plea that the words used 'so far as they were statements of fact, were true, and so far as they were expressions of opinion, were fair comment upon a matter of public interest'.

In court Bosworth Goldman was described by his counsel, Mr T.J. O'Connor KC, as a young man of initiative and energy, aged 26, 'who was looked upon as a responsible essayist, broadcaster and journalist with a knowledge of his subject'. He'd travelled extensively in Russia, in 1930 and 1932, visiting the Arctic prison camps. But he wasn't a *Daily Express* reporter. And he'd never worked for the paper before. It seemed *Forward* was conducting a vendetta against news about Russia which appeared in the *Daily Express*. Added Mr O'Connor: '*Forward*, exhibiting sensitiveness to defamatory news about Russia, attacked the *Daily Express* in no uncertain terms, claiming that much of the news which appeared in the *Express* was inaccurate, and it seems to have had sources of information which enabled it to challenge the *Daily Express*.'

Emrys Hughes told the court that he would describe news about

Russia contained in the *Daily Express* as inaccurate sensationalism. 'Their report of the banishment of Zinoviev and Kamenev contained a number of sensational self-contradictory statements,' Hughes claimed. 'For instance, it said in one place that they had been sent to Siberia. Then it went on to say that they had been sent to Solovetski Island. I know that Solovetski Island was nowhere near Siberia and so I held that this article was a piece of sensationalism, and false. It showed that someone had been inventing things.'

There had been no previous libel action brought against *Forward* in his ten-year association with the paper, Emrys Hughes stated. He denied this was because 'it was almost impossible to get anything out of the company'.

Mr Justice Swift noted, in his summing up, that for some time before the end of 1934 there had been a vendetta between the *Forward* and the *Daily Express* over Russia. 'There was no doubt that by that time Mr Hughes had it well ingrained in his mind that all who wrote for the *Daily Express* were rogues and liars and ought not to be treated with the least consideration; that the paper ought not to be bought, and if it were bought, it should only be so that the person who read it could disbelieve everything that was said.'

He also informed the jury that the defendants had mixed up statements of facts and comment in a way which the law did not permit. Goldman was awarded £575 damages and costs.

In a counter claim *Forward* complained that Bosworth Goldman's solicitors had written to W.H. Smith and Sons saying they could not understand how the company felt able to distribute a newspaper 'so obviously likely to contain libellous matter'. Mr Justice Swift agreed the words were defamatory but added the letter was a privileged communication which had been published without malice. He found in favour of the defendants who were also awarded costs.

Forward had been wrong to discount the main elements of the *Daily Express* story. Tom Johnston later acknowledged that 1934 was the year when things were 'beginning to cook up for the big purge of communist members' four years later.

Zinoviev and Kamenev were among the first to suffer. Following the assassination of Sergey Kirov, another leading Communist Party figure, in a corridor of the Smolny Institute, Leningrad, on 1 December 1934, they were arrested and charged with complicity to murder. Two years later a notorious show trial found them guilty and they were executed, on the orders of the misanthrope in the Kremlin, their old comrade, Iosif Vissarionovich Dzhugashvili, otherwise known as Stalin.

Forward's row with the *Daily Express* peaked just as its former editor and owner was making plans to return to London to resume another old familiar role – Member of Parliament for West Stirlingshire and Clackmannanshire.

Tom Johnston expected his strong stand against military sanctions and war preparations to cost him votes in the 1935 general election. Asked at one constituency meeting if he would not agree to bomb Italian towns if Mussolini bombed Britain he replied: 'I think a world boycott – moral, political, economic – of Italy would do Mussolini greater harm than killing the women and children of Italy.'

'But surely,' his questioner persisted, 'if Mussolini's troops kill British women and children, we should retaliate?'

Johnston disagreed. 'If an Italian rapes my sister, am I expected to rape his sister in retaliation?' he demanded.

'But would you do nothing?' the man asked, puzzled.

'Most certainly,' Johnston replied firmly.

The election had been called by Stanley Baldwin, the Tory leader, soon after he succeeded Ramsay MacDonald as Prime Minister. Johnston claimed the Tories, under Baldwin, were bent upon squandering the nation's resources by spending an extra £150 million on armaments in addition to army, navy and air force budgets previously allocated.

If that happened, he warned the voters of West Stirling and Clackmannanshire, it would be 'goodbye to all hopes of lifting the miseries of unemployment: goodbye to all hopes of progressive improvement in the social conditions of the poor: goodbye to all hopes of raising the scale of old-age pensions, to all hopes of bringing the aged spinster on to the pension lists.

'A race in armaments will blacken out our hopes of prosperity for all,' Johnston added. 'And the end of that race will be war and the complete destruction of our civilisation.' It was abundantly clear, Johnston continued, that the Tory Government, 'while paying lip service to collective peace through the League of Nations, really believes in a programme of great national rearmament at almost any cost'.

He wanted to pursue a different road to peace. 'We must strive for a Tribunal of Equity under the auspices of the League of Nations,' Johnston explained in his election address, 'where nations with grievances may plead their cause: we must remove economic injustice between the nations who have and those who have not colonies, by inviting the League to take supervision of all colonial (non-self-governing) possessions: and the only force that need be permitted for the maintenance of law between the nations is an international police under the control of the League.

'Peace can never be secured through war or preparation for war,' Johnston insisted. 'The last war to end war cost the world 13 million dead in the armed forces and 20 million wounded.' Uncounted millions died of starvation and pestilence and the world was faced with a mountainous and crushing burden of public debt. 'And what have we got for it?' Johnston demanded. 'Militarism killed? Not so! There are more armed men and more devilish weapons of destruction in Europe today than there were in 1913.'

He favoured a total world boycott of Italy, including all diplomatic representation, over the war in Abyssinia. 'This great moral and economic boycott would win in the end,' Johnston promised. 'And if it wins, militarism is finished, for no state would continue piling up armaments after such a demonstration of their futility and ineffectiveness. But even if it should fail in this its first attempt,' Johnston went on, 'there is no sense in our committing the crowning folly of a suicidal war. No war under whatsoever auspices or with whatsoever groupings will get any support from me.'

According to the *Stirling Observer* the Tory organisation in the constituency was among the best in the country. Tom Johnston, who had contested six previous Parliamentary elections in West Stirling, winning three and losing three, remarked drily: 'In a number of villages we had no local organisation whatsoever and in several villages we did not dare put up a local chairman at a public meeting. And yet, despite it all, we got 1,000 more votes than in our peak year of 1929.'

Many of the villages were near-feudal in their ways and the will of the landowner was a major factor in people's lives. With obvious amusement Johnston recorded, for the benefit of *Forward*, how the local gentry turned out in their cars to drive workers to the polls. At Bridge of Allan, a tiny hamlet outside Stirling, the Tory agent had 140 cars at his disposal, Johnston claimed.

'But although the reactionaries have a great electoral machine, and although much political dominance still vests in the baronial estates, they have been crushed by something bigger and more powerful,' Johnston continued. 'Sixteen thousand people, sickened by the callous indifference of the last Parliament to the sufferings of the coal-mining communities and the unemployed, marched indignantly to the polls.'

In a straight fight Johnston defeated his Conservative opponent, A.P. Duffes, by a comfortable margin. Indeed, the size of his majority surprised everyone, including the winning candidate. The final result, in a near 84 per cent poll, showed Johnston with 16,015 votes against 13,053 for his opponent – a majority of 2,962.

Considering the constituency as a whole he questioned whether there was 'anywhere in the country a more solid, loyal, determined, and well-primed Labour–Socialist electorate. No divisions, no splits, no narks or professional girners,' he declared. In addition, however, he also believed the size of his majority showed Labour must have 'picked up in the villages and the hamlets over 1,000 voters who came to us like Nicodemus by night – farm workers, estate hands, butlers, gardeners, maids up at the big house'.

Elsewhere in the country a majority of voters favoured the Tories. Stanley Baldwin, who commanded 387 seats in the new House of Commons, continued as Prime Minister. But the results showed that his predecessor, Ramsay MacDonald, had been defeated in sensational circumstances at Seaham Harbour, Northumberland, by Emmanuel Shinwell, the man who first proposed him as leader of the Labour Party in those far-off, hopeful days of 1922.

'I didn't enjoy it, the idea of fighting a man I once proposed as leader,' Shinwell reflected years later. 'But what could I do, refuse to do it?'

Ramsay MacDonald, defeated in Seaham by more than 20,000 votes, was thrown an unexpected Parliamentary lifeline the following year when the Association of Unionist Graduates agreed to accept him as their candidate in a by-election for a seat representing the Scottish universities. MacDonald won easily. And, on his return to the House of Commons, as a reward for services rendered, he was offered a place at the Cabinet table, as Lord President of the Council.

To many of his old admirers, he presented a sorry sight at the despatch box, performing in his final role, on behalf of a Tory-led Government. Years later, Tom Johnston continued to recall, with detectable anguish, how Labour's first Prime Minister was 'actually put up in the House of Commons to answer questions about arrangements for the Royal Coronation: about precedence in the procession: about how many seats were to be allotted at the ceremony to deserving classes: about the lavatory arrangements, and other humiliations of like kind.'

'Perhaps,' the former Lord Privy Seal in MacDonald's last Labour Government concluded sadly, 'it is unfair to suggest that Mr Baldwin and his Cabinet associates arranged that he should give the answers; probably they were as ashamed as were the rest of the Members of the House at the spectacle he was presenting'.

MacDonald continued to serve as Lord President of the Council until Stanley Baldwin retired as Prime Minister in May 1937: six months later, aboard the liner *Reina del Pacifico*, bound for South America, he died.

In a short assessment of his fallen leader, written on MacDonald's death, Tom Johnston recalled how he walked about the lobbies while old friends turned their backs upon him. 'Perhaps,' Johnston suggested, 'it was not so much his abnegation in crisis in 1931 that caused the embitterments against him, but the fact that he who had been elected general of an army should have silently, and furtively, and without consulting his army, or explaining himself to the ranks, deserted and gone to lead the enemy against the folks who trusted him.'

Johnston believed MacDonald paid dearly for his desertion. The last half dozen years of his public life had been a tragedy, a recantation and a humiliation. At the same time, generously remembering what he considered the good times, Johnston also considered it folly to belittle the great service MacDonald gave in the creation of the Labour Party. 'The MacDonald who died in 1931 was a great and noteworthy figure in the march to the povertyless commonwealth,' Johnston insisted.

CHAPTER EIGHTEEN

TOM JOHNSTON was in politics to change society. Being an MP was never enough. But in company with another 153 Labour MPs he appeared condemned by the results of the 1935 general election to another long, and fruitless, spell in opposition.

He was always an influential figure in Labour circles at Westminster. Following the 1922 election, when he first appeared in the House of Commons alongside the Clydesiders, Johnston finished third in the ballot for a seat on the Parliamentary Party Executive, ahead of Shinwell and Wheatley who were also elected. Nine years later he remained a popular figure with rank and file MPs, finishing fourth, behind Arthur Henderson, J.R. Clynes and William Graham, for a place on the executive. Hugh Dalton, Arthur Greenwood and Emmanuel Shinwell, all former Ministers before Ramsay MacDonald deserted Labour to join the National Government, finished behind him in the 1931 vote. Other prominent names, such as Clement Attlee, Herbert Morrison and Stafford Cripps, failed to win election to the executive on that occasion. And in 1935, on his return to the House of Commons, he finished third in the same poll behind J.R. Clynes and Hugh Dalton. It was, mused Dalton, a future Labour Chancellor with his eye on the leadership held by Clement Attlee, 'a rough measure of our relative standing in the esteem of the Parliamentary party at that time'.

Indeed, Johnston's success encouraged the *Glasgow Weekly Herald* to suggest, in June 1935, that he was now in a position to challenge Attlee for the leadership. Johnston 'has given to his work both scholarship and drive', the newspaper claimed, 'a fortunate combination for most of those whose interest he has always kept in sight'. The *Weekly Herald* considered Johnston 'a man with ideas and the necessary purpose to make them concrete. He is one of the none too large number of Labour men in Scotland whose future one will follow with interest.'

Johnston might have beaten Attlee in a ballot of MPs for the Labour leadership in 1932. But he wasn't an MP at the time and the opportunity didn't present itself. It is hard to imagine him not competing if the circumstances looked favourable. Of course, it is just as difficult to contemplate the awkward Scot appealing to English voters in numbers which would ensure victory for Labour. Later, as a cynical Hugh Dalton assessed his chances, Johnston was 'marooned' in Scotland.

His old chief, William Adamson, was no longer an MP when Tom Johnston returned to the House of Commons in 1935: the former Secretary of State for Scotland had been defeated in a bitter contest in Fife by the veteran communist, Willie Gallagher. In his place the Labour leader, Clement Attlee, invited Johnston to assume responsibility for Scottish affairs in the House of Commons. Short of achieving real power, it was a role he cherished.

Johnston had been an ardent supporter of self-government for Scotland and a Parliament, with meaningful tax-raising powers, sitting in Edinburgh, all his life. But he was never a nationalist in the modern, narrow, separatist sense of the word. He never wavered in his belief that Scotland should remain inside the United Kingdom and with it the British Empire. And he was careful, in his public utterances at least, not to encroach on Westminster's wider responsibilities.

Although he supported the Rev. James Barr's 1927 self-government for Scotland Bill, which promised the withdrawal of all Scottish MPs from Westminster following Home Rule, he hoped this particular clause might be changed at a later stage. In his view Britain was a partnership of free nations with each of the partners enjoying the same rights and privileges within the Union. Hence his belief that MPs from Scotland should be entitled to attend Westminster, to speak and vote on matters outside the remit of the Scottish Parliament which affected the United Kingdom as a whole; at the same time adding a Scottish voice, and a Scottish perspective, to debates concerning the Empire for as long as the Empire existed.

Almost two-thirds of a century later, a similar argument could be applied, just as easily, to Britain's membership of the European Union and the future role of the Westminster Parliament in a devolved United Kingdom.

Tom Johnston would have been happy to support the idea of regional assemblies serving the whole of Britain, with a Parliament at Westminster, representing the United Kingdom, applying itself to wider issues. The legislature he favoured for Edinburgh would have been unbeholden to Westminster solely on matters of domestic importance to Scotland; including job creation, health, housing, tourism and pensions.

During the abdication crisis of 1936 he was against an election on the issue of Republicanism versus the Monarchy. His old friend, James Maxton, wanted the monarchy abolished entirely following the enforced departure of King Edward VIII. Maxton believed the King's refusal to part with Mrs Simpson presented the country with a perfect opportunity 'to establish a completely democratic form of government that does away with the monarchial institution and the hereditary principle'.

Johnston disagreed. He admitted his belief in the inevitability of Scotland becoming a republic one day. 'But suppose we got it this year, or next year! Suppose that in disgust the bourgeois classes and the Churches had decided to cut out the hereditary monarchy and the plush and gilt of Buckingham Palace, and all the silly, stupid, childish lies which are required to keep up the appearance of the divinity of the King – suppose the whole contraption had gone, and we had secured a President – what then? Would we be any nearer a socialist commonwealth?' Johnston demanded.

Johnston was prepared to vote against the ex-King and his wife becoming a charge on the public purse, to be set against the next Civil List. But he rejected the idea of an election on the single issue of Republicanism versus the Monarchy because he believed it would mentally submerge 'the great economic questions which the Labour Party has sought to make fundamental in national politics'.

Writing in *Forward* on 19 December 1936, only days after the Prime Minister, Stanley Baldwin, informed a tense House of Commons that King Edward VIII, later the Duke of Windsor, had put his signature to a Deed of Abdication, Johnston conceded: 'The shocks of the past month to the monarchy system have just about destroyed the one argument many socialists — myself included — had even for the temporary continuance of that system.

'Many of us believed that the monarchy might be a useful buffer for a socialist government endeavouring to achieve a transfer to socialism without an insurrection or sabotage by the propertied classes.

'So long, we thought, as the King had touched a new law with his sceptre,' Johnston explained, 'there would be at least some measure of respect paid to that law, and any rebellion against it would be a rebellion against the King.'

According to Johnston it had been assumed that, so long as the King was by the side of his constitutionally elected socialist Ministers, the army, the navy, the air force, the law and civil service would continue to function. He offered a pragmatic view of the civilising influences of kingship, and the electoral advantages which accrued to those who subscribed to the notion of monarchy; not least the wealthier supporters of the departed, and seriously lamented, King Edward VIII and his reluctant successor, King George VI.

Previously, wrote Johnston, 'the King business was a partial guarantee of peaceful transition. But one is not so sure of the validity of such an argument now. The hierarchy of the Church, and the aristocracy of wealth and its Press have shown that they no longer yield unconditional obedience to a King, especially when they could appeal to deeply entrenched moral sentiments against him.'

Sometime later, at a public meeting in his constituency, he silenced a persistent advocate of republicanism, who objected to Labour MPs swearing an oath of allegiance to the Crown, by suggesting the first president of a Scottish republic, chosen by popular vote, would be the wife of George VI, Queen Elizabeth, later the Queen Mother. She would win by a margin of ten to one against all-comers, Johnston asserted, to a roar of applause from the audience. He remembered the moment long after with satisfaction. For it 'finished the interrupter, who indeed took it as a notice to quit'.

Johnston's interest in achieving the best and fairest method of governing Scotland lasted a lifetime. But by his own admission the means he favoured throughout most of his Parliamentary career altered considerably with the years.

Prior to the Second World War he helped found the Saltire Society, which sought to link cultural development to social reform, and the London Scots Self-Government Committee, a radical nationalist body, which favoured planning as the principal means of curing Scotland's ills. Many of the committee's proposals, contained in a pamphlet published in December 1937 with a foreword by the Labour leader, Clement Attlee, bear a marked resemblance to some of the structural changes in the governance of Scotland which Johnston endeavoured to introduce when he became Secretary of State, little more than three years later.

Plan for Scotland, written by the committee's treasurer, Thomas Burns, argued in favour of a federal Britain, 'with individual legislatures for the internal affairs of each nation and a Federal Parliament at Westminster, in which Scotland would still be represented'. On the question of constituent Parliaments for all the member nations of the United Kingdom a note to the London Scots' proposals conceded 'whereas in Scotland there is a widespread and growing demand for such decentralisation, in England such an idea is little canvassed except in purely political circles'.

It was essential to the London Scots argument that Scotland was a wealthy country, rich in natural resources, food and technical skill, 'reduced to poverty by unchecked individualist greed and an out-of-date bureaucratic system of government. Manifestly,' the committee claimed, 'if there is to be any hope of getting a better livelihood, full work, plenty to eat, good houses, good health for the ordinary Scotsman, there is urgent need of planned socialised development of the country's resources.'

Author Burns and his fellow London Scots sought no jurisdiction over matters affecting the Crown, the armed services, foreign affairs, imperial affairs, sterling and the Post Office. It would have been impossible then for anyone to imagine a UK government prepared to privatise the Post Office.

What they wanted was not dissimilar to the proposals submitted to Parliament by George Buchanan and the Rev. James Barr – both seconded by Tom Johnston who was now president of the London Scots Self-Government Committee – more than a decade earlier. A single chamber legislature, with 148 members representing 74 constituencies, was once again the preferred option for the proposed Scots Parliament.

But the committee's answer to the question of Scottish representation at Westminster looked like a compromise between the views of the president, Tom Johnston, and the committee chairman, the Rev. James Barr, from their differences on the subject all those years ago. The latest proposals supported a separate group of Scottish MPs continuing at Westminster to safeguard Scottish interests in the imperial Parliament. The level of representation which should be allowed at Westminster was unspecified. However, the London Scots were prepared to concede a reduction in numbers, in advance of negotiation, and the withdrawal of all voting rights in English affairs from anyone representing a Scottish constituency.

Their proposals envisaged the head of the new Government assuming the title Prime Minister. 'He would, as in most democracies, be the leader of the Government, and co-ordinate and formulate the Cabinet's policy. His Secretariat would form the chief channel of communication between the Scots Cabinet and the Westminster Cabinet.'

The London Scots also anticipated the need for a Minister of Finance, with responsibility for the Scottish Treasury, the Scottish Central Bank and the Scottish National Investment Board; a Minister of Planning, with a wide variety of responsibilities, including imports and exports, internal trade and wages, agriculture, industry, transport and the public utilities; a Minister of Health and Food Controller; Lord Advocate; Minister of Education and Arts; and a Minister of Public Works.

'Each Minister would be assisted by advisory planning committees for each main industry and aspect of national life,' the pamphlet, *Plan for Scotland*, continued. 'These committees would be democratically elected and representative of the whole community as producers and consumers.'

Attlee, in his preface, acknowledged 'nationalism has an immense attractive force for good or evil. Suppressed,' he warned, 'it may poison the political life of a nation. Given its proper place it can enrich it.' He commended the London Scots Self-Government Committee for 'having got down to practical proposals as a basis of discussion. Nothing is easier,' the man later famous for his perfunctory manner continued, 'than to make windy speeches on the right of self-government, in which little attention is given to construction, but much to the fomenting of ill-will between nations.'

Johnston had been developing a view that the Scots Grand Committee could be used as a staging post on the road to devolution. It would be to everyone's advantage, he suggested, if all purely Scottish Bills were heard, at second reading, in the Scots Grand Committee instead of the floor of the House of Commons. Similarly, there was no reason why the Scottish Estimates shouldn't be considered, and voted upon, by members of the same committee.

As a member of the 1937 Gilmour Committee on the Administration of Scotland Johnston added a note to the report expressing his 'regret that our terms of reference precluded us from considering the question of Parliamentary examination and control of the Scottish estimates. Such examination and control as is annually attempted under existing arrangements of public business is manifestly inadequate.'

A Bill to reorganise the workings of the Scottish Office was given its second reading in the House of Commons in December 1938. Johnston wanted Crown Lands and the Forestry Commission brought under Scottish Office control. Neither was included in the proposed new measures. Johnston offered an amendment which claimed, unsuccessfully, that 'more far-reaching measures were required for the administration of affairs in Scotland'.

In fact, there was a useful precedent to support his view about the estimates. In 1919 all departmental estimates, excluding the army, navy and air force, had been sent to the appropriate committee for approval. Johnston's proposals went further, however. He wanted the Scots Grand Committee to hold its meetings in Edinburgh; with local authority representatives and members of the general public encouraged to attend. According to Johnston, writing in 1937, 'Parliamentary control of the Scottish Estimates has, to all intents and purposes, disappeared'. If the money debates were subjected to Scottish public scrutiny there would be 'a widening of the area of popular criticism and control', Johnston claimed. By appearing in Edinburgh the committee would help to increase people's knowledge of the issues under discussion and encourage a more general interest in the administration. Added Johnston: 'The governors would be nearer the governed.'

A total of 11 hours of parliamentary time had been set aside recently for the discussion of public health in Scotland; with another three hours allocated to the activities of the Herring Industry Board. 'Agriculture, education and all the myriad affairs under the Scottish Office vote got nothing at all,' Johnston wrote. 'This means that the estimates for all these undiscussed departments and services, with their almost boundless ramifications, and their supreme importance to the well-being of Scots folk, were ultimately passed by Parliament *en bloc* and without one moment of examination. No one surely can defend a system like that,' Johnston protested.

Because of the sheer weight of work burdening the imperial Parliament Johnston feared there was a danger of handing over the control of affairs in Scotland to a civil service bureaucracy. 'In theory, of course, this bureaucracy is itself under the control and direction of the Secretary of State for Scotland,' Johnston noted. 'But what can that poor Pooh-Bah do?' he demanded. 'His area of administration is 400 miles away from his office. He has his Cabinet duties to perform. He has four large ministries to supervise and with the best will in the world he cannot do it. The machine is indeed already far beyond his control.'

He also anticipated a time when a government with a majority in the House of Commons might be in a minority in Scotland. In his view this did not entitle the Government to weight the Scots Grand Committee in accordance with its overall majority. 'A purely Scots Bill should be a matter for determination during the committee stages by the Scots representatives, and the Scots representatives alone,' he argued. 'Should a government ever be in a minority among Scots representatives it ought not to attempt legislation solely affecting Scotland and opposed to the wishes of her elected representatives.'

Writing in the political magazine *Fortnightly*, in October 1937,

Johnston suggested there was one possible route by which large-scale devolution might be achieved. Demonstrate that England would benefit, and that it would be good for business, he urged. That way, Johnston explained, 'we might reasonably hope that the propositions will be discussed upon their merits and without the introduction of any unnecessary political prejudices or catchwords'.

He believed all steps in devolution required consent. In particular, English apprehensions should be removed. As Johnston saw it: 'The English must be convinced that the proposed Government and administrative changes inure to their advantage as well as to the advantage of the Scots. Any proposals in the direction of self-government, to be acceptable to Westminster, must not only be evolutionary, they must be clear, businesslike, and evoke the minimum of opposition, both in England and Scotland.' Otherwise, Johnston warned, 'the majority in both Houses of Parliament is unlikely to permit any complete severance in Scottish affairs'.

According to Johnston, 'sudden cut self-government propagandists' had been unable to surmount another major difficulty. There were only two methods by which a Parliament in Edinburgh could be re-established. 'Either the English and the Welsh must be persuaded to it, or they must be compelled to it,' he wrote. 'There is no third method.

'Compulsion on the Irish model, even were it desirable in itself, can be ruled out as a sheer impossibility, since neither the gunmen, nor the supporting public opinion for the gunmen, exists,' Johnston continued. 'We are left, therefore, with persuasion.'

He also noted that, although the sentiment for a greater devolution of economic and administrative power from Whitehall to Edinburgh was undoubtedly wide and growing, 'neither the Labour Party nor Big Business shows the slightest sign of adopting any course which might involve severance from their class associates south of the border'.

In his view 'the Scot in Parliament may not be loved by the Englishman; he may be tolerated as a sort of disagreeable and sometimes rather incomprehensible brother-in-law; but the English will not evict him from Westminster. If and when he wants to run his own establishment at home he will only be allowed to go when the

Englishman is thoroughly satisfied that the severance is, and to the extent that it is, in the economic and political interest of both Scotsmen and Englishmen,' Johnston insisted.

A paper, written by Walter Elliot in December 1937, when he was Secretary of State, showed the Government knew about the seriousness of Scotland's problems. Elliot utilised figures which had been available to his colleagues for at least a month. They knew unemployment in Scotland was 15.2 per cent compared to 9.7 per cent in England. It could hardly escape their notice that 'notwithstanding the recent improvement in the position of the heavy industries, unemployment in Scotland is nearly 70 per cent more severe than in England;'. It was also a matter of considerable concern to Elliot that 23 per cent of all families in Scotland lived in conditions of gross overcrowding compared to four per cent in England and Wales. Infant mortality in Scotland also exceeded the figure for England and Wales by 35 per cent; with maternal mortality in Scotland half as high again as the comparable rate for England and Wales. 'In proportion to population,' Elliot observed, 'twice as many cases of pneumonia and of scarlet fever were notified in Scotland as in England over a recent five-year period, while the diphtheria figure was higher by a third; and in each case the disparity between the two countries had worsened as compared with ten years earlier.'

Elliot followed his figures with a warning for his Cabinet colleagues: 'It is the consciousness of their existence which is reflected, not in the small and unimportant nationalist party, but in the dissatisfaction and uneasiness amongst moderate and reasonable people of every view or rank, a dissatisfaction expressed in every book published about Scotland now for several years.

Elliot's report was a damning indictment of the contrast in living standards which could be found in different parts of the United Kingdom at the time. Coming from a well-respected member of the Cabinet it would have been reasonable to expect the Government to take serious heed of his findings. But it didn't. 'Circumstances were unpropitious,' Elliot confided in a letter to Tom Johnston dated 30 April 1942, 'and the vigorous action I had hoped for was not secured.'

Years of unexpected power and opportunity lay ahead for Johnston.

For the moment, however, as he prepared for the next meeting of the well-meaning, and highly ambitious, London Self-Government Committee, he could still fret at the knowledge unemployment was always five to seven per cent higher in Scotland compared to England and Wales. Nor did it escape his notice that, out of a total of 3,217 new factories built in Britain between 1932 and 1937, the year the London Scots Self-Government Committee was launched, only 127 were located in Scotland. This dismal statistic Johnston compared to a total of 133 factories which closed in Scotland during the same period – 'so we actually lost on balance', he commented.

Writing after the war, with his usual regard for statistics, and a passionate recall of the circumstances which governed many people's lives little more than a decade earlier, he was also able to record: 'We had serious emigrations of our healthiest stocks of citizenry; we had 300,000 houses without water closet; our maternal mortality was 50 per cent higher than in England and Wales, our infant mortality was 25 per cent worse; our army rejects were six per cent higher; control of some of our banks was moving south to Lombard Street.'

But long after he resigned as Secretary of State for Scotland, and retired as an MP, he felt especially uneasy about Scotland obtaining political power without first ensuring there was an adequate economy in place for a new Parliament to administer. He believed people who argued in favour of self-government should direct some part of their propagandist energy towards securing an aircraft industry, a motor industry and restoring transatlantic shipping services. There would be little purport in Scotland obtaining its own Parliament in Edinburgh, Johnston suggested darkly, 'if it has to administer an emigration system, a glorified Poor Law and a graveyard!'.

CHAPTER NINETEEN

THEY WERE, TOM JOHNSTON reflected grimly, the years the locust ate; that period between the general election of 1935 and the outbreak of war in 1939.

'Almost everywhere in Europe,' he wrote, 'the caveman arose and clubbed his neighbours; the lamps of liberty flickered and went out; the Jews ran hither and thither seeking escape; in Hitler's Germany the trade unions and co-operative societies were smashed, their funds plundered, their leaders exiled or driven to concentration camps. Appeasement, surrender, abasement, humiliation, dirt eating were all offered to placate the fascist leaders: in vain!'

Munich, as Winston Churchill told the House of Commons in a memorable speech, delivered on 5 October 1938, was 'only the beginning of the reckoning. This is only the first sip, the first foretaste of a bitter cup which will be proffered to us year by year unless by a supreme recovery of moral health and martial vigour, we arise again and take our stand for freedom as in the olden time.'

Not many men on any side of public life earned enconiums from history for the part they played then, Johnston later observed. 'We all sensed the shame and humiliation of Munich, but most part of us hoped secretly that Chamberlain was right and that Hitler could be bought off at the expense of our acquiescence in his villainies towards the smaller nations.'

In 1936, on a visit to Danzig, the Free City already threatened by Hitler, Johnston watched with growing dismay as ardent pro-Nazis among the local citizenry stood respectfully to attention while Hitler's voice blared at them from loudspeakers attached to telephone poles on roadways and streets. *Der Sturmer*, the wickedly anti-Jewish propaganda paper condemned as a rag by Johnston, was difficult to obtain in Danzig. As propaganda Johnston thought it probably had little effect. 'Some decent Germans in Danzig were thoroughly ashamed of it and openly denounced it as a low pornographic sheet,' he wrote. 'There was, however, in the streets, much marching and counter marching and heil Hitlering, and there was a general apprehension of a pogrom of some kind in the near future.'

Writing in *Forward* on 1 August 1936, following the outbreak of the Spanish Civil War, he declared angrily: 'Some dirty money gangs are financing this horrible coup, but if it fails Spain will emerge with a proletarian dictatorship, and the old order will go out, not in an evolutionary, peaceful way, but in a welter of blood and in a generation of hunger and misery. If the coup succeeds there will be a White Terror, with repercussions even in this country, the end of which no man can foresee.'

As the volunteer workers and their womenfolk marched out to meet the well-equipped armies of the feudal lords, Johnston went on, 'we catch again a whiff of the heroism and sacrifice of the brave boys in the Russian revolution. An epical enthusiasm stirs Spain and moves the onlookers in other lands.'

He disagreed with Rousseau that, in Spain at least, the working class had nothing to lose but their chains. 'The Spanish people have something to lose,' Johnston insisted fiercely. 'They have a political democracy now, achieved in the teeth of every obstacle from Church, Press, Landownership and Money, and there is no instance in history of a people which, having secured political freedom, continues to accept economic servitude. Viva España!'

Despite the ridicule he knew the idea attracted in many quarters, the war in Spain reinforced his belief in the need for a world police force, operating under the control of the League of Nations, as the only hopeful barrier to another all-out war involving all the major nations. On 12 September 1936 he declared: 'Sooner or later statesmen in the different countries will listen: sooner or later there will be *pourparlers*: sooner or later the machinery of peace and security will be created.'

The force he envisaged could be used, Johnston explained, to prevent a gangster raid, in defiance of law and arbitration, upon innocent civilians. Once established this force could be used to protect frontiers from attack by violence; guaranteeing security, Johnston suggested. 'If we got security, we could get disarmament; if we got disarmament, there would be no war; if we got no war there is no call for the intervention of the international force and, therefore, not even by accident, the loss of an innocent civilian anywhere.'

The force he proposed would be far from passive. 'It would attack the attackers and prevent the success of their efforts,' Johnston declared. 'It would doubtless search out and destroy their aerodromes, their aircraft, their armies and their battleships. It would defend the law-abiding from the assassin, but not by the barbarous and wholly irrational and foolish method of destroying the assassin's children and grandparents. That is,' he added hopefully, 'if it ever had to go into action at all.'

On 30 June 1937 he also committed himself to the belief that an international police force, operating under the command of the League of Nations, could provide 'the conditions in which national disarmament becomes practical politics; indeed, the creation of the international force renders national armaments obviously and palpably useless'.

The extent of Hitler's ambitions in Europe were soon obvious. 'No use now calling for international boycotts, or an international police to restrain the warmongers,' Johnston reflected later.

The League of Nations had been allowed to slither to decrepitude. 'The only alternatives left,' Johnston observed, 'were a cowardly acquiescence in the death of democracy or a desperate resistance in a war for which we were unprepared with arms, until these arms could be procured.'

But there was probably even less chance of Johnston persuading a majority of MPs that, in order to ease international tension, Britain should agree to 'internationalise' Gibraltar and the Suez Canal. 'Why should a private company of British, French and Egyptian financiers be permitted to exploit, for huge dividends, the great maritime highway to the East?' Johnston demanded. 'And why should we stick our guns at Gibraltar, and camp our forces upon Spanish soil, and place ourselves in a position of sealing up the Mediterranean sea at both its eastern and western exits?'

Johnston was anxious to stress he wasn't suggesting handing over these two key Mediterranean ports to any other power. 'Not at all,' he insisted. 'I am only suggesting that they should be brought under international ownership, and that, until we do so, peace and security will elude us.'

Startling though it seemed to less adventurous minds he also suggested this idea could be further developed to include colonial interests around the world, starting with the half-dozen nations who ruled in Africa. 'An international board administering the non-self-governing territories and the primitive races, primarily for the benefit of the native inhabitants without any trade or strategic or financial privileges to any single governing nation, would certainly remove from the German mind the great grievance which has existed since the Versailles Peace Treaty,' Johnston suggested.

Writing in *Forward* on 25 March 1939 he also maintained: 'We get nowhere by merely denouncing Chamberlain and his past and present policy. Mere evasions or side-stepping or word-spinning will not serve us. They solve nothing. They protect us in no way whatsoever.'

On 8 April 1939 he warned his readers: 'The Jew is now fleeing hither and thither in Central Europe as he has not had to run since the Middle Ages; the co-operative society funds have been annexed; the trades unions abolished; the socialist leaders are dead or in jail; there is no liberty of meeting or Press. Pledges mean nothing and outside Central Europe we are all living in terror of a coming holocaust.'

Johnston was already convinced there could be no escape from the war through a policy of non-resistance. 'It is no use appealing to the Nazi leaders to be merciful and moderate,' he wrote.

However, in accordance with Labour Party policy, he argued against conscription. As a socialist and a citizen, Johnston claimed, he could cite half a dozen good reasons for opposing compulsory call-up. He disliked the idea of conscription partly because it could be used 'as the means of breaking political or economic movements of the working class'. But he was also against any enforced call-up because it placed businesses and commerce under the control of the military mind 'with disastrous consequences to the nation. Officers commanding and military service tribunals are frequently incapable of wise decisions in selecting the men whom they believe should be compulsorily withdrawn from industry and commerce,' Johnston added.

Those in favour of conscription claimed it offered equality of sacrifice, but it didn't, said Johnston. People who urged conscription of life didn't argue in favour of conscription of capital wealth, he noticed. Nor, in his view, could there be 'equality of sacrifice between the man who has no dependent children and the man who has several dependent children, the man who has a widowed mother to maintain and the man who has no aged relatives to support'.

Anyway, he suggested, the next war might well be decided 'by insurrections stimulated in the enemy countries, by sabotage, blowing up bridges, railway tunnels, electricity pylons, water pipes. Against this form of warfare,' Johnston argued blithely, 'conscription serves no obvious purpose. It may indeed be about as useful as a fifth wheel on a coach.'

News of a non-aggression pact between Germany and Russia, signed by Stalin and the German Foreign Minister, Joachim von Ribbentrop, on 23 August 1939, took Johnston, like everyone else in Britain, by surprise. A statement issued by the duplicitous partners explained: 'Both High Contracting Parties obligate themselves to desist from any act of violence, any aggressive action, and any attack on each other, either individually or jointly with other Powers.'

Forward's headline was typical of the prevailing mood: 'Tovarish Ribbentrop, Kamarad Stalin! Who would have believed it?' In his reaction to the shock agreement Tom Johnston reserved his heaviest fire for communist supporters living in Britain. They had been 'declaiming bravely that this Stalin-Ribbentrop deal is a death blow to fascism and that it was an honourable, straightforward, upright transaction!' he wrote. 'Nevertheless, one may speculate upon the transports of invective that the same "coms" would have thrown over any British government caught negotiating a surreptitious deal with Ribbentrop, while it was at the same time ostensibly in friendly negotiations with Russia.'

On 2 September 1939, in the absence of any renewed attempts to secure his international peace force, with time running out and the war about to begin, Johnston declared himself totally against the idea of non-resistance. 'I do not believe in the idea of non-resistance. If we had a socialist government in this country tomorrow we would be faced from the word go with an attempted seizure of power by the fascists. We should then have only two choices: surrender or resist.

'If we surrendered,' Johnston went on, 'we should be handing over the Jews to the bludgeon or exile; every known and active socialist and trade unionist to the concentration camp; we should be surrendering what liberties we have of thought, speech, publication, association; our trades unions would be broken up, our co-operative societies plundered. Surrender would neither give us peace nationally nor internationally.'

It was the war that kept Tom Johnston at Westminster. At the annual meeting of West Stirlingshire Labour Party on 22 May 1937 constituency officials were told he would be retiring at the next election. His Parliamentary duties, his work with the City of Glasgow Friendly Society, journalism and book writing, as well as dealing with a vast correspondence and undertaking regular public speaking engagements on behalf of the Labour Party, were collectively too much for him, Johnston explained.

He would be nearing 60 at the time of the next election. Eleven of the last 15 years had been spent at Westminster. For all but three of these years he had been fretting on the opposition benches. Two years as a Minister, between 1929 and 1931, were the acknowledged high ground of his Parliamentary career. Time spent as a member of the Cabinet, within sight of real power, totalled barely five months, however.

Johnston believed his time could be put to better use. Free of Westminster, and its attendant travel, he would be able to concentrate on his business affairs and devote whatever time was left to writing and historical research; activities he much enjoyed.

However, he also promised to make himself available to assist the new candidate. Whoever succeeded him would start with conditions set fair for a long and happy partnership. 'There is more good comradeship and absence of sectional fissure or bickering in West Stirlingshire than in any other constituency in Britain,' said Johnston.

As a valedictory address the brief speech Johnston delivered to his supporters on 22 May 1937 was hopelessly premature. He never appeared as a candidate in a Parliamentary election again. But eight years later he was still there.

Johnston didn't agree with people who argued, during the months immediately preceding the Second World War, that anyone who believed in civil defence also committed themselves to the entire murderous equipment of war. It was widely recognised that Britain's civil defence capability was hopelessly inadequate. But there was a widespread view, especially in Labour Party circles, that a country which prepared for war invited war.

'A man may urge protection of the civilian population and at the same time urge national and international policies designed to remove the causes of war,' Johnston insisted. 'There is no contradiction whatever between the two activities.' Anyone who paid tax, pacifists included, contributed 'willy-nilly to war preparations', Johnston added. 'There is no escape from that under existing conditions except suicide.'

He was in favour of providing food, water and shelter for the civilian population. 'I am in favour of organising food, water and shelter in advance,' wrote Johnston. 'I am in favour of ambulances and fire brigades for the protection of the worker and his family, and that whether in peace or in war.'

Invited by the Prime Minister, Neville Chamberlain, to become Regional Commissioner for Civil Defence in Scotland, Johnston declined on the grounds he did not want 'to run the risk of being associated even indirectly with an administration capable of a second Czech humiliation'.

Pressed further by Sir John Anderson, then Minister for Home Security, and Arthur Greenwood, deputy chairman of the Labour Party, he finally agreed to co-operate with the Lord Advocate, T.M. Cooper, in trying to make civilian Scotland ready for war. But not until Britain was formally at war with what he called the 'Fascist-Nazi assassins' did Johnston accept full responsibility for these arrangements and become Regional Commissioner.

The decision to concentrate his energies on civil defence encouraged him to consider whether or not he should continue as an

MP. Even Johnston acknowledged there were only so many hours in a day. Also, keeping in mind his previous plans, he had been due to retire from the House of Commons the following year.

However, there were serious arguments against incurring the upheaval of a by-election during wartime. Emergency legislation allowed Parliament to continue and the main parties had agreed not to contest by-elections. But that didn't exclude the possibility of a candidate from another party appearing in West Stirlingshire and Clackmannan. Hostilities hadn't ended when Dr Robert McIntyre won Motherwell for the SNP in 1945. Pressed by the Labour Party Executive to stay in his seat, Johnston agreed.

CHAPTER TWENTY

WHITEHALL WAS PRIVATELY, and fearfully, forecasting that nearly two million people would be injured in bombing raids over Britain in the first few weeks of the war. A third of that total would die. And five per cent of all property would be destroyed.

But few people paid much attention to the Government's early attempts to interest them in civil defence. Emergency Committees had been introduced by the Chamberlain Government early in 1939 and given wide powers over resentful local authorities. 'At that time,' according to one official, 'few authorities fully realised the problems with which they would be faced after an air attack.'

In Scotland, for example, at the start of the war, 33 counties and 191 burghs were responsible for their own fire-fighting arrangements. Several attempts had been made, without success, to standardise equipment and co-ordinate the various brigades in a single service. But it took nearly two years of bickering and indecision, during the worst bombing of the war, to establish the National Fire Service.

A letter of appointment issued by the Ministry of Home Security to Regional Commissioners was certainly clear in its intent. 'In case of sudden emergency involving a complete or partial breakdown of communication the Regional Commissioner will, in the absence of the Secretary of State for Scotland, have full authority to give urgent decisions in the name of the Government.

'In such circumstances,' each Regional Commissioner's letter of appointment continued, 'you will, on behalf of the Government, take such steps as in your judgment are necessary for the public safety and you will be entitled to expect all persons to give you facilities or assistance in pursuance of their duty to co-operate in defence of the realm. Such action, duly recorded, will be supported by the Government and the Government will ask Parliament to give you whatever indemnification may subsequently be found necessary.'

He was expected, Johnston later explained, 'to supervise Air-Raid Precautions and Civil Defence arrangements generally: he was to persuade and convince the laggards among the local authorities: he had to remove difficulties and jarring edges: he had to keep up civilian morale: he had to prepare for the worst and hope for the best'.

One lesson from the First World War which Johnston, as Regional Commissioner for Scotland, was determined not to repeat this time: there would be no scrambling for food and all possible precautions would be taken to avoid price 'ramps' arising from any shortages. 'We must either have control or anarchy and profiteering,' Johnston declared, 'with the weaker and poorer sections of the nation crushed to the wall.'

A statement issued in September from his headquarters at 25 Palmerston Place, Edinburgh, promised that supplies of commodities required by the nation would be carefully distributed. The country had been holding great reserves of canned herring, whale oil, sugar, wheat and canned meat when the war started. Rationing would begin with meat, butter, margarine, sugar, bacon, ham and cooking fats. 'We are determined to see that what supplies are available will be reasonably spread over every household,' Johnston explained.

Steps were being taken to increase supplies of home-produced foods. But it would help, Johnston suggested, if as many people as possible grew their own vegetables. 'We must avoid waste and all unnecessary dependence upon foreign imports if there is to be sufficient food and proper nutrition for everybody. The Scottish people can be trusted to see that there is no waste,' the Regional Commissioner added hopefully.

Three months after the war started Johnston was able to demonstrate a marked difference between the price of food under Government control, including certain grades of flour, margarine, tinned herring and canned meat, and commodities which had been allowed to continue in what he called 'the smash and grab of the competitive system'. As an example he claimed the wholesale price of unregulated oatmeal was 60 per cent higher. He also rebuked the chairman of the National Farmers

Union in Scotland for saying he hoped barley producers would 'enjoy the going while the going was good. That is a dangerous doctrine and it is one which I hope the farmers in this country will insist on repudiating,' Johnston added.

The war was already costing £6 million a day and Johnston was expressing concern about the dangers of inflation. 'We must prevent a repetition of the inflationary processes which nearly wrecked the country in the last war,' he warned.

Johnston recognised it would be impossible to pay for the war by taxation and savings on current levels of production. Assuming half the money needed to fund the war could be raised from taxation it would be necessary to raise another £3 million a day in loans, he estimated. At the time of the last war banks had been allowed to issue credits to private customers who then made loans to the Government; stoking inflation. If people failed to subscribe to the proposed defence loan from genuine savings, 'we will be taking steps that will lead us irrevocably on the same road as Germany went at the conclusion of the last war', Johnston added.

He proposed raising all credits necessary to fight the war in the name of the Prime Minister and the Chancellor of the Exchequer, acting for the nation. Whatever interest was due would then accrue to a national account, saving the country from the burden of paying unnecessary dividends and interest upon inflated credit.

In theory, at least, Regional Commissioners had been granted considerable powers over local authorities. A review of their duties and performance, prepared early in the war, stressed: 'Local authorities should be in no doubt about the extent to which Regional Commissioners are held responsible to central Government for the general direction and control of the work of restoration after a heavy attack.' As Tom Johnston described his duties during this period of the war, if the Germans landed in Scotland, and communication with central Government in London ceased, as Regional Commissioner for Civil Defence he would have been expected to take charge of civic affairs until he was 'either shot or concentration camped by the enemy'. In practice, however, so long as communication with London was maintained, the Regional Commissioners were virtually powerless. 'That is certainly the case in regard to pre-blitz precautions and post-blitz emergency measures,' Sir Hugh Elles, Regional Commissioner for south-west England, based in Bristol, complained. 'We can exhort, persuade, suggest, advise, co-ordinate by agreement,' he added, in a letter addressed to the Minister responsible for Home Security, Herbert Morrison, 'but we cannot compel, and everybody knows it.'

This view was supported by a highly contentious article, clearly from a well-placed source, which appeared in *The Times* on 16 May 1941. It claimed central Government had shown a marked reluctance to trespass upon local authority powers in the cause of efficiency. It also suggested local Emergency Committees had been formed on a party basis regardless of administrative efficiency. 'The tangle of competing local bodies and their officials must be cut away and power concentrated on one responsible unit,' *The Times* article continued. 'But appointments must be made with entire disregard of seniority, or of any consideration save that of efficiency, and be subject to ruthless scrapping if efficiency is not achieved.'

Although they were empowered to assume full control and direction of civil defence services during an emergency the Regional Commissioners couldn't dismiss officials of any of these services or make changes in the membership of the Emergency Committee responsible. In Scotland the town clerk of a royal burgh couldn't be dismissed without the approval of the Court of Session. And a public row of that kind, in the middle of a war, was unthinkable.

Johnston, from his headquarters at 25 Palmerston Place, Edinburgh, instinctively favoured persuasion; unlike Sir Hugh Elles, in Bristol, who wanted statutory powers to help 'hasten the processes of suggestion and advice'. Some councils might be tempted to strike if the Government was persuaded to restrict their freedom of action even further, Johnston warned. Others might simply choose to do nothing and leave everything to the Regional Commissioners.

Johnston knew relations with local authority grandees could be difficult. But he was also the first to admit that, in many areas, their experience, influence and local knowledge could be vital to the war effort. It was a view supported by an official report, from inside the Scottish Office, following the five major bombing raids which devastated large areas of Clydebank between March and May 1941. This claimed: 'It can be confidently stated that, apart from a few exceptions, the local government organisation has stood up remarkably well to the very heavy strain which has been put upon it.'

Johnston's passion for devolution was evident in the appointment of five district commissioners, centred on the main areas of population, to assist him. The Mass Observation Unit, which had been established to monitor civilian reaction to the war, believed this system 'gave a closer tie to the major civic authorities, and worked better than, for instance, running south-east England from Tunbridge Wells'.

Johnston provided his services as Regional Commissioner for Civil Defence at no charge to the state. It was an example followed by all the district commissioners and their deputies. In fact, as Johnston later noted, only one in 13 Civil Defence workers in Scotland accepted payment for their services and sacrifices during the war. Between 1939 and 1940 there was 'greater community of feeling and greater goodwill among ourselves than probably at any time in our history', Johnston maintained.

There was no limit to the 'urgent and sticky problems' he was expected to solve during the 17 months he spent as Regional Commissioner for Scotland. These ranged from finding billets and transport for thousands of mothers and children evacuated from crowded industrial areas to billets in the country at the height of the bombing threat, to ensuring the safety of the Scottish Crown regalia and jewels. The precious regalia were finally built into the wall of Edinburgh Castle. Only four men knew their exact whereabouts. 'I often wondered,' mused Johnston, 'what would happen had a bomb hit the four of us. The chances were that the regalia might have been lost until judgment day.' Whatever else, finding them could have been the source of sublime comedy! Like the hilarious outcome of another day's executive action at 25 Palmerston Place, Edinburgh.

On this occasion Tom Johnston was endeavouring to find a safe hiding place for thousands of gallons of whisky. The whisky didn't pose any kind of threat to the Regional Commissioner's teetotal habits. But it was a potential fire hazard if stored in a major area of population. It was also a valuable export, worth millions of dollars in the United States, and as such an asset nobody wanted to lose.

An attempt to bury the precious amber liquid deep beneath the surface of the earth, in a disused lead mine at Wanlockhead, was rebuffed by Customs and Excise. The men in starched shirts were probably right to worry that although the whisky might be safe from enemy bombers, it was unlikely to survive inquiry from foraging packs of British citizenry if ever news of its whereabouts leaked out.

Johnston finally ordered one huge load, valued at £1 million, to the United States for sale, or safekeeping. A ship was found, the SS *Politician*, with sufficient space in its hold to accommodate the additional cargo. A route to the Atlantic was planned by way of The Minch. And it was there, in thick fog, that the SS *Politician* ran aground on the tiny island of Eriskay.

Unlike the teetotal Regional Commissioner for Civil Defence in faraway Edinburgh, the people of Eriskay and neighbouring Barra were happy to accept a drop of the hard stuff occasionally. But especially if it came their way free, in thousands of cases, compliments of the Government.

Sir Compton Mackenzie, who immortalised the incident in his comic novel *Whisky Galore*, treasured the reaction of important visitors from the mainland when they entered his house on Barra and 'saw the bottles of whisky in a long row all round the top of the bookshelves'. One such important guest was Tom Johnston who visited Barra not long after the loss of the SS *Politician*. Johnston declined his host's offer of whisky but said he would drink half a glass of sherry. 'I'm sorry you won't sample some of our whisky,' an amused Sir Compton Mackenzie reported himself as saying at the time. 'After all you are the man we have to thank for giving us whisky galore.'

His guest was entitled to feel perplexed. The famous author enjoyed the moment. 'Tom Johnston looked at the bottles of whisky round the top of the bookshelves,' Sir Compton recalled, in *My Life and Times*, 'and then quickly swallowed that half glass of sherry as if it were firewater.'

One of Johnston's last duties, as Regional Commissioner in charge of Civil Defence for Scotland, was to arrange a dinner party in the North British Hotel, Glasgow, for two of the most powerful men in the world. One of the principal guests was instantly recognisable; cigar-smoking, scowling, pugnacious. The other, slim and frail, was barely known outside the United States.

It was the strength of his guest's contacts that interested Winston Churchill. For the stranger in the room to whom the Prime Minister of Great Britain himself even deferred was the special envoy of the President of the United States, Roosevelt's close friend and loyal aide, Harry Hopkins. Hopkins had been in Britain a week. He arrived at Poole Airport on 9 January 1941 carrying the highest credentials. 'Telegrams had been received from Washington stating that he was the closest confidant and personal agent of the President,' wrote Churchill.

He and Hopkins lunched alone next day. Their first meeting lasted nearly three hours. 'I soon comprehended his personal dynamism and the outstanding importance of his mission,' commented Churchill. Two days later he cabled Roosevelt: 'Former Naval Person to President Roosevelt – Hopkins and I spent the weekend together, and he is coming with me on a short tour of Fleet bases, so we shall have plenty of time to cover all points at leisure. I am most grateful to you for sending so remarkable an envoy, who enjoys so high a measure of your intimacy and confidence.'

Their tour of the battleships was scheduled to include a visit to Scapa Flow. Britain's ambassador to the United States, Lord Lothian, had died suddenly the previous month. Churchill had chosen Lord Halifax as his successor. Halifax was an old political foe, a survivor in the Cabinet from the days of Chamberlain, who might yet succeed Churchill in Downing Street. Churchill, not surprisingly, wanted rid of him. The vacancy in Washington provided the perfect opportunity. However, the Prime Minister also wanted Britain's new ambassador to arrive in the United States 'with every circumstance of importance'. So it was arranged 'our newest and strongest battleship, the *King George V*, with a proper escort of destroyers, should carry him and his wife across the ocean'. Tom Johnston was among those who suspected the real reason for the visit, by special train and ship, to Scapa Flow, was 'less to see Halifax off on his voyage than to show Hopkins the might and majesty of the British fleet'.

On the return journey to London the Prime Minister was scheduled to visit Glasgow. He wanted to see for himself how the city was coping with the requirements of the Civil Defence regulations. Tom Johnston was summoned to await his arrival at Edinburgh and accompany him on the last stage of his journey across Scotland.

When the special train, with its important cargo, arrived at Waverley Station the Regional Commissioner nipped on board and was taken immediately to a private compartment to see Churchill. And there he was told that 'nothing had been got out of Hopkins; he was poker-faced and dumb as an oyster', Johnston recalled.

Railway whistles, tramway gongs and cheering crowds greeted the Prime Minister on his arrival in Glasgow. 'Everywhere,' wrote Johnston, 'the greatest enthusiasm and affection for the national wartime leader was made manifest, and Hopkins I am sure was keenly observant of it all.' Following his tour of Civil Defence installations the Prime Minister addressed a meeting of 300 councillors, officials and other prominent citizens in the City Chambers. 'His summary of the war situation, at home and overseas, was masterly,' T.J. Honeyman, who was present, recalled.

Before he left London for Scapa Flow the Prime Minister had been suffering from a heavy cold. His doctor, Lord Moran, advised him not to travel. Thus hampered he assured his listeners in the City Chambers: 'I have absolutely no doubt that we shall win a complete and decisive victory over the forces of evil, and that the victory itself will only be a stimulus to further efforts to conquer ourselves, and to make our country worthy in the days of peace as it is proving itself in the hours of war.'

The presence of his American guest, Harry Hopkins, was explained with the words: 'He has come in order to put himself in the closest relation to events here and he will soon return to report to his famous chief the impressions he has gathered in our island.' Hopkins' response, for the moment, was nothing more than a noncommittal acknowledgment of his welcome and a passing boast about his Scots ancestry.

Over dinner, in Room 21 of the North British Hotel, he told Tom

Johnston that either his grandmother, or his great-grandmother, had been born in Auchterarder. Johnston immediately promised 'to get his pedigree hunted out for him'. Johnston also recalled: 'When the dinner was about over, the PM sidled up to me from the other end of the table and whispered an injunction to remember to propose the toast of the President of the United States immediately I had proposed the toast to the King.' Johnston went further. He told the assembled guests that Hopkins, a friend from overseas, was particularly welcome in their midst 'for the sake of his old grandmother from Auchterarder'.

The expected applause brought Hopkins, frail and thin, to his feet. He wasn't there to make speeches, the man of the moment apologised. 'But now that I am here and on my feet,' Hopkins went on, 'perhaps I might say in the language of the old book to which my grandmother from Auchterarder, and no doubt your grandmother too, Mr Johnston, paid so much attention. "Wheresoever thou goest we go, and where thou lodgest we lodge, thy people shall be our people, thy God, our God, even unto the end".'

Hopkins was looking straight at Churchill as he delivered his final words. Not everyone knew the quotation was from the Book of Ruth. But there was no mistaking its meaning; or the effect Hopkins intended. 'Here,' wrote Johnston, 'was the first news that the United States was throwing its weight upon the Allied side.'

There was total silence when Hopkins resumed his seat. It was a moment nobody present forgot. 'Such indiscreet partisanship came from the heart,' commented Hopkins' biographer, Harry H. Adams. 'Churchill was near to tears and there were damp eyes among others present.'

Churchill's doctor, Lord Moran, also recalled: 'I was surprised to find the PM in tears. He knew what it meant. Even to us the words seemed like a rope thrown to a drowning man.'

However, as Adams also observed, 'It's one unfortunate effect was that it raised hopes that would not be fulfilled, at least for a long time.'

Hopkins returned to Britain, on his second mission from the President, in the summer of 1941. Churchill invited him to attend a meeting of the Cabinet. Duff Cooper, the Minister of Information,

231

resisted informing the newspapers. On 22 July 1941 Cooper was replaced as Minister of Information by Brendan Bracken; and made Chancellor of the Duchy of Lancaster. Two days later he wrote, defending his action, to Churchill: 'Mr Hopkins is, of course, a foreigner, who has no allegiance to the Crown, who is bound by no Privy Councillor's oath and to whom the application of the Official Secrets Act might be questionable.'

Churchill's action could cause trouble in America on two counts, the former Minister for Information suggested boldly. It might be asserted that the President's envoy was being insulted and his integrity questioned; or people might ask why an American citizen was 'sitting in a British War Cabinet, and was this another device for ensnaring America into the war'.

Churchill was unimpressed, it seemed. A scribbled note at the bottom of Duff Cooper's letter testified to his annoyance. 'It was a pity not to state the fact as I desired,' he growled. 'None of these arguments appeals to me.'

Arrangements were also made for Hopkins to broadcast on the BBC. He told listeners: 'I have learned from your Cabinet Ministers what England needs now, and I am returning to America to report this to the President. I have found that there are certain things which you need in order to fight this war. I am confident America can supply them.'

Churchill, in his mammoth *History of the Second World War*, was unstinting in his praise of Harry Hopkins and the assistance he helped bring to Britain during the war. Slim, frail and usually ill, the American absolutely glowed 'with refined comprehension of the Cause. It was to be the defeat, ruin, and slaughter of Hitler, to the exclusion of all other purposes, loyalties, or aims,' claimed Churchill. 'In the history of the United States few brighter flames have burned.'

A team from the Mass Observation Unit, visiting Glasgow early in 1941, shortly after Churchill's tour of Civil Defence installations, reported themselves impressed by the city's preparations to minimise the effects of heavy bombing.

'This great scattered conurbation had enough sense, skill and room for manoeuvre to adapt and improvise so as to offset the worst impacts of the unexpected, by now so familiar from smaller towns,' its leader, Professor Tom Harrison, recalled in *Living Through the Blitz*. 'But, alas for the best laid plans of modern man, the first big impact of 439 planes on two successive nights fell most heavily on the periphery, notably at the smaller, connected shipbuilding community of Clydebank.'

Clydebank, with a staunch Labour council in control, was one of the last local authorities in Britain to turn its attention to Civil Defence. David Kirkwood, the highly popular local MP, provided a lead for the town's recalcitrance. In October 1935 Kirkwood declared: 'I am still out for peace in the real sense and would not send a Clydebank boy to war upon any consideration. No war for me under any circumstances.'

It required the legal obligations imposed on the council by the Air Raid Precautions Act of December 1937 to force a change of policy on the town. Until then Clydebank refused to co-operate with other councils on Civil Defence, as recommended by the Scottish Office. Thereafter, however, according to the town's official historian, I.M.M. Macphail, the council set about making up for lost time and lost opportunities. 'By the time that war came, probably little, if anything, had been lost.'

Clydebank was famous throughout the world as a centre of shipbuilding excellence. During the first few months of the war the world's largest liner, the *Queen Elizabeth*, towered above the town, nearing completion in the fitting-out basin at John Brown's yard. A direct hit and the huge vessel could have been destroyed, blocking the River Clyde to all shipping and seriously affecting Britain's war effort. The Admiralty, headed by Churchill, wanted the *Queen Elizabeth* moved. And at precisely 12.32 GMT on 26 February 1940 the biggest ship in the world left Clydebank in secret, to begin an epic voyage to New York – and safety!

Almost exactly a year later, on 25 February 1941, a meeting called by the Town Clerk and local Civil Defence Controller, Henry Kelly, to discuss fire-watching arrangements, was sparsely attended. The authorities had been trying for months to impress upon people everywhere the need for vigilant fire-watching procedures against the ravages of incendiary attack. Following the massive destruction wrought on Clydebank one witness, working for Mass Observation, alleged 'gross neglect of fire watching in many streets' contributed to the devastation.

The bombing continued for two nights. By the time it finished and the Luftwaffe pilots returned home, one-third of the town's 12,000 tenement houses had been demolished. Another third had been rendered temporarily uninhabitable. And in the whole of the town only seven tenements survived the bombing totally unscathed.

Pressed in the House of Commons for accurate information concerning the number of casualties sustained in the two raids, the Minister for Home Security, Herbert Morrison, offered figures for Clydeside as a whole. He wasn't prepared to distinguish between Glasgow and Clydebank for reasons of security, Morrison explained. MPs were told that 1,000 people had been killed and another 1,000 seriously injured.

An official and confidential report, prepared by the Regional Commissioner's office in Edinburgh, now headed by Lord Rosebery, divided the dead as follows: 647 men, women and children had been killed in Glasgow, population 1.1 million; 358 people perished in Clydebank, population 55,000; and another 78 people died as a result of the air-raids in neighbouring counties, mostly Dunbartonshire. The figures for those seriously injured were: 973 in Clydebank; 390 in Glasgow; 219 in Dunbartonshire; and 20 elsewhere.

Tom Johnston, who had been appointed Secretary of State for Scotland five weeks earlier, attended a mass funeral for the unidentified dead at Dalnottar Cemetery, Clydebank, on Monday, 18 March 1941. 'Of the population of 55,000 only 2,000 could find any kind of habitation, however ramshackle, in the town,' he recalled in *Memories*, 'and poor, shivering, nerve-racked folk, bereft of their worldly goods and possessions and mourning some loved one torn to bloody rags by massed bombing, had to be sheltered and tended in widely scattered homes all over the West Country; and the stink of the burning oil from the great containers which had been hit: the smoke from the smouldering tenements: in the midst of all the chaos and destruction volunteer vans being driven by women from the Voluntary Services; the handing out of cups of tea in the streets; the massed funerals of the victims – these memories abide!'

But he also remembered with pride 'the workers of John Brown and Company turning up next morning grim and purposeful at the work gates. Within 48 hours three-fourths of the industrial production of the neighbourhood was resumed, although the men had to be transported, some of them for long distances, morning and night to their employment.'

Statistically, he could later claim, after four years of war, that less than one per cent of man hours were lost on Clydeside during the conflict. 'That infinitesimal figure disposes of the legend of Red Clydeside,' Johnston declared.

CHAPTER TWENTY-ONE

CHURCHILL WANTED HIM in the Government – and he wasn't prepared to take no for an answer. His first offer was the Ministry of Health. Johnston baulked at the idea of a London job. Nor, according to his version of events, was he keen to accept the Scottish Office.

Summoned to London to face the Prime Minister he was asked finally to state his reasons for refusing to join the National Government. Johnston explained he wanted to stay in Scotland, abandon politics, and write books. History books. Churchill could hardly believe his ears. 'Good heavens, man,' he growled, 'join me and you can help make history!'

Johnston, who was rarely complimentary, never mind kind, to Churchill in print over many years, likened the experience to a rabbit cornered by a boa constrictor. However, before he agreed to join the Government as Secretary of State for Scotland, he obtained the Prime Minister's support for a cherished idea – a Council of State composed of everyone who had been Secretary of State for Scotland, regardless of party, to advise him. If the Council was unanimous on a Scottish issue he expected Churchill to add his considerable support to whatever action they proposed. To the Prime Minister it seemed he was simply suggesting 'a sort of National Government of all parties idea, just like our Government here'.

Whatever he told the Prime Minister, and continued to claim long afterwards, Johnston was clearly delighted with his appointment. 'Coming down Whitehall I ticked off in my mind several of the things I was certain I could do, even during a war,' he recalled. His priorities included 'an industrial parliament to begin attracting industries north, face up to the Whitehall departments and stem the drift south of our

Scots population. And I could have a jolly good try at a public corporation on a non-profit basis to harness Highland water power for electricity.'

But there was also a frivolous side to his appointment from the Prime Minister's point of view. According to his private secretary, John Colville, it amused Churchill to know the editor of *Forward* and the premier duke of England were both serving in his administration: the Duke of Norfolk, Earl Marshal of England, had been appointed Under-Secretary of State for Agriculture. Colville, in his book *The Fringes of Power*, judged Johnston both dynamic and excellent.

Officials of the Glasgow Friendly Society responded with some style to news of his appointment. A company minute recorded: 'The General Manager reported that he had been appealed to by the Prime Minister to take a Cabinet Office during the present national emergency. He had turned down the proposal upon two occasions when it was offered, but finally a strong appeal had been made to him in the national interest and, subject to the board's agreement, giving him the necessary leave of absence, he was prepared to accept.'

Glasgow insurance men were rarely invited to play a part in Cabinet-making! Moved by the president, seconded by the vice-president, the board of the Glasgow Friendly Society agreed unanimously to release their general manager, without salary, for a period of six months; unless the war was settled sooner, in which case he could return earlier.

His appointment to the Cabinet also meant severing his long connection with *Forward*. On 7 February 1941 he wrote to the other directors: 'For 35 years now with but one brief break I have presided over the affairs of the *Forward*. I need not say how only the most urgent and overwhelming considerations of what I believe to be the Scottish public interest would have induced me to resign again (for what I trust will be but another brief break) from the chairmanship and the directorship of the company.'

Emrys Hughes took a jaundiced view of Johnston's departure to join the wartime Coalition. 'Who would have dreamt that Tom Johnston of *Forward*, who had so scornfully derided the Lloyd George coalition in the First World War, would become Secretary of State for Scotland in a coalition Government headed by Winston Churchill?' he demanded.

It was probably the cause of some anger, and no little embarrassment, to Johnston as a member of the wartime Cabinet that the paper he did so much to create and sustain for more than three decades, was often fiercely critical of the Government for most of the war. Defending his actions later, Emrys Hughes claimed he was simply following the example set by Johnston himself during the First World War. This meant publishing 'some dull right-wing features to camouflage the weekly criticism of Churchill and the war which I wrote on the first page', Hughes explained.

On 8 February 1941 Tom Johnston arrived in the First Division Courtroom of the Court of Session in Edinburgh and handed his letter of appointment, as Secretary of State for Scotland, to the country's most senior judge, the Lord President, Lord Normand. Having satisfied himself that the paperwork was in order the Lord President administered the oath of office. A bench of Scottish judges was in attendance to witness the proceedings as Johnston solemnly swore that he would 'well and truly serve His Majesty in the office of the Lord Keeper of the Great Seal'. He then signed the parchments of office, bowed to the watching judges, and left the Court of Session to begin the most important job of his life.

Hitler and his murderous crew probably hadn't heard of Tom Johnston. But they would have been right to assume anyone chosen by Churchill to take charge of Scotland during the war was an implacable foe. From an ancient Scottish text, *Archaeologica Scotia III*, Johnston borrowed a fierce warning for anyone resembling the Berlin gang. 'He shall be an exile from every place where habitations are built, where the waves mount with the wind, and where the karle sows corn. He shall be driven from the Church and Christian men, and far from every abiding place, save Hell.'

Johnston, who took no salary for his work as Secretary of State, moved speedily, and with considerable determination, to recruit his surviving predecessors to the high-sounding Council of State. His old boss, William Adamson, the only previous Labour politician appointed Secretary of State for Scotland, had been dead since 1936: for as long as it lasted Johnston would be presiding over a Tory-dominated committee.

Officially designated the Scottish Council on Post-War Problems, it was the press, claimed Johnston, who introduced the grander, easier-to-use – and headline! – name for the group. Sounding as it did more authorative, even permanent, Johnston was never likely to complain about the change.

The guidelines he provided for the six-man Council were simple and to the point. 'Individuals among us were free to take their own line upon disputed issues,' Johnston explained. 'As a Council we would concentrate on securing results upon issues where we were agreed about Scotland's interests.' The final result was 'a surprisingly large field of agreement. And none can say but we acted promptly,' Johnston added.

The five who served on the Council of State for the duration of the war, in addition to Johnston himself, were Lord Alness (formerly Robert Munro), Archibald Sinclair, Walter Elliot, John Colville and Ernest Brown who was unable to attend the first meeting of the new Council, held at Fielden House, 10 Great College Street, London, on 29 September 1941. With four civil servants, Sir A.P. Hamilton, P.J. Rose, David Milne and A.J. Aglen also present, Johnston opened the meeting by outlining his plans for the group. It would be their job, he explained, to consider Scotland's post-war problems, set up inquiries, decide on their priority and survey the results. The responsibility for any action which might be taken as a result of their recommendations would remain with the appropriate Ministers, Johnston added; meaning himself, mostly, for as long as he remained at the Scottish Office.

However, he didn't doubt the advice and support of the Council would be of the utmost value. 'At the end of hostilities,' said Johnston, 'the Government should have available authoritative advice on the questions considered and should be in a position to act at once.'

A preliminary list of subjects for consideration by the new Council included hydro-electric development, the hard-pressed herring industry and the unification of hospital services; all proposed by Johnston. Sir Archibald Sinclair considered dairy farming worth the Council's attention. John Colville was concerned about industrial development.

The business of housing and food production was raised by Walter Elliot.

Johnston's control of the Council of State was established immediately. At their first meeting the Council agreed to recommend an inquiry into the provision of hydro-electric power in Scotland. Johnston thought it should be headed by the Lord Justice Clerk, Lord Cooper. At least one member of the Council, Lord Alness, doubted the propriety of the Lord Justice Clerk heading an inquiry into such a contentious subject. In the end, however, it was Johnston's view which prevailed.

At one critical stage in the war he also used the authority of the Council of State to resist key building workers from Scotland being conscripted to the armed forces. Their influence, Johnston claimed, helped local authorities, the Special Housing Association and private builders to complete 36,200 houses, in addition to carrying out repairs on 75,000 houses damaged by bombing.

'It enabled us also,' Johnston went on, 'to secure the erection of Civil Defence hostels in such a manner as would enable their rapid conversion after the war to separate dwelling houses: it gave us labour too for the restoration and rehabilitation in suitable cases of dwellings previously condemned, and for the conversion of empty shops and offices into dwelling houses.'

It was estimated, at the height of the conflict, that more than 400,000 houses in Scotland were without sanitation of any kind. Miles of traditional tenement buildings in Glasgow, in particular, provided an obvious target for improvement. Many were beyond saving. Others were in a state of terminal decline. But there was a community spirit in many of the affected areas which was worth preserving.

A subcommittee of the Scottish Housing Advisory Council, established by Johnston, recommended full modernisation of all properties with a life expectancy of at least 20 years and improvement grants for properties which offered decent accommodation for at least five years. But this committee didn't report until 1947. By then Tom Johnston was no longer in charge at the Scottish Office. And his successors, well meaning but grievously shortsighted, were committed to a policy which failed to discourage the wholesale destruction of Glasgow's tenement townships; and the creation of vast, bleak housing schemes on its periphery.

He was also a good deal less successful with his attempts to upgrade the importance – and public awareness – of the Scots Grand Committee. For a start he failed to pursue his original idea of holding the meetings in Parliament House, anticipating 'much legal and political trouble'.

One meeting of Scottish MPs was scheduled for Edinburgh in October 1941. Only 27 MPs bothered to attend. And more than half of those present were from the Labour Party; demonstrating comradely support for Johnston in a scheme which few people considered important. Robert Boothby probably voiced the opinion of many of those who attended. In a letter to his old crony, Compton Mackenzie on Barra, he described the exercise as 'a pretty dismal disaster'.

Johnston later claimed he was 'really quite pleased to get an attendance of about 40 per cent, especially when the MPs who came had to pay their own rail fares, and give up their vacation in attending'. But it wasn't an experiment he cared to repeat, deciding finally that whenever he considered it necessary to communicate with MPs outside normal Parliamentary business, London could provide the venue. He would also take care to issue the invitations when Parliament was sitting.

Scotland hadn't recovered from the depression of the inter-war years when the Second World War started, Johnston argued, in a paper prepared during his years as Secretary of State. For reasons arising out of social and economic trends in the past few decades, the country's contribution to war industry was not quite fully commensurate with her natural resources and human capacity.

'But it is of a vitally essential kind,' Johnston insisted, 'and it is astonishingly large, for a country that by the time of James Watt had barely recovered from the devastation of prolonged civil war, and whose subsequent prodigious advance was largely frustrated by calamitous all-round depression in the period between the great wars of our day.'

Scottish industry suffered severely from the depression. Work after work was closed down, the country's heavy industrial capacity was reduced and the spirit of industrial and commercial organisation was weakened. 'Prolonged unemployment, on a scale that threatened irreparable ruin to areas so contrasting in character as Clydeside and the Outer Hebrides, reduced the capacity of many workers,' Johnston added.

He had been fiercely critical of British shipowners who placed construction orders with foreign yards before the war. Britain could boast long experience in ship construction, favourably situated waterfronts and shipyards, good designers and craftsmen, and all the latest inventions and appliances, Johnston argued. Yet, during 1937–38, at least £6 million worth of shipbuilding orders went to yards in Germany and Scandinavia. This amounted to a wages loss of around three pounds a week to 30,000 British tradesmen. But it also represented a huge loss in buying power to the British nation, Johnston argued, with less money accumulating to the Treasury from income tax and customs revenues, and more money lost to the national exchequer through an increase in unemployment and poor law expenditure. 'Upon a proper and complete balance sheet the nation is a heavy loser by permitting this sort of thing to develop,' Johnston warned.

Many industries were bound to benefit from the war. Unfortunately for people living in Britain's northern territory the main beneficiaries were in England; as Tom Johnston soon discovered when, on 8 February 1941, he arrived at the Scottish Office as Secretary of State. There was no Board of Trade in St Andrew's House and no machinery of any kind for industrial contacts. Most war-related work had been located in England. Scotland was used to provide storage space and as a source of labour for factories in the south.

According to Johnston's own records, in the course of the war, some 13,000 women were transferred to England because of the shortage of factories in Scotland. This figure included 500 women directed south in a single week in 1942, a year after Johnston was appointed Secretary of State.

'Unless drastic and immediate steps had been taken to correct these drifts to the land beyond the Cheviots, the outlook for Scottish industry and the Scottish nation post-war had been bleak indeed,' Johnston noted later.

Johnston acknowledged the need for planning. But he was suspicious of planners who operated from a distance. During his time at the Scottish

Office he insisted on drawing an imaginary line in chalk at the Cheviots, to separate Whitehall planners from the people he believed should decide Scotland's future: Scots living in Scotland! 'Every now and again some ingenious gentleman in London would exude a plan for a centralised planning of our industries, our housing, our roads, rails, canals, airports, our shops, our churches – yes, the location of our churches! – and our beer shops,' Johnston recalled. 'And you never knew in what rapturous moment some persuasive hierarchy at a Ministry might have been authorised to so plan and blueprint for us.'

His answer was to establish, at Government expense, two regional planning authorities for Scotland, covering east and west of the country. 'Thereafter, when central planning boiled up in London, I could always point to the prior existence of my regional associations and say that centralisation must stop south of the Cheviots,' Johnston claimed.

His cantankerous fellow Scot, John Reith, guiding father of the BBC and a man of considerable self-regard with a reputation for empire building on his own behalf, was for a year and a half Minister of Works and Buildings in the wartime Government. Johnston wasted little time in ensuring he was made aware of the chalk line at the Cheviots. 'He is very bothered by Bevin and other English Ministers who do things affecting Scotland without consulting him,' a disgruntled Reith, dropped by Churchill, later observed.

One senior colleague, Herbert Morrison, also revealed that whenever Johnston looked in danger of losing an argument in Cabinet he didn't hesitate to remind those present that 'there was a strong nationalist movement in Scotland and that it could be a potential danger if it grew through lack of attention to Scottish interests'. It was a useful tactic, as Johnston proved frequently, during his occupancy of St Andrew's House.

His long-cherished idea for an industrial parliament in Scotland was pursued, but never properly achieved, by merging two existing bodies, the Scottish Development Council and the Scottish Economic Committee, into a new, and powerful, pressure group with a cumbersome title, the Scottish Council (Development and Industry). Its membership and funds were drawn from local authorities, the Chambers of Commerce, the Scottish Trades Union Congress, the Development Council and the Scottish banks. 'Its functions,' Johnston explained, 'were the safeguarding, the stimulation, and the encouragement of Scottish industrial development, both during and after the war.'

Under the chairmanship of the Lord Provost of Edinburgh, Sir Will Y. Darling, the new Council wasted no time making its presence felt. The authority with which it argued Scotland's industrial case in what Johnston called 'the proper quarters' was probably its main strength. In three months Government production space in Scottish factories and workshops doubled to 1,000,000 square feet. A month later another 500,000 square feet was added; with another 350,000 square feet confirmed a few weeks later. During the next three years the Council managed to persuade three Government supply departments to spend £12 million on factories and plant in Scotland. In total, between 1942 and the general election of 1945, they were able to secure over 700 new enterprises, or substantial extensions to existing companies, involving 90,000 jobs.

But there was no sign, as the war neared its end, of the Scottish Council (Development and Industry) resting on its record. In its view the wartime central Government didn't direct enough high-priority production work to Scotland. It even proposed sending home mobile workers from England and replacing them with unemployed Scots.

One former senior civil servant, George Pottinger, writing in 1979, thought Tom Johnston was probably overstating its importance when he likened the Scottish Council (Development and Industry) to an industrial Cabinet. However, as Pottinger also noted, the Council 'rapidly became the most effective pressure group in Great Britain and its success is still envied by English regions'. Whitehall departments often complained that in one respect the Scottish industrialist had a positive advantage compared with his competitors in the south, Pottinger added. 'The English firm could approach the appropriate Ministry through the local MP. The Scottish industrialist could also enlist the aid of the Secretary of State, if necessary in Cabinet, and he in turn could cite an impressive consensus of support from the Scottish Council.'

Due to major expansion in a number of key industries

unemployment in Scotland totalled about 20,000 during the war. This figure probably represented an irreducible minimum, Johnston sensed. In his view 'no workers in the world respond more heartily to good management, or co-operate with it to better purpose, than the Scots. Their fine record in the war shows keen appreciation of the great issues involved, and augurs well for our industrial future.'

He also believed: 'The strong self-respect of the Scot may at times intensify into undue individualism and a certain touchiness, while his loyalty to principle and to his fellow workers may occasionally be abused. But self-respect, loyal comradeship, and a passionate love of justice are traits inseparably bound up with his fine qualities as a worker, and they are harmonised and broadened by knowledge and common sense.'

In the national interest, as it affected ordinary people especially, Johnston usually demonstrated uncommon good sense. When he was Secretary of State for Scotland, he anticipated the National Health Service by using hospital beds earmarked for Civil Defence casualties to accommodate ordinary patients who could not afford specialist services.

Everyone knew voluntary hospitals couldn't cope with the demands on their time and facilities at the start of the war. It could take a year for a troublesome appendix to be removed. People with minor complaints, including ear, nose and throat ailments, usually waited months before being treated. Johnston learned of one elderly man who had been waiting seven years for a hernia operation. 'These hospital waiting lists saddened me,' he wrote. When he discovered there were fewer Civil Defence casualties than expected Johnston decided, as an experiment, to make the hospitals, which had been equipped to cope with a rush of casualties, available for free specialist examination and treatment of civilian war workers. 'It was obviously foolish to have well-equipped hospitals often standing empty and their staffs awaiting Civil Defence casualties – which, thank God, never came – while war workers could not afford specialist diagnosis and treatment,' Johnston explained.

The experiment started on Clydeside and was a huge success. Eventually, on Johnston's authority, it covered the whole of Scotland. Waiting lists for treatment at the voluntary hospitals, totalling 34,000 patients, simply disappeared. And, as Johnston testified after the war, there was no friction or antagonism from the voluntary hospitals over any of the lost patients. 'Indeed,' wrote Johnston, 'they made a small monetary payment for every patient taken off their hands, and a vast amount of preventable suffering and pain was simply obliterated.'

Family doctors also contributed to this minor revolution in patient care. They were encouraged, with difficult cases of diagnosis, to seek assistance from specialists paid by the Scottish Office, or refer patients to the Civil Defence hospitals for treatment.

Together with Ernest Brown, Minister of Health in the wartime Government, Johnston was largely responsible for the original White Paper outlining a National Health Service, which was approved by the War Cabinet on 9 February 1944. The original blueprint document had been submitted to the Reconstruction Priorities Committee the previous month. By February 1944, when the White Paper outlining the coalition Government's plans for a National Health Service available to all reached the House of Commons, Ernest Brown had been replaced as Minister of Health by Henry Willink.

In an introduction to the most far-reaching legislation ever attempted in Britain, Willink and Johnston explained that it was the Government's intention that 'in future every man and woman and child can rely on getting all the advice and treatment and care which they may need in matters of personal health; that what they get shall be the best medical and other facilities available; that their getting these shall not depend on whether they can pay for them, or on any other factor irrelevant to the real need – the real need being to bring the country's full resources to bear upon reducing ill-health and promoting good health in all its citizens.' It was an inspiring endeavour and one Tom Johnston was pleased to promote.

The Council of State met for the last time at St Andrew's House on 16 February 1945, four years, a week and a day after Johnston became Secretary of State. Apart from officials only Lord Alness and Ernest Brown joined Johnston for the meeting. Sir Archibald Sinclair, John Colville and Walter Elliot were all busy elsewhere.

It was the 16th occasion on which the Council of State had been convened and the depleted group settled down to consider the usual mixed agenda. Before them were many of the chairman's pet projects, developed over his years in power. These included the future role of Prestwick Airport as an international airport, complete with feeder services to the rest of the United Kingdom, the need for an aircraft industry in Scotland – a dream notion which hadn't been discounted totally by Sir Stafford Cripps, the Minister for Aircraft Production, in a speech delivered in Edinburgh the previous week – local rating, the requirements of a Bill covering hill sheep farming and a review of the latest National Health Service proposals.

The minutes show that, on the controversial subject of the NHS, 'Lord Alness and Mr Ernest Brown congratulated the chairman on the measure of agreement resulting from discussions in Scotland. They felt, however, that progress in England, where the fears of the voluntary hospitals had not been allayed, and where medical politics would play a considerable part, would be more difficult, and that it would be doubtful whether legislation could be introduced in the present session.'

Johnston credited the Council of State with encouraging 'a new spirit of independence and hope in our national life. You could sense it everywhere, and not least in the civil service. We met England now without any inferiority complex. We were a nation once again.'

Unfinished business included the 1945 Education (Scotland) Bill. Tom Johnston maintained a declared interest in education throughout the whole of his political career. 'If a secondary schooling is good for the children of the middle class and the children of the rich,' he once told the House of Commons, 'it ought to be good enough for the children of the working class.' Similarly, when he received the freedom of Kirkintilloch, his acceptance speech included a heartfelt reminder: 'The justification of all educational expenditure is the interests and well-being of our children – the sound mind in the sound body.'

It was as a member of the School Board in Kirkintilloch that he began in local politics. And it was in protest at the decision to make education a county responsibility that he resigned.

He was often vehement in his criticism of a curriculum which sustained historical falsehoods and relied heavily on subjects which were of little practical value except for examination purposes. Some of his views would find little support among feminists. By his own admission Johnston was 'indifferent if the girl students knew nothing about the height of Mount Popocatepetl, provided they could cook a vegetable stew, and could beautify a home, and had been taught the rudiments of health and first-aid and citizenship, and some of the arts and handicrafts'.

Boys, he appeared to believe, should be allowed to concentrate on engineering. Diesel engines, and a grounding in citizenship, provided the basis of more practical learning skills than any amount of parsing. But during the years he spent at the Scottish Office there wasn't a single day school in Glasgow, Renfrewshire or Dunbartonshire with a motor car for engineering instruction purposes, Johnston complained.

His attempts to introduce what he considered the first necessity of all education, a culture of good citizenship, into schools, failed. At a Convention on Juvenile Delinquency which he arranged as Secretary of State, Johnston suggested that any headmaster who succeeded in keeping his school clear of delinquency convictions should be invited to appear before the local authority and publicly thanked by the provost. 'We thank and reward a man who jumps off a bridge to save a child from drowning,' Johnston argued. 'How much more should we congratulate and reward a schoolmaster who, by forethought, exhortation, and organisation of a public school spirit, succeeds in saving perhaps hundreds of pupils from acquiring criminal records and habits and our whole social organism from grave perils.'

Johnston enjoyed an uneasy relationship with the mandarins of the Scottish Education Department. He considered them over-cautious and set in their ways: they disliked his impetuous approach and his affection for *ad hoc* committees outside the established order.

When the Advisory Council on Education in Scotland was reconstituted in 1942 the SED wanted to keep a tight rein on its activities. Johnston, by contrast, favoured giving the Council considerable room to manoeuvre. At its first meeting members of the Council were encouraged by the Secretary of State to survey the whole field of education. Johnston said he hoped they would regard themselves as a parliament on education and do a big job.

Offered such an exhilarating start to their deliberations it is hardly surprising the Council decided they would like to begin by examining the administration of education in its entirety. A possible starting point was the role and attitudes of the Scottish Education Department including, presumably, the position of the Secretary of State in such matters. Johnston, under pressure from inside St Andrew's House, and with a good deal on his mind during the war, abandoned his instincts and refused to allow it.

He was actually out of office, and about to retire from the House of Commons, when Churchill agreed to help him obtain a third reading for the 1945 Education (Scotland) Bill which many people believed should carry his name. Churchill, who was now Prime Minister in the Conservative caretaker Government which followed the end of the war in Europe, offered to support Johnston's Bill on one condition: it must first obtain general agreement in the Scottish Grand Committee.

Johnston worked hard to achieve the necessary accord. At its third reading on 3 June 1945 the Education (Scotland) Bill, complete with 92 clauses and six schedules, required only two hours in the House of Commons before it was sent to receive the Royal Assent. A week later, just days before the 1945 Education (Scotland) Act arrived on the King's desk for signature, the country's teachers showed their appreciation by making Johnston an Honorary Fellow of the Educational Institute of Scotland. His political career was ending where it began.

The first political speech he ever made was about education when he was a member of the local School Board in Kirkintilloch. And the last time he addressed the House of Commons the subject was education. It was a kind of symmetry that was bound to please Johnston.

Two days after he left St Andrew's House as Secretary of State for the last time, and shortly before his deal with Churchill over the future shape of Scottish education, *The Scotsman* appealed for a continuation of consensus politics. In a lengthy leading article the capital's main opinion-former outside the New Club claimed the departing Secretary of State 'accomplished much in his four years of office, not only in legislation but also in stimulating a Scottish spirit of enterprise and determination to overcome the difficulties, social, industrial and economic, with which Scotland is confronted. He laid the foundations and prepared the plans on which her future well-being must largely depend.

'It would be not only deplorable but tragic if all these projects were now to be cast aside or were to become the subject of party bickerings.

'It is to be hoped that the aim of securing progress by basing Scottish schemes on common agreement instead of on merely party considerations will be kept steadily in view. If that is done, Mr Johnston's pioneering work will prove to be of permanent value and good in Scotland.'

Coalition government, as it applied during the Second World War, suited Tom Johnston. It conformed to his long-held views that some problems were above party strife. He favoured an extension of the principle beyond the end of hostilities, with everyone working together to tackle post-war reconstruction on a fair and sensible basis, not least housing, health and the right to work.

'Mr Churchill might indeed have drawn upon the bank of his wartime prestige and preserved a political unity in the country for some time longer,' Johnston suggested. However, as he also told officials from his West Stirlingshire constituency in March 1945, just as 'the war is galloping to a close, political warfare can be expected soon after'.

Johnston confirmed his intention to retire from the House of Commons at the upcoming election with a warning: 'Many people who are eagerly sharpening the swords of political partisanship might live to regret such an excess of zeal.' Added the man who first informed constituency officials of his intention to retire eight years earlier: 'Great issues are waiting to be settled. We must never return to the days of mass unemployment in Scotland.' A month later a leading article in *John Bull* declared: 'His achievements for the good of his country are a challenge to the Sassenach.'

A letter written by the Labour leader, Clement Attlee, in his room at the Clifton Hotel, Blackpool, and telephoned to the Prime Minister at Chequers on 21 May 1945, proposed continuing with the coalition until the autumn. Attlee was attending the Labour Party conference in the seaside town and well placed to judge the mood of his followers. The majority wanted power and a chance to exploit socialist policies, without further delay!

However, the man who had been Churchill's deputy throughout most of the war, was anxious to avoid a rushed election similar to 1918 following the end of the First World War. If the major parties agreed to wait until the autumn, Attlee suggested, the election could be fought on a more complete and effective register. The delay would also allow the full electorate, including voters overseas, 'a fair opportunity of considering candidates and policy'.

Post-war reconstruction was the main issue dividing the major parties. Attlee recognised the Government needed to be 'united on principle and policy. A government so divided that it could take no effective action would be a disaster for the country.'

In his reply dated 22 May 1945 Churchill, who had been prepared to wait until the war against Japan was at an end, didn't favour the two sides 'bickering together till the autumn. Such a process would not be the decent way of carrying on a British government.' The following day Churchill made two visits to Buckingham Palace. At noon he resigned as head of the coalition, five years and 13 days after he first accepted the responsibility. A few hours later he returned and formally accepted the King's invitation to continue as Prime Minister in a caretaker Conservative administration.

During the election campaign which followed Tom Johnston was disappointed beyond anger at reports Churchill had been claiming Labour would introduce Gestapo-style police forces if elected. During the war, Johnston observed coldly, it was Churchill who 'entrusted the supervision of the police forces in England and Wales to Mr Herbert Morrison, and their supervision in Scotland to myself as Secretary of State'.

Before the election, at a thanksgiving rally in the Usher Hall, Edinburgh, he proclaimed himself proud that following the dark days of Dunkirk 'there was not one quisling or surrenderist in the Government'. Unity of purpose took the people of Britain from the brink of destruction. 'It was this corporate all-in national effort, each for all, that enabled us to match the hour, and to withstand – at one period entirely alone in the world – the organised fury of the fascist and Nazi powers of darkness,' Johnston claimed.

'If we could only recapture part of that enthusiasm, élan and common purpose, recapture it for the much-needed reconstruction and betterment of our world – if only we could lift great social crusades like better housing and health from the arena of partisan strife, what magnificent achievements might yet be ours.'

CHAPTER TWENTY-TWO

PEOPLE WERE PUZZLED by Tom Johnston's decision to retire from the House of Commons in 1945. He was in robust good health, not yet 65, and at the height of his powers and considerable prestige. A senior Cabinet role in the Attlee administration was guaranteed. Assuming he wanted to remain in Scotland, the new Prime Minister was bound to agree.

In fact, Labour finishing ahead of Churchill and the Conservatives in the general election was a good deal harder to predict. The scale of Attlee's victory was certainly unexpected. Far from enjoying the delirium of a staggering election triumph, Labour could have been condemned to another five years of dispiriting opposition. After more than four years in almost sole charge of Scotland, at the head of his own mini-coalition, life as an opposition MP, unable to influence the radical programme of national reconstruction which the country desperately needed, would have been anathema to Johnston.

Churchill, in the dissolution honours, and Attlee, when he succeeded to Downing Street, offered him a seat in the House of Lords. Johnston, to nobody's great surprise, declined. Attlee also thought of him as a possible successor to Field Marshal Wavell, as the last viceroy of India, before Mountbatten's appointment. Because of the rising tide of Indian nationalism, there was a strong feeling in Downing Street that Wavell did not possess 'sufficient political nous to deal with the situation. He has not the political training,' Attlee explained in a letter, dated 22 December 1945, to Stafford Cripps and Lord Pethick-Lawrence. Added Attlee: 'Our problem has been to see who else could do the job. There is one man in our ranks of outstanding capacity who has the confidence of people of all political views and who has proved himself a most skilful reconciler of contending factions, Tom Johnston.'

Johnston would have been a surprising choice, first as viceroy and then, following Indian independence, governor-general. A quarter of a century earlier Johnston claimed in the House of Commons that it was 'an insult, at this time of day, to impose anybody with the title of a Governor on a free democracy'. And, in fact, Attlee didn't entertain his own original idea for long. In his letter to Cripps and Pethick-Lawrence the Prime Minister admitted: 'I do not think he would be prepared to take on the vice-royalty. He is too wedded to Scotland.'

However, he wasn't finished with the thought that Tom Johnston could contribute greatly to the development of India in the post-war era. Wavell could be left to carry on the government of India and Tom Johnston could be sent out as a special commissioner with full Cabinet powers, Attlee suggested, to make a settlement with the Indian leaders. 'He would, in fact,' the Prime Minister explained, 'be a plenipotentiary.'

Attlee also believed Johnston's appointment would strike the imagination of the Indians, in part because Johnston 'would be divorced from the machine of Indian administration. It would, I think, make an appeal to Indians as a novel line of development, in which India is recognised by Britain as a political entity with which an accommodation has to be reached,' Attlee added.

Pethick-Lawrence, as Secretary of State for India and Burma, recognised some of the difficulties surrounding the appointment. He wondered if Tom Johnston possessed, or could be expected to acquire, the necessary background on India which would justify such complete confidence in him. In his reply, written on 26 December 1945, he also asked: 'Could the viceroy submit to being superseded, in effect, by anyone other than a Cabinet Minister?'

It was perhaps this consideration, as much as anything else, that invalidated Attlee's bold proposal. Without a seat in the House of Commons, and with his reluctance to accept a peerage, the door to the Cabinet room in Downing Street was now closed against Tom Johnston. But although he was finished with the Palace of Westminster, he wasn't deserting politics entirely. His flair for intrigue at the highest political level would yet serve Scotland well.

On a visit to Inverness the Chancellor of the Exchequer, Hugh Dalton, offered the view that three indigenous industries, forestry, tourism and hydro power, could provide the basis for future prosperity in the Highlands. 'The Highlands must be led into a better future, not by the invisible private hand of Adam Smith, but by the visible public hand of the Labour Party,' Dalton insisted.

The future success of the three industries designated for special attention would be the responsibility of separate boards appointed by the Government. Each, in its own right, offered a distinct challenge for a man or woman of purpose. Dalton, a colleague from the wartime Cabinet, put Tom Johnston in charge of all three. Almost seamlessly, the man who dominated Scottish public life for almost the whole of the war, would continue to plan for the beginning of peace.

Timber was a vital asset, in short supply. Yet, before 1945, anyone appointed to the Forestry Commission enjoyed a rare and privileged existence. Although dependent on Government funding the commissioners were subject to no direct ministerial control. Questions in Parliament were answered by a member of the Commission with a day job in Westminster; always, until good sense and a rudimentary regard for democracy prevailed, a backbench Tory MP. This peculiar arrangement survived the first 26 years of the Commission's existence; although, in the House of Commons, as Tom Johnston once observed, it 'used to excite amazement, and sometimes derision'.

The Commission dated from 1919 and resulted from the report of the Acland Committee, appointed three years earlier, to find ways of conserving and developing Britain's timber resources. It concluded: 'Dependence on imported timber is a grave source of weakness in war.' The same report also maintained: 'Our supplies of timber, even in time of peace, are precarious and lie too much outside the Empire.'

Russia was one such threatened source of future supply. Before the First World War almost half Britain's total imports of wood had been supplied by Russia. Now the Tsar and his family were dead and the Bolsheviks ruled in Moscow. An allied force was in Russia, fighting to thwart the revolution. No one could predict the outcome with any certainty. But it was prudent to assume there might be a suspension in normal trade relations between Russia and the west lasting a long time.

The Acland Committee recommended an 80-year programme of afforestation, mainly involving conifers, covering more than 1.7 million acres of countryside. But even this ambitious plan was subject to the Canadian Government agreeing to maintain its forest reserves. Without a guaranteed supply of timber from Canada it would be necessary, Acland warned, for Britain to embark on an even larger programme of afforestation.

Certainly, as viewed by the Acland Committee, there was no shortage of land available for the purpose. 'The area of land utilised for rough grazing, but capable of growing first-class coniferous timber of the same character as that imported,' their report noted, 'is not less than three and probably more than five million acres.'

Four members of the Acland Committee were among the first members of the new Forestry Commission, appointed by the Prime Minister, Lloyd George, under Royal Warrant in 1919: the committee chairman, F.D. Acland, who happened to be an MP and could respond to questions in the House of Commons concerning the Commission's activities, Lord Lovat, Sir John Stirling-Maxwell and the committee secretary, a burly Australian from His Majesty's Office of Woods, Roy Robinson.

For more than three decades, including 20 years as chairman, Robinson dominated the work of the Forestry Commission. His efforts earned him a knighthood and a seat in the House of Lords. Tom Johnston found him 'energetic, forceful and Napoleonic'.

It was evident, however, as the Second World War neared its end, that Robinson headed an industry on the brink of crisis, and desperately in need of change. An internal Forestry Commission report, dated 12 April 1944, conceded 'in respect of management we are far behind all western European states and many parts of the Empire'.

It had been easier and cheaper to purchase timber from abroad, the report noted, than develop home-grown stocks. As a result 'the normal incentive to manage such woodlands as we had on the most productive and economic lines has been lost'. In fact, forestry in Britain hadn't recovered from the demands of the First World War when the Second

World War started. In 1921 Treasury interference, and Government spending cuts, provided an early threat to the Commission's ambitious plans; even its continued existence. Cuts recommended by the Geddes Committee on National Expenditure were circumvented then. Ten years later, however, there was no escape from the financial crisis which ended the life of the second Labour Government. A cut in its income forced the Forestry Commission to destroy 70,000 young trees valued at £50,000. This sum represented more than ten per cent of the total Treasury grant for the year; now worth more than £90 million. It was, Tom Johnston judged, 'surely one of the most wasteful and indeed criminal decisions ever taken in the name of economy'.

During the Second World War, according to one report, 30 to 40 years of normal felling and manufacture had been compressed into five years of hard accomplishment for the war effort. The use of home–grown timber released more than 17 million tons of shipping space for other purposes. The same report, prepared by the Home Timber Merchants Association of Scotland, also maintained: 'The value of that contribution, in the saving of shipping for other vital cargoes, in the shortening of the war, and in assuring full and final victory, can hardly be realised, and is in no danger of being exaggerated.'

Generally free of the tiresome burden of ministerial accountability, and operating latterly from offices at 25 Savile Row, some members of the Forestry Commission rather flattered themselves, Johnston suggested. Those who didn't recommend change he compared unkindly to P.G. Wodehouse's brilliant comic creation, Jeeves. Others with substantial forestry interests, including Lord Lovat, Sir John Stirling-Maxwell and Lord Mansfield, he praised for their efforts in alerting people to 'the perils that a timber famine would bring'.

But there was never much chance of the Forestry Commission emerging from the war unaffected by the range of new opinions surfacing in Whitehall. On 4 August 1942, less than 18 months after Johnston was appointed Secretary of State for Scotland, the political correspondent of the *Glasgow Herald* suggested that machinery introduced in 1919 was no longer appropriate for its original purpose and that 'the special position of Scotland should now be reviewed in the light of altered circumstances'.

The existing legislation guaranteed Scotland two commissioners and a salaried assistant commissioner. But even this arrangement left Scottish interests in 'the position of a permanent minority, an arrangement whose possible disadvantages so far as Scotland is concerned needed no emphasis'.

In all probability, the sentiments on offer from the *Herald*'s correspondent, writing from Westminster, had been influenced by the Secretary of State for Scotland. But the significance of his words were obviously lost on the men who tailored Britain's forestry needs from Savile Row in a style which was no longer fashionable.

Johnston greeted the Commission's preliminary proposals for the future of forestry, submitted in 1943, with a mixture of admiration and downright fury. At a meeting at the Treasury on 9 March 1943 he criticised Sir Roy Robinson for a speech to the Scottish Forestry Association which 'had evoked protests from all sections of political opinion'. Johnston believed Sir Roy's expansionist philosophy was in serious danger of conflicting with the rights of several government departments, including agriculture, planning and health. The Commission wanted the country round the Moray Firth and the border between Scotland and England designated forest regions. 'In the next five years they proposed to acquire a further three million acres,' Johnston recalled, 'but they offered no estimate of the farms they would acquire in the process.'

The difficulties of reconciling forestry with agriculture and sheep farming accounted for much of the bitterness which surrounded the Forestry Commission's activities. Farmers complained when good land, suitable for growing crops, was purchased by the Commission; or sheep were evicted from hillsides to make room for trees. Wildlife attacking crops was another problem which, farmers claimed, the Commission refused to address with sufficient seriousness. One critic suggested Sir Roy and his colleagues went out of their way to 'promote an unhealthy antagonism between the production of timber and the production of food'.

Their 1943 report suggested the commissioners were prepared to tinker with the idea of devolving some authority from Savile Row, including consultative councils and committees involving the commissioners themselves to deal with executive business. However, wrote Johnston, 'lest there be any mistake or misapprehension, the British commissioners at headquarters reserved to themselves questions of policy, finance, personnel, research, education and publications. All acquisition and disposal of land had to be brought before the commissioners at headquarters for approval. At headquarters also they would deal with estates and holdings, technical matters and National Forest Parks,' Johnston added.

However, he also believed the Commission's determination to maintain its independence served to obscure some 'really splendid sections of the Forestry Policy Report'. This included a carefully calculated plan to increase home production of timber from 4.2 per cent of the nation's requirements in 1935 to 35 per cent of its needs before the end of the century. The Commission envisaged utilising five million acres in Scotland, England and Wales. They also suggested opening one new national park every year for the next ten years at a capital outlay not exceeding £50,000. If the Government wished to make a special feature of national parks, the report added, this could be achieved with the provision of an additional £100,000 which would result in 20 parks being opened by the end of the first post-war decade.

However, the commission appeared to disregard the strength of the political forces ranged against them. To the man excercising wide-ranging powers in Scotland, 'they generally conveyed the impression that without much encouragement they would be prepared to run agriculture, road-making, the meteorological office, and take command of the Channel Fleet in their spare time!'

Essentially, of course, all the commissioners wanted was to be left alone, to continue as before, with sufficient funds and minimum political interference. However, they acknowledged grandly, if the government of the day was determined to extend its influence to include forestry, it might be appropriate for the Lord President of the Council to chair a special committee which could include the Minister of Agriculture and Fisheries and the Secretary of State for Scotland in its membership.

On 15 February 1945 the Chancellor of the Exchequer, Sir John Anderson, announced the Government's intention to continue with the Forestry Commission. MPs wouldn't be allowed to serve on the Commission in future and the chairman would be 'responsible directly to the Minister of Agriculture and Fisheries and the Secretary of State for Scotland for carrying out operations, including training, research and forestry holding'.

Tom Johnston attended his first meeting as a commissioner at 25 Savile Row on 15 August 1945. Sir Roy Robinson had been confirmed as chairman and Johnston agreed to become chairman of the national committee in Scotland on condition 'this might only apply for a limited period'.

The plan for timber already submitted depended on the Commission, with the aid of private landowners, planting 1.1 million acres during the first ten years, followed by another 1.5 million acres by the end of the next decade. On 30 November 1945 the Minister of Agriculture and Fisheries, Tom Williams, announced a ten-year plan covering 365,000 acres during the first five years. He also agreed to accept a Forestry Commission scheme which allowed landowners to continue managing their woodlands in an approved way. 'The alternative to proper management under state aid will be state acquisition,' he warned.

Progress was slower than anyone hoped. 'Private timber growers complained that owing to rising costs of estate management and housing, timber felling at the scheduled rates was a losing proposition,' Johnston recalled, 'and it was made no more acceptable to them when they learned that imports from abroad were being paid for at higher rates'.

Johnston, with his usual interest in making the most of the poorest resources, pressed the claims of low grade peat land as a home for quality grade timber. One experiment, at Currour on Rannoch Moor, conducted by Sir John Stirling-Maxwell, was praised by the chairman of the Forestry Commission, Lord Robinson, as 'the most valuable ever done in Britain and an inspiration to subsequent developments'.

From its headquarters in Edinburgh – a shift from central London, undertaken in 1975, which Tom Johnston would have been the first to welcome – members of the Forestry Commission now control 2.5 million acres of Britain's wooded countryside. A similar amount of prime forest land is in private ownership. Forestry work provides direct employment for 40,000 people; not counting timber-related industries located elsewhere.

The demand for timber, and timber-related products, continues to increase. But the 1945 target of providing 35 per cent of the country's needs from forests in Britain won't be achieved. Imports account for more than 80 per cent of the market: some experts believe a 25 per cent share is about the best that might be achieved. But they warn that won't happen until well into the next century, if at all. As a jubilee account of the Commission's activities, published in 1994, acknowledged: 'British forestry is still some way from realising its full potential.'

Tom Johnston served with the Forestry Commission for less than three years. When he resigned, in June 1948, he claimed eight journeys a year, to attend meetings at 25 Savile Row, as one reason for his disaffection. It was an old complaint which time didn't mend.

Anyone other than Tom Johnston as head of the newly created Scottish Tourist Board would have been hard to justify. He had been arguing for years that tourism was a major industry, long neglected in Scotland, and sorely in need of serious development.

His interest in the wealth-creating potential of Scotland's colourful history and breathtaking scenery was a natural extension of his passion for utilising the nation's resources for the benefit of its people. Not everyone accepted his vision, of course. When he was Under-Secretary of State at the Scottish Office, Johnston felt obliged to complain: 'Within the bounds of Scotland there are great tracts of beautiful mountain and loch scenery, huge acres of health-giving strath and glen and peak, forbidden, or at least difficult of access, to the general public.

'While there is in fact no law of trespass,' Johnston continued, in a BBC radio talk broadcast on 23 November 1929, 'the landlords and sporting agents have created a very effective barrier. They have closed inns and sleeping places. They pull down cottages when the lease expires. In actual fact, if not by formal edict, the great sanatoria and beauty spots of Scotland are closed to the tourist traffic, not only of England and Scotland, but of Europe.'

Johnston didn't doubt the harm this mean-spirited attitude inflicted on the prosperity of the country generally. Commenting on the economic potential of tourism to Scotland he maintained: 'Through it many thousands of people would find employment out of a purchasing power which presently passes our shores.' Five months later, as Lord Privy Seal, he claimed a healthy tourist industry could be used to combat rising unemployment. In a speech to the House of Commons, Johnston acknowledged the subject of tourism could be the cause of some mirth among fellow MPs. But there was nothing frivolous about his argument, or the figures he provided to support his case: foreign visitors to France spent around £120 million annually, Johnston reported.

Anyone who considered the matter carefully could see tourism was fraught with great economic possibilities, Johnston went on. The workforce already totalled 350,000; a larger figure than the number employed in iron and steel, or wool and cotton. But of this great industry, Johnston complained, 'it can be said that Great Britain is the only country which has hitherto not actively taken steps to facilitate its development'.

Before his appointment as Lord Privy Seal he had been able to persuade the Prime Minister to let him form a Scottish Tourist Development Association, independent of the British Travel Association. However, in return for Treasury support, calculated on the Goschen scale, Johnston committed the infant Scottish organisation to donate more than 25 per cent of the money it raised, by subscription and donation, to the BTA. It was an uncharacteristic blunder and, by his own admission, naïve. Allegedly, as Johnston, older and wiser, endeavoured to explain, the money was meant to provide 'a contribution to the general British propaganda abroad, nobody being observant of the fact that Scotland already was paying her share of the British Treasury money through her taxation'. As a result Scotland received £345 18s 7d at the end of the first year. And even this magnificent sum, calculated to the last penny, reduced year by year until 1939 when Treasury support for the Scottish tourist trade amounted to £250.

'Had it not been for the Hitler war, which stopped the tourist business and much else besides,' Johnston later observed, 'the Scottish association might have been induced to return its cheque in disgust to London, and the country thereafter might have been entertained by the spectacle of prominent personages exposing the farce by standing at the Waverley steps with explanatory placards, and with their hats out a-begging.'

The fact he had been duped rankled for years. And the business of making amends was high on his personal agenda during the last year of the war. His aim was a vigorous, well-funded tourist industry, based in Scotland, and unbeholden to London for money. Together with Sir Steven Bilsland, later Lord Bilsland, chairman of the Scottish Council, he selected Dr Tom Honeyman, the energetic Director of Art Galleries and Museums in Glasgow, to produce a plan.

The process started with an urgent telephone call from Bilsland to Honeyman in July 1944. Could he attend a meeting in Bilsland's office, with the Secretary of State, right away? It wasn't long before Honeyman discovered what Johnston wanted. Invited to head a committee on post-war tourism in Scotland he was assured 'the Government would not resist any practical proposals which the committee might include in its report'.

As a local government official Honeyman knew he would require the approval of his employers. 'Tom Johnston, with a smile, said he did not think there would be much difficulty in getting it,' Honeyman recalled.

In fact, there was fierce opposition, within the Art Galleries and Museums Committee of Glasgow Corporation, to Honeyman accepting the role. Glasgow didn't yet consider itself a major tourist attraction in its own right. In addition, relations between the Scottish Office and the country's largest city were sometimes strained during the war. Only the casting vote of the committee's acting chairman saved the Secretary of State for Scotland the bother of finding someone else to take charge of his latest brainchild.

Told by Sir David Milne, head civil servant at the Scottish Home Department, that the Secretary of State wanted his report delivered with all possible speed, Honeyman and his committee completed their work within a year. Six months later the Scottish Tourist Board was created; with Johnston, who was no longer an MP, as chairman. Honeyman, who was rewarded for his efforts with a place on the new board, believed nothing could indicate more clearly the importance the former Secretary of State attached to this new Scottish enterprise. 'Tom Johnston's one mistake was his insistence on financial independence,' Honeyman maintained.

But that was the one firm and inflexible condition Johnston applied to his appointment – 'that we would raise all our funds inside Scotland. No more handing over to London any share of the moneys we raised in Scotland for Scottish tourism,' he added. 'We would be independent in name and in reality.'

There was a glimpse of the combative side of his nature at the board's first meeting which was held in St Andrew's House on 24 December 1945. Johnston had been annoyed to learn that all the railway companies had made arrangements for establishing holiday camps, to be managed by Thomas Cook and Sons, without including Scotland in their plans. He had seen the directors of the London North Eastern Railway and warned them of the deplorable effects this would have on Scottish public opinion. He had also been in touch with Messrs Cook who had 'promised to take no decision about managing the LNER camp until they had considered the Scottish position'.

The ten-man board also heard that the Travel Association of Great Britain would continue to handle tourist publicity for the United Kingdom overseas. The association received a Government subsidy of one pound for every one pound collected. The same conditions would apply to contributions from the Scottish Tourist Board. Johnston was determined to ensure that campaigns organised by the Travel Association of Great Britain in other lands didn't just concentrate on places of interest and beauty in England. 'Scotland's interests will be protected,' he promised.

Scotland had been allocated two places on the UK board. It wouldn't take long for anything discussed at their meetings to reach Johnston's ears. However, a request from the Travel Association of Great Britain for a copy of Tourist Board minutes was put on hold. J. Gibson Kerr, the secretary, was instructed to inform his London-based counterpart that the STB was chiefly concerned with domestic matters. However, as the minutes of the second meeting of the Scottish Tourist Board also recorded, 'any points of interest would be communicated to them'.

Led by Johnston the STB represented the usual trawl of the great and the good, undertaken by the Scottish Council, and confirmed by the Secretary of State. Johnston himself admitted that hotel associations and other interested parties were left 'bewildered and resentful when their applications for membership of the board were politely but firmly declined. It was apparently all but in vain that we explained how membership representation by employers entailed membership representation by employees: that if we had hotels, we must also have shipping and road transport, and rail transport, and air transport, to say nothing about catering, automobile, travel agents, brewers, distillers, soft drink manufacturers, coast landladies, and other interests,' Johnston argued.

His aim was an association which, predominantly, represented consumers. He wanted to develop the country and open up the show places for the benefit of everyone, 'the proletariat and the bourgeois and the plutocrats as well', Johnston explained.

Cheap package holidays to exotic-sounding locations in faraway countries didn't exist. Clyde coast towns, like Rothesay, Dunoon and Largs, competed fiercely with east coast havens such as Portobello, Dunbar and Arbroath for the bulk of the annual family holiday trade. A register was compiled of the various types of holiday accommodation available in Scotland. Local authorities were encouraged to improve the standard of houses which could be used to support the bed and breakfast trade in rural areas. Guidebooks were commissioned and information bureaux established in different parts of the country. Hotels and boarding-houses were encouraged to improve their catering standards and feature native produce.

Contact was also developed with a wide variety of Scots societies overseas. Johnston was fond of claiming there were 20 million people of Scots descent living outside Scotland. 'Who, having experienced it, can ever forget the overpowering intensity of the Scottishness in the gatherings of our folk from Calcutta to Chicago?' he inquired. His own strong streak of kailyard sentiment encouraged the belief that, with its nostalgia for the old birthplace, this greater Scotland beyond the seas was a fact of some importance in the world. 'Folly beyond words not to do all in our power to tighten the bands of racial fraternity and to attract the exiles back to holiday in the land of their birth, or whence their forbears sprang!' he claimed.

By 1950 it was estimated that 40 per cent of the 240,281 foreign tourists who arrived in Britain from countries outside Europe included Scotland in their itinerary. More than 65,000 people were employed in the tourist trade. According to Johnston 'the Scottish economy benefits to the extent of £12.8 million, excluding shares of summer lettings, railway transport, catering and merchandise sales'.

But then as now the railway authorities showed little regard for Scotland. A decade before the Beeching axe destroyed the Scottish rail network, and more than 40 years ahead of the latest threats to the West Highland line and the west coast sleeper service, an information bulletin issued jointly by the Scottish Tourist Board and the Tourist Association of Scotland revealed: 'Proposals by the Railway Executive to close certain branch lines and railway services in Scotland have been causing the board and other authorities considerable concern.'

Johnston campaigned vigorously for the restoration of a transatlantic shipping service between New York and the Clyde. 'It is intolerable that great ships should be built there, sail away and never return,' he complained. Following a meeting in New York an unnamed English shipping magnate conceded he had made 'a splendid case, but please not to forget that he was chairman of an English harbour board'.

Characteristically, he refused to take no for an answer. His persistence was finally rewarded when the Donaldson Atlantic Company introduced a transatlantic service, using the *Lismoria* and the *Laurentia*, and the Canadian Pacific Railway Company carried passengers between the Clyde and the St Lawrence aboard the aptly named *Empress of Scotland*.

There wasn't much he could do about the weather; except insist, with the help of some carefully selected statistics, that it wasn't as bad as people imagined. In the average year, for example, his chart showed the sunniest place in Britain was the Inner Hebrides and not, as many people imagined, the south-east coast of England.

Another negative factor, counting against Scotland ever becoming a major world tourist attraction, was the irksome presence of the dreaded midge. Tom Johnston was horrified to learn Scotland harboured 155 different kinds of midge. Midges didn't exist in Patagonia or New Zealand, he discovered: why was their presence tolerated in Scotland? At the very least, Johnston wanted effective lotions made available at reasonable prices, and without further delay.

His anti-midge campaign earned him an accolade from the Tory-inclined *Glasgow Herald*. A leading article suggested his respect for the midge marked him 'as a man who, having set Scotland's peculiar problems in the right perspective, is determined to mend matters'. Demonstrating its own sure grasp of the seriousness of the problem Johnston now confronted, the *Herald* added: 'He will earn his monument if he adds no more personal achievement than the eradication of the midge which since the wolf went has been the only voracious creature with which the southron visitor could not cope unaided.'

Johnston continued as chairman of the Scottish Tourist Board for more than nine years. His decision to resign was made after he had been 'pressed by the Prime Minister and others to accept a new part-time sphere of activity'. At a dinner in his honour, held in Edinburgh in January 1955, Johnston claimed tourism now contributed £51 million a year to the Scottish economy. In his last year as chairman of the STB the number of visitors to Scotland exceeded 300,000. Measured in terms of employment it was already the sixth largest industry in the country.

'We have kept clear of partisan politics,' said Johnston. 'We have kept clear of group formation. We have kept clear of dependence on grants in aid and subsidies from the trade. We are all proud of the success so far and I am sure the future has even greater successes in store.'

The Earl of Home, then Minister of State at the Scottish Office, and less than nine years away from his surprising transition to Downing Street, described Johnston as 'an outstanding administrator with an original mind and a Scottish bias'. Added the man who followed

Churchill, Eden and Macmillan as Prime Minister: 'A man with ideas is always troublesome, most of all to those in executive authority. But I can safely say I have never met the official or Minister of the Crown who does not value and welcome Mr Johnston's vision and initiative.'

Tom Johnston was the pioneer whose vision helped make tourism Scotland's largest industry. But the numbers involved now would have been unthinkable in his day: 10.25 million visits a year at the last count, including 1.75 million from overseas, helping to support 180,000 Scottish jobs, worth £2 billion a year to the national economy.

In achieving this eminence the collapse of the country's heavy industrial base, and the absence of a motor industry, would have been a matter of profound regret to him. Similarly, he would have been sorry to learn from Derek Reid, chief executive of the Scottish Tourist Board, that Scotland had failed to keep pace with the growth in tourism worldwide due largely 'to a decline in the English market, a lack of cohesion within the industry and a lack of resources for marketing and for capital investment in infrastructure'.

But this was the view expressed by the chief executive of the STB in an article in *The Herald* on 25 May 1995; six and a half decades after Tom Johnston first persuaded Ramsay MacDonald to let him introduce a Scottish Tourist Development Association, independent of the British Travel Association, and more than half a century since Tom Honeyman and his committee began work on a plan for the future development of tourism in Scotland.

For too long, Derek Reid complained, tourism had been regarded as a 'candy floss' industry in Scotland: people engaged in 'real' work hewed coal, built ships, or pressed steel for a living. But in future, he warned, 'if Scotland is to prosper then tourism must become recognised and developed as a serious industry with unfulfilled potential'.

If he was ever convinced the old industries were gone, never to return, it was an argument Tom Johnston, the man who invented Scottish tourism, was bound, reluctantly, to accept. But long before that happened the serious devolutionist, who said an aircraft industry and a motor industry, supplementing shipbuilding and steel, were among the prerequisites of an independent Scotland, would have been at the forefront of whatever fight was going to save Scottish industry from the dismal future that lay ahead.

It had been agreed Johnston would continue as a member of the Scottish Tourist Board following his appointment as chairman of the Broadcasting Council of Scotland, and a Governor of the BBC. This was the post pressed on him by the Prime Minister, Sir Winston Churchill, and the Secretary of State for Scotland, James Stuart. It wasn't a role which matched his status. There was no power, and little authority, attached to his latest appointment and, once again, he would be expected to attend meetings in London on a regular basis; a routine he never much enjoyed and, aged 73, was entitled to consider part of his past. His price for accepting the chairmanship of the Broadcasting Council was a say in the appointment of his successor as chairman of the Scottish Tourist Board, which was also restructured according to his wishes, with the number of deputy chairmen increased from two to four. Even then his commitment to the BBC didn't last long: after only 18 months as chairman of the Broadcasting Council of Scotland, he resigned.

It would have been almost impossible for any public duty to compete, in the post-war years, with Tom Johnston's commitment to the North of Scotland Hydro-Electric Board. Speaking in Glasgow on 24 November 1946, more than a year after vacating St Andrew's House, as Secretary of State for Scotland, he insisted: 'Highland depopulation did not stop at the clearances. In the first 30 years of the present century, in the 205 parishes covered by the operations of the North of Scotland Hydro-Electric Board, there was a decrease in population of no less than 30 per cent. Unless drastic steps are taken to market our resources, to sell our power in such a way as to attract new industries, and to reduce local rates, I cannot see any chance of restoration. Unless we do that the future is black indeed.'

In the course of the same speech Johnston anticipated a time when water power from Highland streams, lochs and rivers would be equal 'to the total amount of power at present produced from steam-coal stations, with a surplus enough left to electrify the railways and provide power to introduce any number of new industries in the Highlands'. It was a dream that started with the report of the Cooper Committee, appointed by Johnston in October 1941. 'It is now or never for the Highlands,' he warned representatives of the Association of County Councils, and the Convention of Royal Burghs, almost a year later.

The problems of post-war reconstruction in the Highlands had been the subject of a joint note by the Scottish Home Department and the Department of Agriculture. It concluded: 'It is in essence how to enable a scattered but huddled population to live tolerably under natural conditions probably more difficult than those existing in any other part of Great Britain.'

A plan to develop water power in Glen Affric had been opposed in the House of Commons on 10 September 1941 by the MP for Twickenham, Edward Keeling, on the grounds it was 'contentious, disturbs national unity, cannot be carried out during the war and may not be suitable or beneficial in the unpredictable conditions prevailing after the war'. Keeling also opposed a suggestion that only Scottish members should be entitled to participate in this particular debate on the grounds English members were also interested in the Highlands – 'they go there quite a lot', he asserted. In any case, Keeling argued, there had been 'so much bitterness in Scotland, both in the press and elsewhere, about the scheme that perhaps only Sassenachs can view it calmly and dispassionately'.

The findings of the committee headed by Lord Cooper, the Lord Justice Clerk, were presented to the House of Commons on 15 December 1942. Tom Johnston considered the Cooper Report 'a masterly production, and a model of terse, constructive and courageous draughtsmanship'.

Barely 14 months earlier the learned judge had been invited to consider 'the practicability and desirability of further developments in the use of water power resources in Scotland for the generation of electricity'. No doubt to Tom Johnston's great delight Cooper's main recommendation was a new public service corporation to be called the North of Scotland Hydro-Electric Board. Among its findings the Cooper Report maintained: 'The committee consider that the complaints which have been made, and the fears which are entertained, on the score of injury to amenity, have been grossly exaggerated, and that the amenity question has too often been used merely as a makeweight in an opposition truly founded upon other grounds.'

Eventually, as Tom Johnston noted appreciatively, for the first time since the Reform Bill of 1832, a Bill based on Lord Cooper's findings sailed through the House of Commons and the House of Lords without a division. At its second reading on 24 February 1943 the Hydro-Electric Development (Scotland) Bill was sponsored by eight Cabinet Ministers, including the Chancellor of the Exchequer, Kingsley Wood. Tom Johnston believed it was the goodwill emanating from the Council of State which ensured its success. As additional insurance, however, he also issued a warning that if anyone was predisposed to oppose the measure he would make it his 'personal business to inform the 51st Highland Division, when it returned after the war, of the names and addresses of the saboteurs'. It is doubtful, of course, if this outrageous proposal in any way affected the outcome. But that didn't stop him claiming in later years that the 'few old Adamites who could not understand anything outside faction fighting for faction fighting's sake' were shocked and warded off by his threat.

But the future authority, and autonomy, of the North of Scotland Hydro-Electric Board was far from settled. The Hydro-Electric Development (Scotland) Act didn't become law until August 1943: five months later a committee headed by Gwilym Lloyd-George, Minister of Fuel and Power in the Coalition Government, recommended bringing all electricity generation under the control of a single authority, the Central Generating Board. This was a clear threat to the Hydro Board's autonomy in the Highland area and Johnston reacted strongly against the proposal. In a letter dated 16 February 1944 he warned Gwilym Lloyd-George that any move to scrap or mutilate the Hydro Board would 'rouse a tremendous and all-party protest'.

Lloyd-George wanted the country's resources regarded as a whole. In the interest of national efficiency he believed 'there must be some adequate machinery for securing proper co-operation between every organisation in the country engaged in the generation of electricity'.

The dispute lasted for months and was unresolved when the war ended. In an official history of the Hydro Board, published in 1988 by Aberdeen University Press, Peter L. Payne observed: 'It is not difficult to imagine a weaker, less committed Scottish Secretary giving up the struggle or fatally compromising the principle upon which the Board had been based.' However, as Payne also noted: 'Tom Johnston had fathered the Board. It was perhaps his proudest creation. He was determined to fight for its survival.'

Johnston's vision of the North of Scotland Hydro-Electric Board was modelled on the Tennessee Valley Authority in the United States which, in the previous decade, 'converted a wilderness, a desolation, and a despair, into a land of thriving prosperity'.

He believed firmly in the principle, advanced in the Cooper Committee report, that large, prosperous schemes could support smaller schemes in rural areas and the islands. When the first sod was cut at Loch Sloy on 11 June 1945 Johnston announced: 'The profits will be used to provide amenity and prosperity for the more remote areas in the country. Otherwise there is no known way under heaven by which this sparsely populated area can be provided with electricity.'

His aim was the reversal of decades of Highland neglect, as Peter L. Payne noted in his official history of the Board. And, although he failed to attain his most optimistic purposes, and was initially vilified for disturbing the fish, despoiling the desolate grandeur of the glens and submerging the grazing of the sheep and the stag, Payne continued, 'harnessing the latent power of the waters and making low-cost energy available for the people of the Highlands was a laudable objective, and one that *was* attained'. According to Peter L. Payne he brought 'little or no technical or economic expertise to the Board, but he did possess enormous political experience and a consummate ability to achieve his objectives'.

It was this ability that probably saved the North of Scotland Hydro-Electric Board from extinction or, at the very least, in the first year of the post-war Labour Government, subordination to the Central Generating Board. Johnston hadn't forgotten his long-running dispute with Gwilym Lloyd-George, during the last months of the Coalition Government, over the future accountability of the Hydro Board. 'There were people at the Ministry of Fuel and Power who could conceive of nothing but a unified centralised control by some gigantic machine covering the whole country from the Shetlands to the Isle of Wight, something perhaps on the model of the National Coal Board,' Johnston recalled.

Herbert Morrison, Lord President of the Council and the man in overall charge of Labour's nationalisation programme, and Emmanuel Shinwell, Minister of Fuel and Power, were invited to Scotland to inspect some of the work in progress. And listen to the case, prepared by their old colleague, Tom Johnston, for leaving the Hydro Board alone.

Encounters of this kind demonstrated the strength and range of Johnston's political contacts. He and Shinwell had been sometime allies, and occasional enemies, in a common cause, for more than 30 years. Morrison had been Home Secretary in the wartime Coalition under Churchill, and a member of the War Cabinet. Morrison went to Loch Sloy and Shinwell visited Pitlochry.

Some of the fiercest opposition to the work of the Hydro Board, orchestrated by a group of prominent landowners, centred on Pitlochry. An Amenity Committee, appointed by the Secretary of State, tried to prevent the Hydro Board building a dam and power station in the area; thus rendering the Tummel-Garry scheme completely uneconomic and useless, Tom Johnston complained. When work on the dam finally started, after a public inquiry found in its favour, Hydro workers were refused admission to all but one hotel in the town. Fifty years later the Pitlochry dam and fish ladder is a major tourist attraction and, as Hamish MacKinven noted wryly, 'there would be a riot in Pitlochry if anyone suggested taking it down'.

MacKinven was present with a group of reporters when Johnston and Shinwell met at Pitlochry. 'Both of them were attended by a team of advisers, six or seven strong,' the former press officer recalled. 'Suddenly it was announced they were going for a walk, alone.' MacKinven shrugged. 'I can't say the men from the Ministry looked terribly pleased when they realised what was happening,' he added. 'But there was nothing they could do about it.'

Those who had been left behind looked on helplessly as the two elderly schemers walked and talked together, on ground where Loch

Faskally, a product of the great new dam under construction, would one day appear. 'They reminded me of two hoodie crows, huddled together,' MacKinven remembered, 'Tom Johnston doing much of the talking, Manny Shinwell nodding and listening, adding a question now and then. Until, finally, on their return, it was obvious Shinwell had been persuaded. When he spoke to reporters Shinwell was emphatic: the North of Scotland Hydro-Electric Board would keep its autonomy!'

It appeared, following his visit to Loch Sloy, that Tom Johnston could also rely on the support of the Lord President; although Herbert Morrison showed greater native caution then Emmanuel Shinwell and 'didn't broadcast his conversion'. But so it proved. And in May 1946 Shinwell, the Minister for Fuel and Power, informed his Cabinet colleagues that the North of Scotland Hydro-Electric Board would be responsible for managing 'both the generation and distribution assets in its area'.

However, the 1947 legislation, which nationalised the electricity industry, also included one important condition which was guaranteed to infuriate Tom Johnston: in future any scheme proposed by the North of Scotland Hydro-Electric Board would be required to obtain authorisation from the British Electricity Authority before it was approved by the Secretary of State for Scotland and the Minister of Fuel and Power. Wrote Peter L. Payne: 'Johnston and his colleagues were determined to resist any erosion of their autonomy. They made it quite clear from the start that they would appeal to the Secretary of State whenever the BEA attempted to use their vetting powers to inhibit the Board's activities.'

Johnston knew the Board could be stopped in its tracks by a change of heart in London; even, after 1950, when Attlee's huge post-war majority collapsed, a change of government. But once a dam was up and functioning, who would dare pull it down?

Johnston's handling of the media, and his sense of public relations, was masterly, according to former press aide Hamish MacKinven. When the power lines reached Iona, 'his mind began thinking historically. Iona was no ordinary little island,' MacKinven explained. 'When most of Europe was black and dark, and the barbarians were sweeping about all over the place, it was the monks on Iona who helped keep the flame of Christianity alive. Tom Johnston knew this was a big thing in Scotland's story and it was a big thing for the Hydro Board.'

His staff was ordered to charter two trains, from Glasgow and Edinburgh, and the steamer *King George V* from Oban, to convey 125 guests to the island for the opening ceremony. Johnston's sense of occasion was well rewarded. The guests included Walter Elliot, an old friend from university days, who had been an important member of the wartime Council of State, and was now Lord High Commissioner to the General Assembly of the Church of Scotland; together with the founder of the Iona Community, the Right Reverend George MacLeod, who was then Moderator of the General Assembly. 'Let there be light in the glens and plains of Scotland,' rejoiced MacLeod, before the wife of the Lord High Commissioner made history with the flick of a switch at an inaugural ceremony in the village hall.

MacLeod's words reflected Johnston's mood exactly. Similarly, he would have been pleased with a report in *The Times* whose attention he valued. In this the highly regarded Bob Brown, who had been singled out by the chairman for a special briefing on the return journey to Oban aboard the *King George V*, described how the North of Scotland Hydro-Electric Board brought electricity to 'sacred' Iona. It was here, Bob Brown informed his readers gravely, that St Columba 'cradled Scottish Christianity 14 centuries ago and kindled on this tiny isle, destined to rank among the historic places of Christendom, a powerful lamp whose rays have shone throughout the troubled centuries since'.

Only 25 houses benefited immediately from the arrival of electricity on Iona. Another 35 houses, as well as the ancient abbey, waited to be connected. Once this had been achieved they would join the 150,000 subscribers, most of them living in difficult-to-reach rural areas, who were already benefiting from the Hydro Board's existence. But the positive publicity which surrounded the arrival of electricity on Iona helped concentrate attention on the enormity of the challenge facing the Hydro Board in other parts of its vast area.

According to *The Times*, if something could be done about providing proper water and sewerage on Iona, Tom Johnston saw no reason why the island couldn't welcome 50,000 visitors a year. 'In a primitive economy where substance can still prove perilous such an influx could yet prove the greatest boon of all,' it added.

Another example of Johnston's clever handling of a major occasion, cited by his former press aide, Hamish MacKinven, involved a visit by the Prime Minister of Australia, Robert Menzies, and a small, brown paper bag, containing a handful of pine seed. Menzies, who was in Britain attending a Commonwealth conference, had been invited by Johnston to perform the opening ceremony at the Gaur dam on the edge of Rannoch Moor. 'Gaur is the heartland of the Clan Menzies,' MacKinven explained. 'It is also one of the few areas where you could find traces of the old Caledonian forest. Following the opening ceremony and the speeches, the chairman reached under his chair and produced a brown paper poke. Nobody knew what to expect. But what it contained was seed taken from cones in the Caledonian forest. Menzies was over the moon! You couldn't think of a more appropriate gift to such a man. But only Tom Johnston could have done it.'

He was chairman of the North of Scotland Hydro–Electric Board for 13 years, during which time the Board commissioned 38 different schemes. Before his long period of service ended the Hydro Board provided electricity to 90 per cent of the population in the north of Scotland; at cheaper rates than those available in the south of England, as a Parliamentary committee of inquiry into the nationalised industries confirmed. And this despite the cost of servicing a vast and sparsely populated area.

On 1 June 1959, two weeks before he retired as chairman, Johnston could also boast that an expenditure of £24 million on a scheme at Loch Awe had been approved by the House of Commons 'without a protest; without a division'. But by then many of the old fierce battles had been won; not least over just how much importance the Hydro Board attached to preserving the amenities. Speaking in Orkney on 9 May 1946 Tom Johnston claimed: 'Every effort that ever attempted change for the benefit of humanity has always been attacked on the grounds of amenities.'

Six years later the *Perthshire Advertiser* conceded that critics of the

Pitlochry scheme had been proved hopelessly wrong. While the Society for the Preservation of Rural Scotland felt able to acknowledge that, far from damaging Glen Affric, 'the Hydro Board had increased the beauty of the glen by some 100 per cent'.

Johnston marked his retirement from the North of Scotland Hydro-Electric Board with an interview on the BBC. He was four months short of 79; in future, it emerged, he would continue to serve as a member of the Scottish Tourist Board and as Chancellor of Aberdeen University. Otherwise he was retiring from public life. Asked by his interviewer, Sir James Fergusson, if he would be going to the House of Lords, Tom Johnston replied: 'I'm not interested in a title. I want to bide among my ain people.'

EPILOGUE

TOM JOHNSTON retreated from public life bearing none of the baubles a political career usually attracts. He wasn't against other people accepting titles. 'But I was so hostile to the idea in my young days, when I was fiery,' he explained to his old friend, Lieutenant-Colonel Thomas Riddell of Fintry, 'that I couldn't really do it.'

He said no to becoming a peer or a viscount, and declined membership of the Order of the Thistle, after telling Churchill that this was the one honour he wanted, because it meant using a title. 'Inquiries were actually made, to see if he could be admitted to the Order of the Thistle, and still remain plain Mr Johnston,' his daughter, Mrs Mary Knox, recalled with a smile. 'But in the end it was decided no, it just wasn't acceptable. So that was the end of that!'

Churchill, who had been installed in the Order of the Garter in return for his services to the nation, pressed him to accept something by way of public recognition. In 1953 Johnston relented and agreed to become a Companion of Honour, to add to the honorary degree bestowed on him by Glasgow University and the freedom scrolls he received from several towns.

He was also Chancellor of Aberdeen University from 1951 until his death 14 years later. However, according to his entry in the *Dictionary of National Biography*, his reserve and modesty was such he only responded positively to Aberdeen's original approach after consulting a few intimate friends 'as to his fitness in the public eye for such an academic post'.

Tom Johnston was just two months short of 84 when he died at his home in Milngavie; still within sight of the Campsie Hills he'd known since infancy. Although he suffered a number of minor strokes during the last years of his life, his wife, Margaret, told reporters he seemed well the previous evening.

In its tribute *The Scotsman* said there was a consensus of opinion that he was 'the greatest Scotsman of modern times and the one who did most for his country'. As Secretary of State for Scotland in the wartime Coalition under Churchill, it added, Johnston had been able to apply 'his great gifts of sound common sense and native shrewdness, his wide experience of public affairs, and of men, to the multifarious problems which beset him, tackling them with a fearlessness and directness that won him the respect and confidence of his fellow countrymen of all shades of opinion'.

In a radio and television tribute broadcast the day after his death, Alastair Dunnett, editor of *The Scotsman* and an old friend, called him 'a man of destiny and all the bigger because he decided to do the job at his own door'.

Long after his death the reputation Johnston gained in St Andrew's House persists. Indeed, according to one leading historian, Professor Christopher Harvie, it has 'endured in Scottish mythology almost as tenaciously as the Red Clyde'. However, according to Harvie, much of this reputation was cultivated by the man himself. In this respect it is worth remembering Tom Johnston was popular with journalists and knew, after years of experience, how to manipulate even the best of them. But journalists rarely create myths: more accurately, perhaps, on the rare occasions such an opportunity presents itself, they will respond with enthusiasm to the sight and deeds of a heroic figure.

Tom Johnston looked and acted and talked the part of a modern-day Scottish hero. But at least one reporter, Wilfred Taylor, assumed there were 'areas of ruthlessness in his character'. The same correspondent, in a curious flight of fancy, also likened the modest, trim bungalow in Milngavie, where Johnston spent his last years, to 'a gubernatorial mansion in all but architecture'.

It is possible, of course, that Tom Johnston succeeded in capturing the popular imagination because people wanted him to succeed. Johnston believed he enjoyed a great advantage as a wartime Minister. 'Political differences were set aside for the common good,' he explained.

But people generally also sensed that he was patently a decent man who wanted the best for people everywhere; not least his own countrymen. As a consequence, as Wilfred Taylor noted, he was 'able to impose his will on the nation and transcend politics because his political basis had been assured and consolidated to the point that his stature was recognised where it counts, among the possessors of power'.

Nor did he use his position, or the trust he enjoyed among all levels of society, to enrich himself. Said Lord Thomson of Monifieth: 'He was absolutely meticulous about expenses. He kept a record of everything, down to the last penny. It was a matter of very deep principle with him that you lived within your means.'

Johnston also worked without salary, as Regional Commissioner for Civil Defence and Secretary of State for Scotland, during the war because of his conviction that 'to do otherwise would amount to profiteering', his daughter, Mrs Mary Knox, explained. 'The war was the only reason he was a member of Churchill's Cabinet. So, in his eyes, if he'd accepted any payment, he would have been making money out of an opportunity which the war created,' Mrs Knox added.

This virtuous attitude didn't commend itself to the tax authorities, however. After the war Johnston was told that, although he took no salary, funds had been allocated for the purpose. 'Technically, it appeared, the money had been gifted by him to the state,' his old friend, Thomas Riddell, recalled. 'It didn't matter to the revenue what he did with his money, he was still liable for tax. In the end, he told me, he was obliged to raise the matter with the Prime Minister. Attlee told him not to worry, he would see to it. Which he did.'

Of course, the scope and success of Tom Johnston's post-war career was wholly dependent on Labour winning the 1945 general election. Even if he had been prepared to accept an offer of employment from Churchill after the war, he couldn't expect to be put in charge of the North of Scotland Hydro-Electric Board, the Forestry Commission and the Scottish Tourist Board simultaneously.

The protracted and bitter opposition, from traditional Tory voters, to hydro power on the scale Johnston envisaged, and pursued with such vigour in the post-war years, also suggests its development would have been seriously curtailed by a Conservative administration; or at the very least subsumed by a central electricity authority based in London. Johnston would have been left on the sidelines of the great post-war reconstruction. Instead, his decision to abandon the House of Commons in 1945 and decline a seat in the House of Lords, which could have led to a Cabinet role in the Attlee Government, was vindicated by events.

Labour in power in the immediate post-war years offered the start he needed. It also allowed him to pursue a policy of action, begun during the war, which enabled him to enlist the talents of people from outside politics to assist in his grand design. Johnston plundered industry, the trade unions, the professions, the universities, the arts, journalism and the community generally, in search of anyone whom he believed could contribute to the future well-being of the country. People who disliked the idea of government by quango were usually disarmed by his enthusiasm and open-mindedness. There was also a touch of the benign dictator about his corporate approach to finding solutions to the nation's ills; and, as more than one observer remarked, 'like many great men he reacted badly to criticism'.

Yet he was the lone Labour voice on the Council of State during the war. Certainly, at meetings, he operated from a position of considerable authority; and there is no doubt the policies it pursued were the policies he wanted to pursue. Nonetheless its existence, together with the fact it survived until the end of the war, and included the redoubtable Walter Elliot, with whom Johnston remained on good terms for more than half a century, suggests he did listen to all sides in an argument and give way if necessary.

Said Lord Thomson of Monifieth: 'If there had been no war and no coalition he would have been bitterly attacked by the ideologues in the Labour Party for co-operating with the other side. But wartime made everything different.'

His lasting legacy is harder to judge. Christopher Harvie blamed Johnston for 'the rather parochial complacency and self-satisfaction which underlay Scottish post-war administration. Faced with the need to plan for fundamental change in the Scottish economy, patriotism and consensus were not enough.'

At the time of his retirement as chairman of the North of Scotland Hydro-Electric Board in 1959 Johnston, by his own admission, was disappointed he had been unable to wipe out the disparity between Scottish unemployment figures and those in England and Wales. But the great dams he helped create are still in place and tourism is now a major Scottish industry; the headquarters of the Forestry Commission is located in Edinburgh and the Secretary of State for Scotland is nowadays the senior UK Minister dealing with forestry matters in the House of Commons; all important developments which Tom Johnston would have welcomed at any time.

It is hard not to conclude, however, that he would have been sorely disappointed to witness the failure of the North of Scotland Hydro-Electric Board to achieve the targets he set for it. Despite its efficiency as an electricity supplier the Board was never allowed to develop in the dramatic way Tom Johnston envisaged. It did not succeed in attracting major industries to the Highlands and, following the years he spent as chairman, its key role as an improver of life in the region was quietly abandoned. Its eventual privatisation, under a Tory Government, would have been the final blow to his ambitions.

His dream of a Parliament in Edinburgh is as yet also unfulfilled. Ironically, it was perhaps his own success as Secretary of State for Scotland, operating within the existing system, which denied the need for serious change: given the status quo, and a powerful, independently minded voice in St Andrew's House, he demonstrated, to the satisfaction of many people, that Scotland's interests could be protected.

John MacCormick admitted the SNP made a mistake in contesting the 1932 Dunbartonshire by-election in opposition to Johnston. 'But who knows whether, if he had become leader of the Labour Party,' MacCormick continued defensively, 'he would ever have had the time or the opportunity, even granting the inclination, to do much for Scotland.' This curious conclusion, published a decade after Tom Johnston vacated St Andrew's House, can be set alongside MacCormick's own acknowledgment, in *The Flag in the Wind*, that his old political adversary was 'the one man above all others who has contributed to the rebuilding of the Scottish economy'.

Sir Douglas Haddow, his private secretary during the war, and later Permanent Under-Secretary at the Scottish Office, supported the popular view that Johnston was Scotland's best-ever Secretary of State. Asked to explain why, Sir Douglas replied: 'He could see through a brick wall!' But the same senior official also believed: 'I don't think he would have been happy, and never as successful, in an ordinary party-divided Parliament. To that extent he was fortunate in his time.'

His daughter, Mrs Mary Knox, maintained: 'We were all very devoted to him. He was so fair, I think that's what I remember most about him.'

It was an epitaph Tom Johnston would have been happy to accept. That and words he borrowed from Macaulay: 'When none is for the party, and all are for the state, we get home.'

Select Bibliography

Henry H. Adams, *Harry Hopkins: a Biography* (New York, 1977)

Paul Addison, *The Road to 1945* (London, 1975)

John Boyd Orr, *As I Recall* (London, 1966)

Gordon Brown, *Maxton* (Edinburgh, 1986)

G.D.H. Cole, *History of the Labour Party from 1914* (London, 1948)

John Colville, *The Fringes of Power* (London, 1985)

Colin Cross, *Philip Snowden* (London, 1966)

Hugh Dalton, *The Fateful Years* (London, 1957) and *High Tide and After* (London, 1962)

Patrick Dollan, unpublished autobiography

Alastair Dunnett, *Among Friends* (London, 1984)

Michael Fry, *Patronage and Principle: a Political History of Modern Scotland* (Aberdeen, 1987)

Kenneth Harris, *Attlee* (London, 1982)

Tom Harrisson, *Living Through the Blitz* (London, 1976)

Christopher Harvie, *Scotland and Nationalism* (London, 1977)

T.J. Honeyman, *Art and Audacity* (London, 1971)

Jack House, *The Friendly Adventure* (Glasgow, 1962)

Emrys Hughes, *Rebels and Renegades*, unpublished autobiography

Andrew Jeffrey, *This Time of Crisis* (Edinburgh, 1993)

Thomas Johnston, *Our Noble Families* (Glasgow, 1909), *The History of the Working Classes in Scotland* (Glasgow, 1920), *The Financiers and the Nation* (Glasgow, 1934) and *Memories* (London, 1952)

Michael Keating and David Bleiman, *Labour and Scottish Nationalism* (London, 1979)

Dr William Knox (ed.), *Scottish Labour Leaders 1918–1939: a Biographical Dictionary* (Edinburgh, 1984)

Gilbert McAllister, *James Maxton: Portrait of a Rebel* (London, 1935)

John M. MacCormick, *The Flag in the Wind* (London, 1955)

Compton Mackenzie, *My Life and Times: Octaves Six and Eight* (London, 1967)

I.M.M. Macphail, *The Clydebank Blitz* (Clydebank, 1974)

David Marquand, *Ramsay Macdonald* (London, 1977)

Robert Keith Middlemas, *The Clydesiders: a Left-Wing Struggle for Parliamentary Power* (London, 1965)

Lord Moran, *Winston Churchill: the Struggle for Survival* (London, 1966)

Sir Oswald Mosley, *My Life* (London, 1968)

Peter L. Payne, *The Hydro* (Aberdeen, 1988)

Sir Harold Nicholson, *King George V: His Life and Reign* (London, 1952)

Henry Pelling, *Origins of the Labour Party* (Oxford, 1965)

George Pottinger, *The Secretaries of State for Scotland 1926–76* (Edinburgh, 1979)

Peter Rowland, *David Lloyd George: a Biography* (New York, 1976)

Emmanuel Shinwell, *Lead with the Left* (London, 1981)

Robert Skidelsky, *Oswald Mosley* (London, 1975)

Philip Snowden, *Autobiography* (London, 1934)

T.C. Smout, *A Century of the Scottish People* (London, 1986)

Tom Steel, *The Life and Death of St Kilda* (London, 1975)

Arthur Turner, *Scottish Home Rule* (Oxford, 1952)

Cedric Watts and Laurence Davies, *Cunninghame Graham: a Critical Biography* (Cambridge, 1979)

INDEX

Acland, F.D., 256
Adams, Henry H., 231
Adamson, William, 85, 109–10, 129, 141, 153, 164, 173, 177, 205, 238
Addison, Christopher, 153
Aglen, A.J., 239
Alexander, A.V., 153
Alness, Lord, 239–40, 246–47
Amulree, Lord, 153
Anderson, Sir John, 221, 260
Asquith, Brig.-Gen. A.M., 64
Asquith, H.H., 38, 64–67, 75, 82, 196
Astor, Viscountess Nancy, 63
Attlee, Clement, 13, 60, 166, 190, 204–5, 208–9, 250–51, 253–54, 274, 280–81

Baird, John Logie, 41
Baldwin, Stanley, 65, 71, 76, 93, 124, 147, 151, 159, 186, 199, 201–2, 206
Banbury, Sir Frederick, 71
Barclay, Nurse Williamina, 129
Barr, Rev. James, 80, 177–78, 179, 205, 208–9
Beaverbrook, Lord, 124
Benn, W. Wedgwood, 153
Bevin, Ernest, 101
Bilsland, Sir Steven (later Lord), 263
Blake, Thomas, 184
Bondfield, Margaret, 152–53, 164
Boothby, Robert, 241
Boyd Orr, John, 117
Bracken, Brendan, 232
Bradbury, Lord, 33–34
Brockway, Fenner, 98
Brown, Bob, 275
Brown, Ernest, 239, 246–47
Brown, Gordon, 86, 102, 115

Brown, James, 83–85
Bruce, King Robert the, 55
Buchanan, George (historian), 14
Buchanan, George (MP), 71, 79, 91, 107, 171–72, 175, 177–78, 208
Burns, John, 44
Burns, Robert, 12
Burns, Thomas, 208

Camden, William, 14
Campbell, Miss Emily, 183, 186
Campbell, John Ross, 91, 102
Carlyle, Thomas, 12
Chamberlain, Neville, 31, 33–35, 151, 157, 215, 218, 221
Churchill, Winston S., 7, 13, 23, 42–43, 46, 104, 150, 215, 229, 232–33, 236, 238, 249–51, 253, 268, 278–80
Clynes, J.R., 64, 66, 153, 204
Cochrane, A.D., 23, 187–89
Cochrane, Margaret Freeland (Mrs Tom Johnston), 8, 279
Cole, G.D.H., 76, 86, 101, 103–4, 112, 138, 146–47, 154, 160–61, 164–66, 182
Colville, John (Churchill's wartime secretary), 13, 37
Colville, John (former Secretary of State for Scotland), 239, 246
Connolly, James, 18
Conrad, Joseph, 44
Cook, Arthur, 102, 104–5
Cooper, Duff, 231–32
Cooper, T.M. (later Lord), 221, 240, 270–71
Cripps, Sir Stafford, 164, 204,

247, 253–54
Cunninghame Graham, R.B., 8, 44–47, 180
Curzon, Lord, 26

Dale, David, 49
Dalton, Hugh, 204–5, 255
Darling, Sir Will Y., 244
Davies, Laurence, 46–47
Derby, Lord, 65
Dickens, Charles, 15
Dickson, Tom, 79
Dollan, Patrick, 8, 18, 113–15
Duffes, A.P., 201
Dunbar, John, 196
Dunnett, Alastair, 10, 13, 18, 279

Eden, Sir Anthony, 268
Edward VIII, 206–7
Elizabeth (wife of George VI), 207
Elles, Sir Hugh, 226
Elliot, Walter, 23, 25, 72, 213, 239–40, 246, 275, 281

Fanshawe, G.D., 93
Ferguson, Neil, 135
Fergusson, Sir James, 277
Flandin, P.E., 148
Fuad I, 95

Gallagher, William, 205
Geddes, Sir Eric, 43
George V, 83, 109
George VI, 207, 251
George, David Lloyd, 20, 26–27, 38–9, 40–44, 47, 57, 80, 109, 116, 119, 123–25, 146, 160, 237, 256
George, Gwilym Lloyd, 271–72
Gilbert, Martin, 104

Gladstone, W.E., 47
Goldman, Bosworth, 196-98
Graham, William, 153, 163, 204
Gray, Robert, 188-89
Greenwood, Arthur, 9-10, 69, 153, 204, 221
Grieve, C.M., 180

Haddow, Sir Douglas, 283
Halifax, Lord, 229
Hamilton, Sir A.P., 239
Hardie, James Keir, 18, 25-27, 78, 100, 112-13
Harris, Kenneth, 166
Harrison, Prof. Tom, 233
Hartshorn, Vernon, 141, 147
Harvie, Prof. Christopher, 279, 281
Hastings, Sir Patrick, 91
Henderson, Arthur, 150, 153, 164, 166
Henderson, George, 128, 131-32
Hitler, Adolf, 12, 215, 217, 232, 238, 263
Home, Earl of, 267
Honeyman, T.J., 230, 263-64, 268
Hope, Sir Harry, 43, 47, 57-58, 75
Hopkins, Harry, 229, 232
Horne, Sir Robert, 89
House, Jack, 192
Hudson, W.H., 44
Hughes, Emrys, 12, 19, 22-23, 78-79, 85, 94, 96, 100, 120-4, 126, 175, 195-98, 237-38
Hutchison, Tom, 40

Inchcape, Lord, 124

Jack, Bailie Daniel, 29
James IV, 167
Johnston, David (father), 8
Johnston, Margaret (wife), 8, 279
Johnston, Mary (mother), 8
Johnston, Rt Hon Thomas, CH, 'Uncrowned King of Scotland', 7, 13
  parents, 8
  image, 8
  defending Scotland's interests, 9
  moderate extremist, 11
  early days, 14

(Johnston cont.)
launches, edits Forward, 17
Our Noble Families, 19-24
Glasgow Univ, 25
supports Keir Hardie as Rector, 25
Kirkintilloch: School Board, 27;
  councillor, 29;
  Scotland's first municipal bank, 31;
  freeman, 35
opposes WWI, 37
clashes with Lloyd George, 38
Forward banned, 40
1918 general election, 42
The History of the Working Classes in Scotland, 48-56
1922 MP West Stirlingshire, 57
maiden speech, 60
Prime Minister apologises, 63
clashes with Asquith, 64-67
targets Empire trade, 68
campaigns against 'sweated' labour, 69
defends Maxton's 'murderers' speech, 72
Labour's radical identity, 73
1923 holds West Stirlingshire, 75
no pact with Liberals, 76
Emrys Hughes joins Forward, 78
tea at Miss Cranston's, 79
first Labour government, 82
ignored by MacDonald, 82
Labour ministers and Court dress, 83
working man becomes Lord High Commissioner to the General Assembly of the Church of Scotland, 83-86

(Johnston cont.)
warns against vested interests, 88
appointment of Lord Advocate, 88
Tories to blame for Sterling's fall, 89
defends Labour budget, 89
supports Wheatley's housing policy, 90
Britain and Soviet Union, 90
John Ross Campbell, 91
Zinoviev letter, 92
loses West Stirlingshire, 93
supports MacDonald as Labour leader, 94
wins by-election Dundee, 95
visits India, 97-100
role of ILP, 100-103
TUC and general strike, 104
coal owners' profits, 105
quits Dundee, 106
regains West Stirling-shire, 108
member second Labour government, 109
at odds with ILP, 111-15
Under-Secretary of State for Scotland, 117
rows with Wheatley, 120-23
seeks all-party programme on unemployment, 137
Mosley memorandum, 138
Lord Privy Seal, 141
angers MacDonald, 144
co-operates with Liberals, 146
sterling in trouble, 147
Labour blameless, 148
meets French premier, 148
money crisis unfolds, 149-53
collapse of second Labour government, 154
against government by Wall Street, 156

(Johnston cont.)
denies pressure from
  TUC, 156
doesn't vote on gold
  standard, 159
opposes early general
  election, 159
Snowden betrays
  Labour, 161
defeat in West Stirling-
  shire, 164–5
Home Rule for
  Scotland, 167
Auld Scots Parliament,
  167
disagrees with R.E.
  Muirhead, 175
National Party of
  Scotland, 180–82
rebukes nationalist
  candidate in St
  Rollex by-election,
  183
loses by-election in
  Dunbartonshire, 189
becomes head of City of
  Glasgow Friendly
  Society, 191
visits Soviet Union,
  192–94
discounts chances of
  communist-led
  revolution in
  Scotland, 194
no longer editor of
  Forward, 195
Forward for sale, 195
against bombing Italy,
  199
favours strong League of
  Nations, 200
regains West Stirling-
  shire in 1935 general
  election, 201
MacDonald great and
  noteworthy figure,
  203
PLP elections, 204
future of Monarchy, 206
Saltire Society and
  London Scots Self-
  Government
  Committee, 208
Gilmour Committee on
  Administration of
  Scotland, 210
Scotland at Westminster,
  211

(Johnston cont.)
years locust ate, 215
international police
  force, 216
opposes conscription,
  218
condemns non-
  resistance, 220
civil defence, 221
Regional Commissioner
  for Scotland, 221–28
visit from Harry
  Hopkins, 229
mass burial at Clyde-
  bank, 234
Secretary of State, 236
Council of State, 239
appoints Cooper
  Committee on hydro
  power, 240
Scottish Housing Advis-
  ory Council, 240
Scots Grand Committee
  meets in Edinburgh,
  241
Scotland and war effort,
  241
Scottish Council
  (Development and
  Industry), 243
anticipates NHS, 245
1945 Education
  (Scotland) Bill, 247
relationship with SED,
  248
helped by Churchill,
  249
retires as Secretary of
  State, 249
annoyed with Churchill,
  251
Usher Hall Thanks-
  giving Rally, 251
considered as viceroy,
  253
Forestry Commission in
  Scotland, 255–61
Scottish Tourist Board,
  261–68
BBC governor, 269
North of Scotland
  Hydro-Electric
  Board, 269–77
seeks and declines Order
  of Thistle, 278
Companion of Honour,
  278
political legacy, 279–83

Jowitt, William, 109

Kamenev, Lev, 196, 198
Keeling, Edward, 270
Kelly, Henry, 233
Kennedy, John A., 186
Ker, J.C., 165
Kerr, J. Gibson, 265
Keynes, J.M., 104, 124, 149
Kirkwood, David, 8, 59, 60,
  63, 80, 113, 174–75, 233
Kirov, Sergey, 199
Knox, Mrs Mary (daughter),
  8, 13, 278, 280, 283

Lansbury, George, 137, 139,
  153, 166, 190
Larkin, James, 45
Laski, Harald, 18
Laval, Pierre, 148
Law, Andrew Bonar, 41, 43,
  47, 57, 59, 63, 67, 71
Leishman, Walter, 80
Leonard, William, 186
Lothian, Lord, 229
Lovat, Lord, 256–57

MacAlister, Sir Donald, 27
McAllister, Gilbert, 117, 147
Macauley, Rev. Kenneth, 128
Macauley, Lord, 283
MacCormick, John M., 9, 10,
  187, 189–90, 282
MacDonald, Ramsay, 11, 18,
  21, 58–59, 66–68, 72–73,
  75–78, 82–84, 86–88, 90–
  96, 100–2, 105, 107–10,
  116–17, 119, 120, 123,
  125, 137, 139, 141–42,
  144–46, 149, 151, 153–60,
  162, 164, 173, 175, 182,
  186–90, 199, 201–4, 268
McGovern, John, 112
MacGregor, Alasdair Alpin,
  134–35
MacInnes, R.I.A., 75
MacIntyre, Hugh, 188–89
MacIntyre, Dr Robert, 222
Mackenzie, Sir Compton, 81,
  131, 180, 228, 241
Mackinven, Hamish, 20, 24,
  273–74, 276
Maclean, John, 195
Maclean, Neil, 80
MacLeod, Rt. Rev. George,
  275
Macleod, Sir Reginald
  Macleod of, 130, 132

MacManus, Arthur, 92
Macmillan, Harold, 268
MacMillan, Hugh, KC, 88
McNeill, Ronald, 64
Macphail, I.M.M., 233
Maitland, Sir Arthur Steel, 124
Mann, Tom, 91
Mannin, Ethel, 18
Mansfield, Lord, 257
Markievicz, Countess Constance, 63
Marquand, David, 59, 71, 73, 82, 146
Martin, Martin, 128
Marx, Karl, 80
Mavor, O.M., 25
Maxton, James, 7, 41-42, 58, 71-72, 77-80, 86, 94, 101-5, 110-11, 113, 115, 117, 119-20, 123, 147, 169-70, 177, 205
Menzies, Robert, 276
Middlemass, Robert Keith, 19, 39, 60, 83, 100
Milne, Sir David, 239, 263
Mitchell, Rosslyn, 40, 80, 88, 196
Mond, Sir Alfred, 124
Montieth, Harold, 162-63
Montrose, Duke of, 58
Moran, Lord, 230-31
Morel, E.D., 94
Morrison, Herbert, 153, 189, 204, 226, 234, 243, 251, 273-74
Mosley, Sir Oswald, 137-39
Mountbatten, Lord Louis, 253
Muirhead, R.E., 17, 167, 175-77, 180-81
Munro, Dugald, 129
Mussolini, Benito, 199

Nicholson, Sir Harold, 83
Norfolk, Duke of, 237
Normand, Lord, 238

Northcliffe, Lord, 18

O'Connor, T.J., KC, 197

Passfield, Lord (Sidney Webb), 153
Patiala, Maharajah of, 97
Paton, John, 111-12, 114
Payne, Peter L., 272, 274
Pethick-Lawrence, Lord, 253-54
Poincaré, Raymond, 63
Pottinger, George, 244

Ramsay, T.W.B., 131
Reid, Derek, 268
Reith, Sir John, 243
Ribbentrop, Joachim von, 219
Riddell, Lt-Col. Thomas, 278, 280
Roberton, Hugh S., 80
Robinson, Sir Roy (later Lord), 256, 258, 260
Roosevelt, Franklin D., 229
Rose, P.J., 239
Rosebery, Lord, 234
Rousseau, Jean-Jacques, 216
Russell, Bertrand, 18

Sankey, Lord, 153
Shaw, George Bernard, 18, 44
Shaw, Thomas, 153
Shinwell, Emmanuel, 9, 26, 59-60, 63, 75, 80, 86, 111-12, 164, 201-2, 204, 273-74
Sime, John, 97
Simon, E.D., 95
Simon, Sir John, 66, 109
Simpson, Wallis, 206
Sinclair, Archibald, 239, 246
Skidelsky, Robert, 140
Smith, Adam, 255
Smith, H.B. Lees, 158
Snowden, Philip, 60, 62, 69-70, 105, 139, 149-50,

152-53, 155-64
Stalin, Joseph, 199, 219
Steel, Tom, 134-35
Stephen, Campbell, 71, 80
Stevenson, James Verdier, 27
Stevenson, W.H., 195
Stewart, James, 183, 185
Stewart, William, 75
Stirling-Maxwell, Sir John, 256-57, 260
Stuart, James, 268
Swift, Mr Justice, 197-98

Taylor, Wilfred, 279-80
Thom, J.G., 186-87
Thomas, J.H., 94, 137-38, 147, 153, 156-57
Thomson, George (Lord Thomson of Monifieth), 11-12, 107, 280-81
Turner, Ben, 143

Watt, James, 241
Watts, Cedric, 46-47
Wavell, Lord, 253-54
Webb, Beatrice, 62, 126
Webb, Sidney (Lord Passfield), 124
Wedgwood, J.C., 164
Weir, L. MacNeill, 72
Wells, H.G., 18, 192
Wheatley, John, 7, 18, 58, 60, 69, 71-73, 77-79, 82, 86, 89-90, 102, 105, 110-12, 119-23, 126, 177, 204
White, W.E., 108
Whitley, John, 175
William III, 168-69
Williams, Tom, 260
Willink, Henry, 246
Wodehouse, P.G., 257
Wood, Kingsley, 271

Younger, Lord, 58

Zinoviev, Grigory, 92, 196, 198